W9-AUC-645

DECEIVED

Books by Peter R. Limburg

DECEIVED

The Story of the Donner Party

Peter R. Limburg

Copyright © 1998 by Peter R. Limburg

All rights reserved. No part of this book may be reproduced or transmitted in any form or by any means, electronic or mechanical, including photocopying, recording, or by any information storage and retrieval system, without permission in writing from the publisher.

Requests for permission to make copies of any part of the work should be mailed to: Permissions, International Publishing Services, 1149 Grand Teton Drive, Pacifica, California 94044

Manufactured in the United States of America

ISBN 1-890988-00-6

IPS Books is an imprint of International Publishing Services, a division of Words To Go, Inc.

Library of Congress Cataloging-in-Publication Data

Limburg, Peter R.
     Deceived : the story of the Donner party / Peter R. Limburg
       p.   cm.
     Includes bibliographical references and index.
     ISBN 1-890988-00-6
     1. Donner Party.   I. Title
F868.N5L55 1998
978' .02—dc21   98-14253
                                      CIP

To my wife, Maggie, who hated this story when I began it, but in the end found it almost as absorbing as I do—and to the memory of the members of the Donner Party, who suffered, succumbed, and survived in the snows of the Sierras.

CONTENTS

Illustrations follow Page 130

THE PEOPLE OF
THE DONNER PARTY

(Most ages are approximate, as of the late spring of 1846)

From Springfield, Illinois:
George Donner, 62
Tamsen Donner, 45, his wife
> Children of George and Tamsen:
>> Frances E. Donner, 6
>> Georgia A. Donner, 4
>> Eliza P. Donner, 3
> George Donner's children by his deceased second wife (whose
>> name is not known):
>> Elitha Cumi Donner, 14
>> Leanna C. Donner, 12
Jacob Donner, 65
Elizabeth Donner, about 45 (birth date not known), his wife
> Children of Jacob and Elizabeth:
>> George Donner, Jr., 8
>> Mary Donner, 7
>> Isaac Donner, 5
>> Samuel Donner, 4
>> Lewis Donner, 2 or 3

Elizabeth Donner's children by a former husband:
Solomon Hook, 13
William Hook, 11
James Frazier Reed, 45
Margaret Reed, 32, his wife
Their children:
Virginia E. Backenstoe Reed, 12 (Margaret's child
by her first husband)
Martha J. (Patty) Reed, 8
James F. Reed, Jr., 5
Thomas K. Reed, 3
Sarah M. Keyes, 70 (Margaret Reed's mother; died May 29, 1846,
on the trail in Kansas)

Teamsters for the Donner Brothers:
John Denton, 28
Noah James, 20
Hiram Miller, age unknown (left Donners at Fort Laramie)
Samuel Shoemaker, 25

Employees of Reed:
Milford (Milt) Elliott, 28, teamster
Walter Herron, 25, teamster
James Smith, 25, teamster
Baylis Williams, 24, handyman
Eliza Williams, his sister, 25, hired girl

Joined the Donner Party at Independence, Missouri:
Antoine or Antonio (last name unknown), 23; hired by the
Donners as a cattle herder at Independence, Missouri

Joined the Donner Party at Fort Bridger:
Jean-Baptiste Trudeau (also known as Bateese and Trubode), 23;
hired as a teamster
William McCutchen, 30
Amanda McCutchen, 24, his wife
Their child:
Harriet McCutchen, 1

Joined the Donners and Reeds at Little Sandy Creek in Wyoming to take the Hastings Cutoff:

Patrick Breen, 40
Margaret (Peggy) Breen, 40, his wife
    Their children:
        John Breen, 14
        Edward J. Breen, 13
        Patrick Breen, Jr., 11
        Simon P. Breen, 9
        Peter Breen, 7
        James Breen, 4
        Isabella Breen, 1
Karl (Dutch Charley) Burger, 30, probably a teamster for Keseberg
Patrick Dolan, 40
William H. Eddy, 28
Eleanor Eddy, 25, his wife
    Their children:
        James P. Eddy, 3
        Margaret Eddy, 1
Luke Halloran, 25; died at Great Salt Lake
— Hardkoop (first name unknown), 60; died in desert west of Great Salt Lake.
Lewis Keseberg, 32
Philippine Keseberg, 22, his wife
    Their children:
        Ada, 3
        Lewis, Jr., 1
Lavina Murphy, 50
    Her children and extended family:
        John Landrum Murphy, 15
        Mary M. Murphy, 13
        Lemuel B. Murphy, 12
        William G. Murphy, 11
        Simon P. Murphy, 10
        Sarah Murphy Foster, 23
        William M. Foster, 28, Sarah's husband
            Their child:
                George Foster, 4

Harriet Murphy Pike, 21
William L. Pike, 25, Harriet's husband; died of accidental
       gunshot wound on Truckee River
       Their children:
               Naomi L. Pike, 3
               Catherine Pike, 1
Joseph Reinhardt, 30
Augustus Spitzer, 30 (believed to have traveled as partners)
Charles T. Stanton, 35
— Wolfinger (first name unknown), 30?; died in desert, probably
       murdered)
Doris Wolfinger, 30, his wife

Joined the Donner Party in the Wasatch Mountains:
Franklin Ward (Uncle Billy) Graves, 57
Elizabeth Graves, 47, his wife
       Their children:
               Sarah Graves Fosdick, 22
               Jay Fosdick, 23, Sarah's husband
               Mary Ann Graves, 20
               William C. Graves, 18
               Eleanor Graves, 15
               Lavina Graves, 13
               Nancy Graves, 9
               Jonathan Graves, 7
               Franklin Ward Graves, Jr., 5
               Elizabeth Graves, Jr., 1
John Snyder, 25, teamster for the Graves family; killed by Reed on
       the Humboldt

Trapped with the Donner Party in the Sierras:
Sutter's Indian *vaqueros:*
Luis, 20?
Salvador, 20?

THE SURVIVORS

The Breen family
Elitha Cumi Donner*
Eliza P. Donner*
Frances E. Donner*
George Donner II*
Georgia A. Donner*
Leanna C. Donner*
Mary Donner*
William H. Eddy
Sarah Graves Fosdick
Sarah Murphy Foster
William M. Foster
Eleanor Graves*
Elizabeth Graves, Jr.**
Jonathan Graves*
Lavina Graves*
Mary Ann Graves
Nancy Graves*

William C. Graves*
Walter Herron
Solomon Hook*
Noah James
Lewis Keseberg
Philippine Keseberg
Amanda McCutchen
William McCutchen
Mary M. Murphy*
Simon P. Murphy*
William G. Murphy*
Harriet Murphy Pike
Naomi Pike*
The Reed family
Jean-Baptiste Trudeau
Eliza Williams
Doris Wolfinger

* Indicates a child
** Died after reaching California

THE DEAD

Died in the Sierras:

Karl Burger
John Denton
Patrick Dolan
George Donner
Tamsen Donner
Jacob Donner
Elizabeth Donner
William Hook*
Isaac Donner*

Elizabeth Graves
FranklinWard Graves, Jr.*
Ada Keseberg*
Lewis Keseberg, Jr.*
Harriet McCutchen*
Lavina Murphy
John Landrum Murphy*
Lemuel Murphy*
Catherine Pike

Lewis Donner*

Samuel Donner*

Eleanor Eddy

James Eddy*

Margaret Eddy*

Milford Elliott

Jay Fosdick

George Foster*

Franklin Ward (Uncle Billy)
   Graves

Joseph Reinhardt

Samuel Shoemaker

James Smith

Augustus Spitzer

Charles T. Stanton

Baylis Williams

Antoine

Luis

Salvador

* Indicates a child

Died on the Trail West:

Sarah M. Keyes, of illness and old age, in Kansas

Luke Halloran, of tuberculosis, at Great Salt Lake

— Hardkoop, of exhaustion and dehydration, in western Nevada

William Pike, by accidental gunshot at Truckee Meadows (the site
      of present-day Reno, Nevada)

John Snyder, killed by Reed along the Humboldt River, Nevada

— Wolfinger, probably murdered by Reinhardt and Spitzer in the
      desert near the Humboldt Sink, Nevada

THE RELIEF PARTIES

The First Relief

Adolph Brueheim (a.k.a. "Greasy Jim")

Ned Coffeemeyer

Billy Coon

Jotham Curtis

William Eddy

Aquila Glover**

Riley Septimus Mootrey

M. D. Ritchie

Daniel Rhoads

John Rhoads

Joseph Sels (a.k.a Joe
      Foster)

John Tucker

Reasin P. (Dan) Tucker

Joseph Verrot (or
      Varro)

The Second Relief

Charles Cady
Nicholas Clark
Matthew Dofar
Joseph Gendreau (spelled Jondro
   in some accounts)

William McCutchen
Hiram Miller
James Frazier Reed**
Charles Stone
John Turner

The Third Relief

William Eddy**
William Foster**
Hiram Miller
Howard Oakley

John Starks
Charles Stone
— Thompson (first
        name unknown)

The Fourth Relief

Ned Coffeemeyer
"Captain" William Fallon**
William Foster
— Keyser (first name unknown)

John Rhoads
Joseph Sels
Reasin P. (Dan) Tucker

** Leaders

MAPS

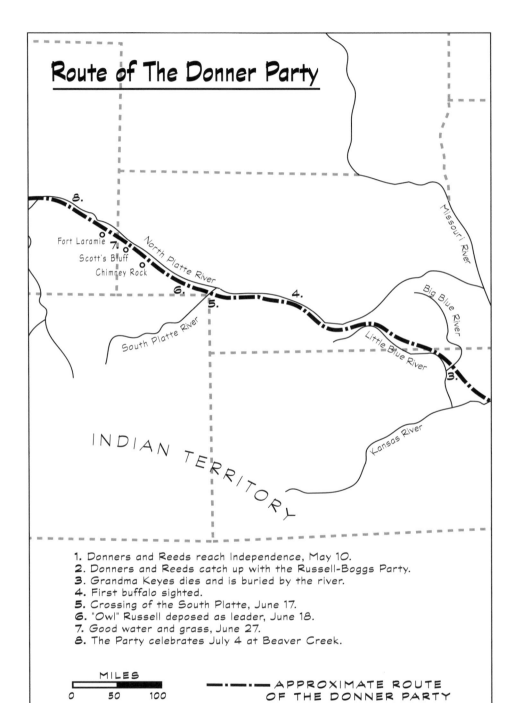

Route of The Donner Party

8.

Fort Laramie
7.
Scott's Bluff
Chimney Rock

North Platte River

6.

5.

South Platte River

4.

Missouri River

Big Blue River

Little Blue River

3.

Kansas River

INDIAN TERRITORY

1. Donners and Reeds reach Independence, May 10.
2. Donners and Reeds catch up with the Russell-Boggs Party.
3. Grandma Keyes dies and is buried by the river.
4. First buffalo sighted.
5. Crossing of the South Platte, June 17.
6. "Owl" Russell deposed as leader, June 18.
7. Good water and grass, June 27.
8. The Party celebrates July 4 at Beaver Creek.

MILES

0   50   100

—·—·—·—· APPROXIMATE ROUTE
OF THE DONNER PARTY

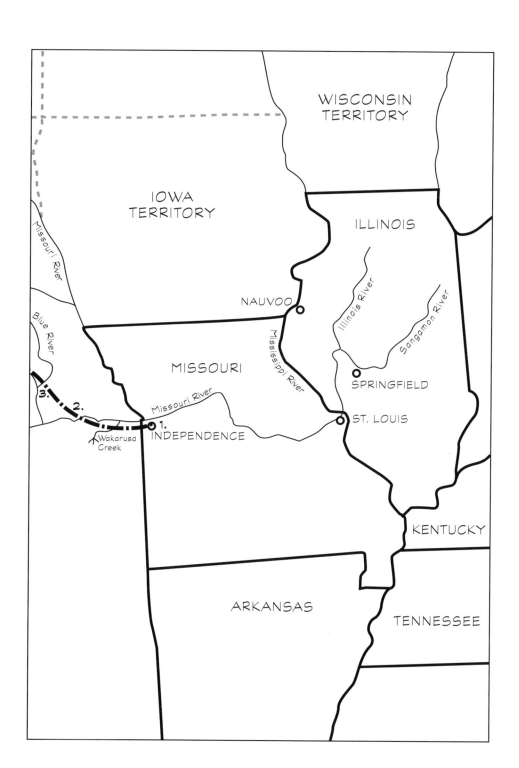

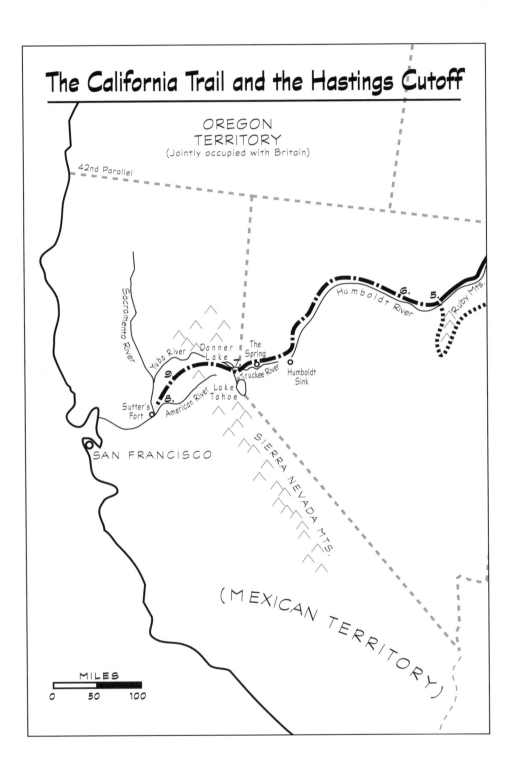

The California Trail and the Hastings Cutoff

OREGON
TERRITORY
(Jointly occupied with Britain)

42nd Parallel

Sacramento River

Humboldt River

6.

5.

Ruby Mts.

Yuba River

Donner
Lake

The
Spring

Truckee River

Humboldt
Sink

9.

7.

8.

Sutter's
Fort

American River

Lake
Tahoe

SAN FRANCISCO

SIERRA NEVADA MTS.

(MEXICAN TERRITORY)

MILES

0   50   100

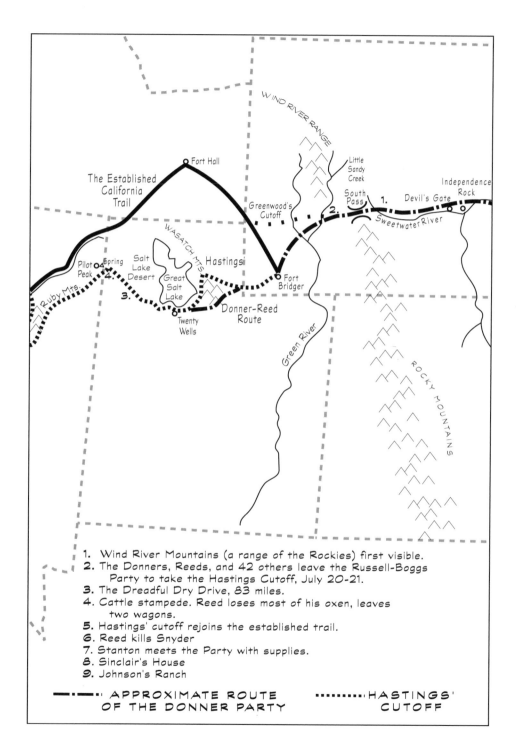

1. Wind River Mountains (a range of the Rockies) first visible.
2. The Donners, Reeds, and 42 others leave the Russell-Boggs Party to take the Hastings Cutoff, July 20-21.
3. The Dreadful Dry Drive, 83 miles.
4. Cattle stampede. Reed loses most of his oxen, leaves two wagons.
5. Hastings' cutoff rejoins the established trail.
6. Reed kills Snyder
7. Stanton meets the Party with supplies.
8. Sinclair's House
9. Johnson's Ranch

▬ ▪ ▬ ▪ APPROXIMATE ROUTE
     OF THE DONNER PARTY

•••••••••• HASTINGS'
          CUTOFF

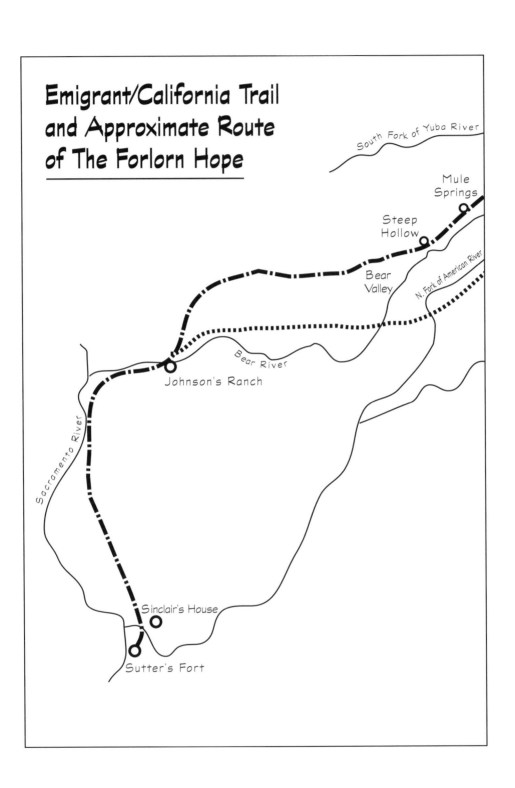

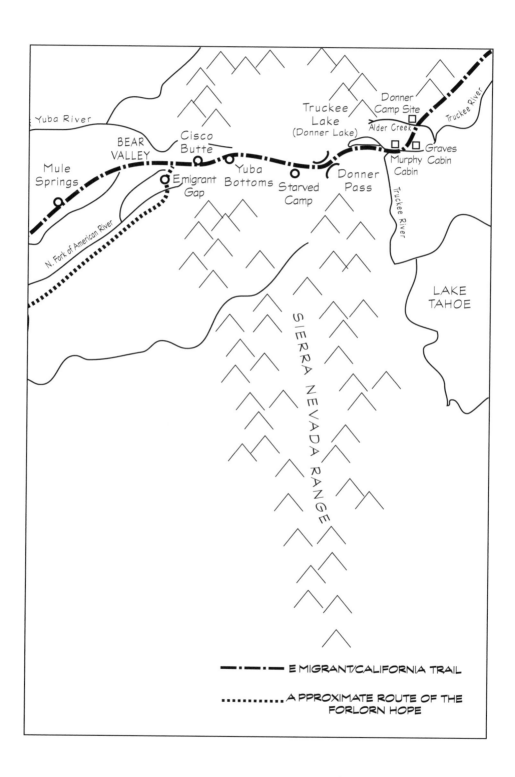

Yuba River

Truckee
Lake
(Donner Lake)

Donner
Camp Site

Alder Creek

Truckee River

BEAR
VALLEY

Cisco
Butte

Mule
Springs

Emigrant
Gap

Yuba
Bottoms

Starved
Camp

Donner
Pass

Graves
Cabin

Murphy
Cabin

N. Fork of American River

Truckee River

LAKE
TAHOE

S
I
E
R
R
A

N
E
V
A
D
A

R
A
N
G
E

—··—··— EMIGRANT/CALIFORNIA TRAIL

·············· APPROXIMATE ROUTE OF THE
FORLORN HOPE

PROLOGUE

Christmas Day 1846.

The snowstorm, which had begun the day before, raged on with unabated force as the little group of ragged, emaciated travelers sat huddled in their makeshift tent of blankets under the deep drifts. Sunk in their misery, they barely realized that it was Christmas Day. Except for being alive, they had little enough to celebrate. They were lost somewhere on the uncharted western slopes of the Sierra Nevada—the mountains which they should have crossed to safety in California three months ago—and they had been without food for the past two days. Their campfire had gone out during the night. There were twelve of them now—seven men and five women. Their leader, the only one who knew the way, had died four days ago of exhaustion, hunger, and exposure, and two more men had died during the night.

They were the remnant of the Forlorn Hope—the younger and stronger adults of the Donner Party—and they had left their families and friends holed up in the snow on the other side of Truckee Pass while they themselves made a desperate push to bring help from the American settlements down in California.

One of the men, Patrick Dolan, became delirious. He struggled free from his companions and staggered out into the storm. Pulling off his boots and most of his clothes, he bawled an incoherent message to William Eddy, the de facto leader of the group.

"Eddy, come with me to the settlements! You're the only one here I can depend on! We'll be there in just a few hours!"

The others left their warm shelter and threw themselves on the raving Dolan, dragging him back beneath the protection of the blankets. He thrashed violently for a bit, then lapsed into a coma and soon ceased to live. It was ironic that Patrick Dolan should die thus, for only the day before he had been the one to break the unspoken taboo and suggest that one of the group must die in order that the others might eat him and live. Now Dolan himself was dead.

When the storm at last died down the following day, someone suggested that the living eat the flesh of the dead, for otherwise they would all perish. And so they cut strips of flesh from Dolan's arms and legs and roasted them on sticks over the rekindled campfire, weeping with grief and guilt as they choked down the loathsome repast. It was the first episode of the cannibalism for which the Donner Party would become notorious—but it was far from the last.

How had they come here, these wretched beings on the edge of death?

It was not what they had expected when they set out confidently on the California Trail, leaving Independence, Missouri, on a beautiful mid-May morning. But they had taken a new and untried cutoff which, they were assured, would save them precious weeks of travel. The cutoff turned out to be a roundabout way through grueling deserts and mountains, and it delayed them disastrously. Tired, demoralized, and barely able to tolerate each other's company, the Donner Party arrived at the crest of the Sierras just in time to be trapped by an early winter storm. Only half of those who had taken the shortcut survived to reach the fabled delights of California. The rest perished of cold, malnutrition, exhaustion, accident, or murder.

The tragedy of the Donner Party gripped the heart of the whole nation. Even today it holds a grim fascination. But, although the final episodes of the tragedy were played out in the towering, rugged peaks of the Sierras, the story really begins on the gently rolling prairies of central Illinois, where the two elderly Donner brothers had their farms just outside Springfield.

CHAPTER 1

The California Fever

The general reason assigned for emigration to the Pacific, by those from the frontier settlements of Illinois and Missouri, is the extreme unhealthiness of those districts. . . . during the summer and autumnal months they are afflicted with the ague and fever. . . . They emigrate to the Pacific in search of health, and if they can find this with a reasonable fertility of soil . . . they will not only be satisfied but feel thankful to Providence for providing them with such a retreat from the miseries they have endured.

—Edwin Bryant, *What I Saw in California*

"California fever" had been sweeping the country for at least two years before the Donner Party left their homes. It was not a medically recognized disease; it was a mania for moving to California. And nowhere was it stronger than in Illinois and Missouri, themselves only recently settled and emerging from the raw frontier.

California promised much to ambitious Americans: limitless prime farmland practically free for the taking, healthy conditions, and a climate of perpetual spring. Or so people read in travelers' accounts in books and magazines and newspapers, and in letters back home from the little group of Americans who had already settled there. These letters were printed and reprinted in newspapers all around the country, not least in *The Sangamo Journal*, the local newspaper of Springfield, Illinois.

What did it matter that California lay two thousand miles away from the Mississippi Valley and that the way there led through deserts and mountains and lands where hostile Indian tribes still held sway? Americans were a restless people, forever moving on to something newer and better, just as their forefathers had done since the nation's beginnings. Neither distance nor obstacles discouraged them; they were sure they could conquer both.

And what difference did it make that California belonged to Mexico? Most people who thought about it at all figured that Americans had a natural right to take all the land they could get. A hundred politicians had boomed this message at them in florid speeches in Congress, duly reported to their constituents. Was it not the Manifest Destiny of the United States—part of God's master plan for mankind—to expand from sea to sea? And who could doubt that once the Mexican residents of California saw the superiority of the American way of life they would clamor to become Americans themselves? If those benighted people failed to grasp that wonderful opportunity, well, there was always the example of Texas, which the U.S. Congress had just annexed after a long and acrimonious controversy.

And so, in the steaming summers and raw winters of the Midwest, people read and talked and dreamed of California, that fabled land on the far-off shore of the mighty Pacific Ocean. And among those readers were George and Jacob Donner and their good friend James Frazier Reed.

Mostly, it was people in their twenties and thirties who heeded the siren call of California. Some sought a better life for themselves and their families. Many had lost their money and homes in the business depressions that periodically swept the country, and hoped for a fresh start. Some honest souls hoped to make enough money to pay off their creditors. A surprising number of "movers" were invalids who thought their health would improve with a change in climate. And there were some who went simply for the adventure, as a well-to-do Englishman might make the Grand Tour of Europe.

George Donner was one of the last people one might expect to pick up and emigrate to California. For one thing, he was sixty-two years old, an old man by the criteria of his time. At his age, most men were getting ready to retire to the rocking chair and turn over the hard work of the farm to their sons or their daughters' husbands. For another, George was a successful man: a notably prosperous farmer, beloved in his community, and a respected member of his church. People called him "Uncle George," a country way of showing affection and respect.

Almost anyone might have thought that Uncle George had had his fill of change and traveling. Born in North Carolina just after the Revolutionary War, he had been taken to Kentucky and then Indiana by his parents. As a young man George had moved to the Springfield area; in middle life he moved to Texas for a year or two; then returned to his old farm at Springfield. By any reasonable yardstick, Uncle George should have stayed quietly at home on his farm to enjoy his sunset years, surrounded by his large and loving family. Yet here he was preparing to emigrate across half a continent to a strange country.

His brother Jacob, "Uncle Jake," was three years older. He had followed George on all his moves—George was always the one who got things rolling; Jake followed along.

Both Donner brothers were gentle, kindhearted men. Friends and acquaintances agreed that they really seemed to get pleasure from helping people. The brothers were of Pennsylvania German stock—their great-grandfather (who spelled his name Dohner) had come to Pennsylvania in about 1700.

George, still vigorous and black-haired, had been married three times. This was not at all unusual for his day, for both women and men often died young in accidents or of diseases that the doctors had no idea how to treat. Women bore the added and constant risk of death in childbirth or its complications. It often happened that people married four or five times in a lifetime.

George's third and present wife was named Tamsen, a form of Thomasine. She came from Massachusetts by way of South Carolina. A small, slight woman, barely five feet tall, Tamsen Donner had an apparently inexhaustible supply of energy and determination. There seemed to be nothing she could not do if she set her keen, inquiring mind to it. She was a born organizer and a voracious reader—it was she who had organized the local reading society that met weekly at George's comfortable farmhouse, an innocent and respectable activity that was to have fateful consequences.

Tamsen had been married once before, to a South Carolina farmer named Tully Dozier. They lived happily on his farm until an epidemic carried off both her husband and their baby son; in the aftermath Tamsen had a miscarriage. After these tragedies, she supported herself for several years by teaching school, then came north to visit a brother who had settled in Sugar Creek, Illinois, about a day's journey from Springfield. There she met the twice-widowed George Donner and in 1839 they were married. Despite the seventeen-year difference in their ages, the marriage was happy. By the time they set out for California they had three children, all girls: six-year-old Frances; four-year-old Georgia, frail and sickly; and Eliza, a toddler of three. By his first wife George had five children, now all grown and independent; by his second wife he had two daughters, Elitha, fourteen, and Leanna, twelve. Tamsen herself was forty-five.

Jacob Donner lived near George with his second wife, Elizabeth, whom everyone called Betsy. Jacob's first wife had died young, leaving no children, but with Betsy he had five young children, ranging from eight to two or three. There were also two stepsons, Solomon and William Hook, from Betsy's first marriage. Less energetic than George, Jacob had been in bad health for years.

George Donner's farm lay about three and a half miles outside Springfield, but George and Tamsen had many friends in town. One of their closest friends was a well-to-do local businessman named James Frazier Reed. It was an unusual sort of friendship, for Reed was almost young enough to have been George's son, and the two men were very different in temperament. Where George was gentle and easygoing, Reed was aggressive and hard-driving. A shrewd entrepreneur, Reed was intelligent, imaginative, a fluent talker, and ambitious. Although a natural leader, he had qualities that would make enemies for him at a time when he desperately needed friends. He was hot-tempered, imperious, opinionated, and impatient. But then, Reed was no ordinary Illinoian, and decidedly no common man.

Born in the north of Ireland in 1800, he was descended from Polish aristocrats—his father's family had fled Poland a generation earlier when that nation was divided up among its more powerful neighbors. On his mother's side he was Scotch-Irish, like Andrew Jackson, John Calhoun, and thousands of lesser-known folk who settled along the frontier and fought bloody feuds with the Indians and sometimes with each other.

Reed came to Virginia with his mother as a young child—his father must have died early. At age twenty he went off to make his fortune mining lead in northwestern Illinois, and in 1831 he came to Springfield. There he settled down to the life of a merchant and businessman. In time, he had a sawmill, a shingle factory, and a starch factory. He was also active in politics as an ardent Democrat.

Still a bachelor in his early thirties, Reed interrupted his business career to enlist in the Black Hawk War in 1832. During this brief and inglorious episode in American history, which occurred when a group of Indians tried to reclaim some land in Illinois from an illegal land grab by greedy white squatters, Reed never came near an Indian. However, he made a good and useful friend, a rising young lawyer named Abraham Lincoln, who served in Reed's company and ate in the same mess.

After the war, Reed courted and wed a young widow named Margaret Keyes Backenstoe, whose family were among the leading citizens of Springfield. Twenty-year-old Margaret had a baby daughter, Virginia, by her late husband. Reed always considered Virginia as his own child; she, in turn, loved him as her own father and always called herself Virginia Reed. James and Margaret had other children: Martha (usually called Patty), aged eight; little Jimmy, aged five; and Tommy, aged three.

Mrs. Reed, born and raised as a Virginia aristocrat, was a semi-invalid, suffering from chronic headaches. Nevertheless, Margaret Reed would show great courage and resourcefulness when disaster struck the family.

Here, then, was the core of the Donner Party: no horny-handed pioneers, but families of wealth and some refinement, definitely ranked among the upper stratum of Springfield's small society. To better understand the kind of people they were, let us take a quick look at the community they were leaving.

♦

The Black Hawk War

In 1829 the Sauk-and-Fox Indians moved from their ancestral lands in Illinois to escape the harassment by white settlers, settling across the Mississippi River in Iowa. White squatters, mostly Indian-hating Kentuckians, moved into the vacated Indian lands in violation of federal treaty obligations. In 1832 an aged chieftain, Black Hawk, confident that the whites would treat him justly once they heard his cause, led a thousand members of his tribe back across the Mississippi from their refuge in Iowa.

Black Hawk was mistaken in his faith in the squatters' sense of fairness. Far from returning the land, they greeted him with ugly threats, then panicked and screamed for the State Guard to come and defend them.

Many men who had been too young to fight in the War of 1812 rushed to join up, eager for a chance to win glory in battle and parade in splendid uniforms. Many surely welcomed the opportunity to escape the boredom and drudgery of life on the family farm.

Black Hawk quickly saw that his cause was hopeless and tried to surrender. The whites opened fire on his truce party. With fewer than 400 warriors (the rest of his band were women and children), Black Hawk took to the woods and launched occasional raids to frighten off the whites. In all, about 200 were killed on each side. At summer's end, a large force of the State Guard trapped the exhausted remnants of Black Hawk's band and slaughtered all but about 150 of them. Except for an occasional skirmish, the gallant volunteers spent most of their time lolling about camp, drilling, boasting, and electing new officers to replace those who displeased them by trying to enforce discipline or putting on other airs. Like Reed, many never came near an Indian. Reed, brave and honorable, must have been disgusted by the "war."

In 1846 Springfield was a boom town, as one would expect of a young state capital. A mere thirty years earlier, it had been merely a part of the rolling, wooded prairie of central Illinois. Not even an Indian village had stood there, although the Indians found it a good place to hunt. Eventually, white settlers found their way to the area and began farming the rich, black soil.

The first settlers were mostly of the rootless frontier type who could not get on in a settled community. Usually brave, tough, and resourceful, they did not like regular work or civilized ways. Frontier folk had little use for education and even less for such sissified refinements as government and law. They felt the proper way to settle a quarrel (and they quarreled frequently) was with fists and teeth; if really aggravated, they went for knife and gun.

These squatters, as they were called, would take possession of a piece of land without bothering with the legal niceties of purchase, clear off some of the trees, and build a crude log cabin. The cabin was crude because the squatter did not intend to live there permanently, and what was the use of building a proper house if you weren't going to stay there anyway? In the clearings the squatters planted an acre or two of corn and a vegetable patch that was left for the women and children to tend. The men spent most of their time hunting and fishing.

Frontiersmen did not appreciate close neighbors. They had a saying that when you could see the chimney smoke from the next cabin it was time to move on. And so, when a serious farmer showed up, the squatter would sell him the land and move west with the frontier.

Real farmers followed the squatters into the rich Sangamon country, and soon flatboats laden with wheat, corn, butter, and other farm produce were floating down the shallow Sangamon River to the Illinois, into the Mississippi, and down to the great markets of St. Louis and New Orleans. In 1821 an enterprising Kentuckian named Iles put up a tavern-plus-general-store in a log house and began selling lots to later arrivals. In the same year the little settlement of Springfield was chosen as the seat of Sangamon County. Other merchants and craftsmen arrived to serve the needs of the farmers. Brick stores and office buildings sprang up in place of the old log huts. Springfield was fast losing its raw frontier character. The stores began to offer fine imported textiles and chinaware along with the homely necessities of daily life. Thanks to adroit politicking by Abraham Lincoln and the other state legislators from Sangamon County, Springfield was chosen as the state capital of Illinois in 1837.

By 1846 life was pretty pleasant in Springfield. The seasons came and went; the farmers raised corn and hogs and sheep and sold them for the best price they could get. Farm work was hard and still done mostly by hand, but the land was rich, and there was plenty of leisure time for hunting and fishing and visiting. For religious folk, the churches provided the comforting regularity of Sunday services and a chance to get together and socialize. Now and then an evangelist would add some excitement by holding a revival meeting, where emotionally overwrought people would confess their most secret sins, jerk uncontrollably, and babble in "unknown tongues."

Politics was another major source of entertainment. Political feelings ran deep and strong, and people supported their parties as today we might root for a favorite sports team. Newspapers belonged to one party or the other, and their political editorials, packed with passionate invective, sometimes took up more space than the news. Then there were such rousing political activities as mass rallies and torchlight parades with the marchers dressed in fancy uniforms.

Closely linked to politics and business were the Freemasons. Masonic lodge meetings provided a welcome diversion from daily drudgery. To the lure of companionship they added resplendent mystical regalia, impressive rituals, and mystery; their proceedings, cloaked in secrecy, were a source of envy to outsiders. Masons were also known for their obligation to help a fellow Mason in distress. The Masonic Lodge in any town or city was an elite organization. Ambitious men eagerly sought membership; it was a mark of distinction, of achievement. James Frazier Reed was a Mason.

There was plenty of cultural life in Springfield, too. During the winter—the slack season for farmers—there were lectures on religion, history, and especially science. There was a local band, and singing societies filled the air with melody. The Thespian Society (an amateur theatrical group) presented plays of high moral tone, and professional acting troupes occasionally visited Springfield for a week or two of highly dramatic performances. But the puritanical element in town, which believed that the theater and novels were sinful, prevented the establishment of a full-time theater. The blue-noses, however, were not powerful enough to suppress Tamsen Donner's reading society. One night a week, at George and Tamsen's home, the members took turns reading aloud from the latest novels, poetry, and nonfiction.

For at least a year before the Donners and Reeds pulled up

stakes and went West, the chief topic of interest at these weekly sessions had been California. Every scrap of information on California was eagerly read and studied. There were books by travelers and long, enthusiastic letters to the newspapers from Americans who had already settled in that far-off, fascinating fairyland. Most of all, the Donners and their friends studied the excellent *Topographical Report* written by dashing John Charles Frémont after his explorations in 1842, and *The Emigrant's Guide to Oregon and California*, by Lansford W. Hastings. The latter book, unfortunately, was their main source of information. Why this was unfortunate will become clear later in the story.

CHAPTER 2
A Promoter and His Puff

In view of their increasing population, accumulating wealth, and growing prosperity, I can not but believe, that the time is not distant, when those wild forests, trackless plains, untrodden valleys, and the unbounded ocean, will present one grand scene, of continuous improvements, universal enterprise, and unparalleled commerce.
— Lansford W. Hastings, *The Emigrant's Guide
to Oregon and California*, p.151

Mr. Lansford Warren Hastings was a young lawyer from Ohio who had himself made the overland trek to California and had grand ideas of enriching himself by land speculation. He seems also to have dreamed of packing California with American settlers who would, sooner or later, revolt against Mexico, as the Texans had done ten years earlier. At that crucial point, waiting on the scene would be the charming, popular, clever Mr. Hastings, an obvious choice for president of the new republic. Of course, to accomplish either of these objectives he first had to entice Americans to California; so in his guidebook he described Oregon as a dreary domain where it never stopped raining, while California shimmered forth as an earthly paradise.

Listen to Hastings's description of California:

"The climate of the Western section [of California] is that of perpetual spring, having no excess of heat or of cold, it is the most uniform and delightful. Even in the months of December and January, vegetation is in full bloom, and all nature wears a most cheering and enlivening aspect . . . you may here enjoy perennial spring, or eternal winter at your option."

How this must have appealed to people who endured the hot, steamy summers and cold, raw winters of central Illinois!

"No fires are required, at any season of the year," continued Hastings's seductive description, "in parlors, offices or shops, hence fuel is never required, for other than culinary purposes." To farmers and their sons, that meant—almost—an end to the tedious, constant chore of cutting, splitting, and stacking firewood, and carrying it into the house even in the worst of rain or snow.

Furthermore, Hastings went on, many kinds of vegetables could be planted and harvested at any and every season of the year. Several kinds of grain yielded two crops annually. And such crops! Hastings spoke in the most factual way of oats six feet tall, with stalks half an inch thick, that yielded seventy bushels to the acre with very little effort on the farmer's part. This agricultural richness by no means exhausted California's resources. The mountains were covered with valuable timber, and there were reports of gold and silver ore—this four years before gold was actually found in the tailrace of Sutter's mill.

Rain hardly ever fell in California (by which Hastings meant the great central valley), and sickness was almost unknown. This in itself was a powerful lure to Americans in those days before modern medicine. Perhaps in that beneficent climate old Uncle Jake Donner's health would return, Mrs. Reed's never-ending headaches would cease, and frail little Georgia Donner would grow to be a healthy young woman instead of dying young.[1]

There was more in Hastings's book than a sales pitch for California. The reader could follow Hastings step by step on his adventurous journey across the mountains in 1842. There was dramatic suspense, as when Hastings, captured by a party of Sioux, talked his way to freedom with the aid of an English-speaking halfbreed. There were thrilling battles with Indians, with the whites emerging victorious. Readers shared the excitement of the buffalo hunt, wept with Hastings at the tragic death of a young blacksmith in a gunshot accident, and marveled with him at such strange sights as the great monolith of Independence Rock, rising like a monument from the undulating prairie, and the majestic mountains of the West.

But Hastings also packed his book with practical advice for emigrants. He told them how much food to take: 200 pounds of flour per person, 150 pounds of bacon, 10 pounds of coffee, 20 of sugar, and 10 of salt. Children would eat as much as adults on the prairie, said Hastings; so don't skimp on their rations. He advised against relying on the buffalo herds for fresh meat; instead, he counseled, drive some beef steers along with you and eat them as you go. Each traveler should be equipped with a good rifle, with at least 5 pounds of powder and 20 pounds of lead to make bullets. If possible, he should also take a pair of revolvers, which were unsurpassed for the close-range work of shooting buffalo from horseback. The rifles were better for shooting marauding Indians.

"Travel light" was another bit of sound advice, for it was vital not to overburden the teams that pulled the wagons. Extra weight also increased the chances of a wagon's bogging down at a river crossing or snapping an axle in a pothole. The wagons themselves should be sturdy and in good condition, and should be thoroughly inspected and repaired before beginning the overland journey. There were no wheelwrights or wagonmakers' shops on the Great Plains.

The teams that pulled the wagons, Hastings counseled, should be oxen, not horses. Oxen could live free of charge on grass along the way, while horses would soon break down, exhausted, if not fed costly grain. And you couldn't take enough grain to feed a team of four draft horses all the way from Independence, Missouri, to California, even if your wagon carried nothing else at all. This was unfortunate, for horses were considerably faster than oxen, which plodded along at two or three miles an hour, about as fast as a man could walk if he weren't in any particular hurry. On the other hand, said Hastings, the very slowness of the oxen made them less liable to be stolen by the Indians.

Hastings also listed the kind of tools and equipment that an emigrating family would need, plus the sorts of goods they should take for trading with the Indians along the way. He described the management of a wagon train and gave instructions for making an easily defensible camp. Furthermore, he furnished character sketches of the various Indian tribes a traveler might meet between Missouri and California, and offered advice on how to deal with each of them.

Most of Hastings's trail information was sound. He had learned it either from personal experience on the trail or from seasoned trappers familiar with the country. Indeed, he had even been a temporary leader of his own wagon train in 1842. Of course, in the old frontier tradition of storytelling, he hadn't been above throwing in a few tall tales of his own, such as a description of hunters capturing buffalo calves and driving them tamely into camp. These lapses his readers might well have pardoned for the entertainment they afforded.

There was one crucial point, however, on which Mr. Hastings, the bright and promising young lawyer, departed from fact and truth. He told of a newly explored trail south of the Great Salt Lake that was much shorter than the established trail and offered much easier going for wagons. The fact was that Hastings had made the whole thing up. He had probably based his statement on a careless misreading of Frémont's report of his explorations, for he had never traveled this trail himself and knew nothing about it at the time he wrote his guidebook. But this casual piece of dishonesty was to lead eighty-seven people into disaster.

But no one in the Donner family was thinking such gloomy thoughts when the Donners left home on April 15, 1846.[2] They had been preparing for the journey for months. Way back in September 1845 George Donner had put his farm up for sale: 240 acres with 80 acres cleared and cultivated, an orchard with bearing trees (peach,

---

The most direct route, for the California emigrants, would be to leave the Oregon route, about two hundred miles east from Fort Hall; thence bearing west southwest, to the Salt Lake; and thence continuing down to the bay of St. Francisco, by the route just described.[Lansford W. Hastings, *The Emigrant's Guide to Oregon and California,* pp. 137–138]

pear, and apple), a good house with two brick chimneys, a first-rate well of

water, and 80 acres of good timber. George had some trouble selling this desirable piece of property because Illinois had been suffering from a long business depression, and few people had much money to spend.

But the plans went on anyway. Tamsen spent the fall and winter sewing clothes for the trip. She also laid in apparatus for preserving botanical specimens (she was a keen amateur botanist) and school supplies, for she planned to start a young ladies' seminary in California. To this end she also packed ample quantities of books, watercolors, oil paints, and materials for women's handiwork, for painting and fine sewing were two accomplishments that every well-bred young lady was expected to master.

In late March 1846 George Donner placed an advertisement in *The Sangamo Journal.* "WESTWARD HO! FOR OREGON AND CALIFORNIA," it declared in capital letters. "Who wants to go to California without costing them anything? As many as eight young men, of good character, who can drive an ox team, will be accommodated by gentlemen who will leave this vicinity about the first of April. Come boys! You can have as much land as you want without costing you any thing. The government of California gives large tracts of land to persons who have to move there. . . ."

Hiring on as a teamster or handyman to do the tedious camp chores was about the only way a poor man could get to California, for it took a good deal of money to buy wagons, teams, and supplies. But somehow the advertisement must have lacked appeal, because George and Jacob ended up with only four teamsters between them. Ox driving was not a popular job. For starters, the driver did not ride on the wagon as he would with horses. Instead, he plodded along beside the leading yoke of oxen in the dust or mud, guiding them with shouts of "Gee!" for the right and "Huoy!" for the left, reinforced with sharp cracks of the long whip he always carried. Evidently the thought of a two-thousand-mile slog was not alluring to the adventurous sort of youth who might want to pick up and head west.

During the last few weeks the tasks of preparing for the trip were interrupted frequently by friends and relatives dropping in for a last-minute visit. But George Donner's three big wagons, specially built for the journey, stood ready at dawn on April 15 when the family roused itself for an early start. It was an impressive little expedition in itself. The oxen were young and strong, well trained, and fast walkers, and there were three spare yoke of oxen for emergencies. (A yoke was a pair of oxen, so called because they were yoked together for work.) There were cows to provide milk and fresh butter along the way, plus a few young beef cattle, five saddle horses, and a good watchdog. Saddle horses could manage quite well on grass alone as long as they were not ridden too much, and they were useful for hunting on the plains, for scouting the country ahead, and for delivering messages.

The first wagon was crammed with merchandise for trading, as Hastings had advised. For the Indians there were bolts of cheap cotton prints, red and yellow flannels, handkerchiefs with colorful borders, glass beads, necklaces, brass rings, pocket mirrors, and other knickknacks dear to the simple hearts of the aborigines. For the more sophisticated Spaniards of California, there were laces, muslins, silks, satins, and other fine fabrics, which George and Tamsen planned to exchange for land. There were also the things the family would not need until they reached California: farm equipment, seeds, furniture, and Tamsen's school supplies.

The second wagon held clothing, tools, camping gear, and ample provisions. Uncle George had sat down with *The Emigrant's Guide* and calculated how much food his family and the hired hands would need, not only for the journey but also for their first few weeks in California.

The third wagon was the family home-on-wheels. Comfortably fitted out, it carried feed boxes on the end for the two favorite saddle horses. It also carried $10,000 in cash, sewn into a quilt. Beyond this, George and Tamsen each carried a large sum (how much is not known) in a money belt.

The first two wagons left promptly after sunup. The family wagon, however, did not get away until almost noon, as friends kept coming by for a final, tearful farewell. At last all the good-byes were said, and the last pieces of baggage stowed on board. The children, neat in their new traveling outfits of linsey-woolsey, climbed up. As the wagon rolled off , they looked back for a last glimpse of the comfortable farmhouse on its little rise.

Heading west, they rumbled through Springfield, past the imposing bulk of the State House, which was still unfinished after nine years. A few blocks beyond, on the outskirts of the town, they halted and made an early camp for the night. Uncle Jake, with his three wagons, was already at the rendezvous, as was James Frazier Reed with his own three.

Hard times still gripped Illinois, but you would never have known it to look at the Reed outfit. All three of the Reed wagons were custom-built, and the family wagon was a marvel of traveling luxury. It was a double-decker, with comfortable spring seats on the lower level and regular bunks on the upper level, much like a modern camper. There was even a little sheet-iron stove for the chilly nights they expected to encounter in the mountains. For safety, the stovepipe ran up through the canvas top of the wagon through a tin plate that shielded the cloth from the heat. In contrast, ordinary folk slept in tents. Those who could not afford a tent slept in a blanket roll on the ground; when it rained (which it often did on the plains), they huddled in the wagon on top of the load. However, James Frazier Reed was not an ordinary man, and he didn't mind if people knew it.

Nor did the Reed family have to scramble into their wagon over the tailgate. They entered graciously by a door with folding steps on one side of the family home-on-wheels, just like a stagecoach. Opposite the door hung a five-foot mirror, a gift to Margaret Reed from her women friends, "so that she would not forget her good looks on the plains." In her memoirs, decades later, Virginia Reed called the ponderous, top-heavy wagon "The Pioneer Palace Car." It took eight oxen to pull it.

In the Reed family baggage were a heavy iron cookstove for California (Hastings had warned against taking even so much as an extra frying pan because of the weight), fine wines, and a library of the books that respectable families were expected to read.

Reed wished the people of California to know that he was a man of some distinction, so with him he took all his Masonic regalia—he held the high rank of master Mason—and a letter of introduction signed by both his own congressman and the governor of Illinois.

The letter testified to his admirable qualities as a citizen and a businessman.

Reed had hoped that his good friend Abraham Lincoln would stop by his house to say good-bye, but the lanky lawyer was handling a case in a distant court and could not come. Mrs. Lincoln and their eldest son, Robert, did come, however.

The three families settled down by their campfire for a social hour. Hardly had they made themselves comfortable than they were startled by the sound of clattering hooves. Eight men on horseback galloped up to the campfire and flung themselves from their panting mounts. Bandits? Hooligans? No—they were all members of the Reading Society who had come for a last reunion. They stayed long after dark, chatting with the departing friends they might never see again. Not that they were worried about the perils of the trip —had not Hastings assured his readers that they were perfectly safe as long as they followed his instructions? But no one made the four-month journey to or from California just for a social visit.

The next morning the caravan started off in earnest. Traveling with Reed was his aged mother-in-law, Sarah Keyes. Grandma Keyes was seventy years old and in bad health. Her doctor had given her only a few months to live. But she insisted on making the trip, for she wanted desperately to see her son Caden, who had gone to California with a herd of cattle the year before. Caden, unhappy in California, had written that he planned to start back to the States in the spring of '46.[3] They expected to meet him on the trail.

The hired hands completed the party. Working for the Donner brothers were two local young men, Noah James and Samuel Shoemaker; Hiram Miller, a blacksmith; and an English gunsmith, John Denton. Reed's chief driver was Milford Elliott, who had worked in Reed's sawmill and was devoted to the family. Everybody called him Milt. James Smith and Walter Herron helped with the driving. Then there was the Reeds' hired girl, Eliza Williams, who was fat, deaf, and possibly retarded. Her younger brother, Baylis, came along as handyman.

The nine wagons rolled leisurely across Illinois and Missouri (under good conditions you could count on oxen making ten to twelve miles a day—more would tire them). They reached Independence,

Missouri, on May 10. This was a little late to get started across the plains: the favored date was May 1, or even earlier, if possible, for timing was very important to a successful crossing. The idea was to leave as early as possible, so that you could get a head start on the other emigrants and your animals would have first chance at the grass. Late in the season, the chances were that other emigrants' teams would have eaten it down to the ground, and you would have to make wide, time-wasting detours to find pasturage.

It was also crucial to reach the California mountains before the dreaded snow fell. And you had to make allowances for flooded rivers, broken axles, and other mishaps that almost inevitably caused delays. Experts said that September was the last safe month to cross the Sierras, although with luck you might make it across in October.

On the other hand, if you started too early, the prairie would still be wet and marshy from the spring thaws, and your wagons would almost certainly bog down. And pasturage would be scanty, for the grass had not yet started to grow.

In any case, most emigrants stayed over at Independence for several days to check over their wagons and get them repaired if needed, replenish their supplies, and trade animals. Some arrived by steamboat and bought their entire outfits at Independence.

CHAPTER NOTES

1.   The Sangamon country was known as an unhealthy place. Each fall the ague, a type of malaria, broke out, striking most of the population with chills, shakes, fevers, and aches. Other diseases flourished, too. Invalids dosed themselves with quinine and horrid chemicals or with largely ineffectual herbal remedies, and dulled their aches and pains with whiskey and opiates. To people facing these realities, California seemed especially attractive.

2.   Some historians argue that the date was really April 14, while others contend it was the sixteenth. Eliza Donner, who was only three years old at the time of departure, recalled it years later as April 15.

3.   Robert Caden Keyes was a roving, restless, perpetually dissatisfied ne'er-do-well. He wrote home that California had no water or timber, that the natives were dishonest, and that he was lumps all over from flea bites. Obviously Reed did not take these complaints seriously. Surprisingly, Caden eventually settled in California, buckled down to work, and made a success of himself.

CHAPTER 3

Farewell to the States

All persons were remarkably cheerful and happy. Many were almost boisterous in their mirth. We were nearly all strangers, and there was manifestly an effort on the part of each, to make the most favorable impression he could upon every one.

—Jessy Quinn Thornton, *Oregon and California in 1848, p. 21*

Today Independence, Missouri, is hardly more than a suburb of Kansas City. In 1846, however, Kansas City was a mere village, and Independence was the last bridgehead of civilization on the great road to the West. Located a few miles east of today's Missouri-Kansas line and a few miles south of the Missouri River, it was a frontier metropolis where all kinds of people met and mingled.

There were Mexican and New Mexican muleteers, resplendent in blue jackets with brass buttons, conical black hats with a red band, and white duck pantaloons; shabbily dressed Indians on their sturdy ponies; skin-clad American and French-Canadian trappers from the Rockies; and the bold Santa Fe traders who took American goods to the Mexicans of Santa Fe and brought home silver coins, gold dust, and fine Spanish mules in exchange. But above all there were the emigrants, by the hundreds and thousands. And there were the resident merchants and craftsmen who made a good living by taking care of the assorted needs of all.

In 1846 westbound Americans did not call themselves "pioneers." They were *movers* or *emigrants,* for they were emigrating from their homes to a new country. Tamsen Donner wrote to her sister that about seven thousand wagons full of emigrants were reckoned to be leaving Independence for Oregon and California that May.

The Donners and Reeds did not stay long in Independence. They had heard that a large company of wagons (they were called wagon companies then, not wagon trains) was waiting for latecomers on Wakarusa Creek in Kansas, about two and a half days west of Independence. On May 12 the Donner-Reed contingent were on their way to the rendezvous, for they did not want to miss their chance of joining the wagon company. Experience had shown that numbers gave safety against hostile Indians. And there were more helping hands in difficult situations, such as a tricky river crossing.

The company had already left the Wakarusa when the Donners and Reeds arrived, but they caught up with it at Soldier Creek, in Indian territory, on May 19. Reed hastily washed off the mud of the trail, shaved, and called upon the commander of the company, Colonel William H. Russell, to request admission for his party. Some wagon companies were quite choosy about whom they would allow to travel with them. This was a reasonable precaution: Travelers did not want drunkards, thieves, or anyone who would stir up trouble with the Indians. Armed with his letter of recommendation from the governor of Illinois, Reed was welcomed by Russell as a fellow gentleman, the Donners likewise.

Russell was a tall, amiable, talkative fellow, rather pompous, the very incarnation of a western politician. A native of Kentucky, he was drawn to politics at an early age and spent some years as secretary to Henry Clay, who was a master politician and one of the most powerful men in the U.S. Senate. Later Russell moved to Missouri and went into politics on his own. This was an age when political oratory was a top-ranking public entertainment, and Russell could speechify with

---

Frontier Political Humor

Behind the affable colonel's back, people told an irreverent story. It seems that the great man had been practicing a speech one evening by the edge of a woods, and during a pause heard the owls calling "Whoo! Whoo!" Russell, who was nearsighted but too vain to wear eyeglasses, could not make out who was querying his identity. He drew himself to his full height, swelled his mighty chest, and shouted back, "Colonel William H. Russell of Kentucky, a bosom friend of Henry Clay! That's who!" Ever afterward he was known as "Owl" Russell.

---

the best. His high-flown rhetoric, delivered in a booming giant's voice, brought him success, and he got himself appointed as U.S. marshal.

Russell was not the only dignitary in the company. There was Lillburn Boggs, a former governor of Missouri. During his term of office, Boggs had been instrumental in driving the Mormons from that state in a reign of terror. But that was eight years earlier, and Boggs had moved to Independence and gone into business outfitting the Santa Fe traders and the Rocky Mountain fur trappers. His wife died, and he married a granddaughter of the famous Daniel Boone. At the moment he was waiting for Boone's son Alphonso to join the company.

Another of the gentry was Jessy Quinn Thornton, a thirty-five-year-old lawyer from Quincy, Illinois. Virginia-born Thornton had studied law in London and practiced in Virginia and Missouri before moving to Illinois to get away from slavery. He was a friend of Lincoln's great rival, the rising politician Stephen A. Douglas, and of Senator Thomas Hart Benton of Missouri, the great champion of Manifest Destiny and the westward movement. Thornton also corresponded with the well-known New York newspaper editor Horace Greeley.

Thornton and his wife, Nancy—they had no children—were painfully refined and genteel. Both invalids, they were headed for Oregon in the hope that their health would improve. Both were energetic diary-keepers in spite of their illness, and they were keen observers. That was fortunate, for it is to Jessy Thornton that we owe the best and most complete contemporary report of what happened to the Donner Party.

Then there was Edwin Bryant, a Massachusetts-born journalist who had until recently edited a newspaper in Louisville, Kentucky. A bachelor, the forty-one-year-old Bryant was bound for California mainly for the adventure of the trip. Like a good journalist, Bryant wandered about the encampment talking to the emigrants and sizing them up. On the whole, he was favorably impressed.

Thornton, too, despite his genteel snobbishness, thought well of the group. In his diary he noted, "The majority were plain, honest, substantial, intelligent, enterprising, and virtuous. They were, indeed, far superior to those who usually settle a new country."

That evening Owl Russell took a census of the company for whose safety he was responsible. He counted 72 wagons, 130 men, 65 women, 125 children, 155 guns, mostly rifles, 104 pistols, 1,100 pounds of powder and 2,672 of lead, 69,420 pounds of flour, 40,200 pounds of bacon, and an estimated 710 head of cattle and horses.

The wagons, as Thornton reported, were mostly new, strong, and well painted. All of them had tops of sturdy canvas, some of them painted to make them more waterproof. Some of the wagontops bore the painted slogan "California"; others announced to the world that they were headed for Oregon.

Some of the Oregon wagons carried political slogans: "The whole or none" or "54° 40'." These referred to the still-simmering quarrel between the United States and Great Britain over the Oregon Territory, which both countries claimed. "Oregon" was the name for the huge area that lay between the Rocky Mountains and the Pacific Ocean, from the forty-second parallel of latitude on the south (the line that today marks the northern boundaries of California, Nevada, and part of Utah) and 54° 40' on the north (the southern tip of Alaska). Back in 1818 the United States and Britain had agreed to a joint occupation of the remote area. But now President Polk and his fellow expansionists were making ferocious noises about claiming all of it, by force if necessary.

Alarming rumors were flying around the wagon camp. The local Kanza Indians were said to be organizing to wipe out the emigrants!

Britain was egging on Mexico to fight the United States over the recent annexation of Texas! British officers were scouring the prairies to incite the Indians to attack wagon companies all along the trail! But worse than any of these imaginary dangers was the Mormon Scare.

Founded in upstate New York in 1830 by a young man named Joseph Smith, who saw strange visions and claimed to be instructed by angels, the Mormon faith had prospered and gained thousands of converts. The Mormons were hardworking, sober, and helpful to one another. But somehow they managed to arouse the hostility of their neighbors wherever they went. Their clannishness and outspoken claims of superiority to the "Gentiles," as they called all non-Mormons, angered many. As Mormon wealth and power grew, many "Gentiles" came to fear that the Mormons would push them out. There were rumors that Joseph plotted with his followers to establish a Mormon dictatorship.

From New York State the Mormons moved to Ohio, where a Gentile mob tarred and feathered Joseph and threatened him with worse. Next, guided by one of Joseph's visions, they settled in western Misssouri. In 1838 Governor Boggs called out the state militia against the Mormons. His orders declared: "The Mormons must be treated as enemies and must be exterminated and driven from the State."

Joseph led his beleaguered flock across the Mississippi to the Illinois town of Nauvoo. There he set up a tightly disciplined, church-ruled community, and once more the hardworking, thrifty Mormons prospered. But Joseph sold their votes to both political parties, and he made the further mistake of creating a well-armed private army. Once more anti-Mormon hysteria flamed up, fueled by high-handed actions on Joseph Smith's part. In a show of strength, Joseph mobilized his well-drilled private army, the Nauvoo Legion. The governor responded by calling out the State Guard. To avert a bloodbath, Joseph surrendered to the authorities and was jailed at Carthage, Illinois. There, on June 27, 1844, a mob murdered Joseph Smith and his brother Hyrum.

Brigham Young, Joseph's successor, realized that his people's safety depended on moving them out of reach of the Gentiles. He planned to lead them to a safe refuge in the West. But the Mormons were not moving fast enough to suit the Illinoians, and vigilante groups committed atrocities against them almost daily to hasten their departure. The pressure was too great, and the Mormons began their exodus from Nauvoo in the dead of winter—February 1846—amid great suffering.

Now, in May, it was rumored that a large army of heavily armed Mormons were ready and waiting to avenge themselves on their persecutors. This was not true, but it gave the emigrants some very nervous moments, particularly former governor Lillburn Boggs. Indeed, they were more afraid of the Mormons than of all the Indian tribes together.

But on this evening before departure, the members of Russell's company forgot their worries. There was a holiday atmosphere. Some folks were almost boisterous in their good humor and excitement. Everyone was on his best behavior, trying to make a good impression on the strangers with whom he would be traveling for the next four months.

> Emigrants should, invariably, arrive at Independence, Mo., on, or before, the fifteenth day of April, so as to be in readiness, to enter upon their journey, on, or before, the first day of May, after which time, they should never start, if it can, possibly, be avoided. [Lansford W. Hastings, *The Emigrant's Guide to Oregon and California,* p.147]

On May 16 the company moved out by sections. They began the routine they would follow each day, at least until discipline and cooperation broke down.

At sunup or thereabouts a bugle would blow to arouse the camp. The men and boys on night herding duty would bring in the cattle and horses, which had been grazing on the prairie near the wagons. (When Indian raids were expected, the stock were driven inside the wagon circle, but this was an emergency measure only.) The women made their cooking fires and prepared breakfast, consisting usually of bread and bacon washed down with strong coffee.

After the meal, the men took down the tents and stowed them in the wagons while the women packed the cooking utensils. Men and boys hurried about the encampment catching their oxen and yoking them to the wagons. This could be a vexatious, time-consuming procedure. The oxen resented the whole business and showed their displeasure by trying to kick, gore, or step on the feet of their drivers. The drivers retaliated by beating the oxen over the head with a whip handle or jabbing them viciously in the ribs. On the other hand, many emigrants were fond of their oxen and treated them like pets. These kind masters had much less trouble.

Once the oxen were yoked up, the wagons got under way. The whole wagon company was supposed to be rolling by six or seven o'clock to take advantage of the morning coolness and to make a good distance before the noon halt. At nooning, the wagons would draw up in a neat column while the people ate and the animals rested and grazed. Nooning was supposed to take an hour but usually lasted longer. The oxen were yoked up again, and the train rolled on for another four or five hours until the captain signaled a halt for the night.

In companies that had an experienced "pilot," or guide, the guide would estimate the distance the company could make each day and select the campsite in advance. In practice, this did not always work, nor did every company have a guide. The Donners and Reeds had to rely on the judgment of Russell, who was a responsible captain but as new on the trail as everyone else.

At the evening halt, the wagons were drawn up in a circle, just as they are in Western movies, and chained together front to rear. This formed a fortification that Indians were seldom foolhardy enough to attack, although they often rode around it putting on a threatening performance. When Indians did attack a wagon company—which happened rarely at this period—it was usually when the wagons were on the move and hard to defend. However, Indians often did pick off careless emigrants who strayed away from the company, and when the opportunity offered itself they stole horses and stampeded oxen for the fun of it. Part of the Plains Indian way of life was raiding other tribes, and they behaved toward the white man's tribe as they did toward each other.

With the wagon circle formed, the captain assigned guard duty for the night, the animals were turned out to graze under guard, and the women cooked dinner. After dinner there would be visiting back and forth among the campfires, and the young people might sneak in some courting under the brilliant prairie stars. Perhaps someone would bring out a mouth organ or a violin, and there would be a dance. But the merriment seldom lasted late. People were tired, and another day's wearisome journey lay ahead. So the camp slumbered, except for those who had been assigned to guard duty.

In theory the captain determined every move of the wagon company. He chose the line of march and called the halts. He assigned each wagon its place in the column. This was supposed to go by rotation so that everyone got his turn at the head of the line and didn't have to breathe dust all day. The duties of gathering wood and water were also doled out by the captain, as were the two or three shifts of night guard.

In theory, again, the captain was supreme. In practice, he had little power. Freeborn Americans did not like to take orders, even from their own freely elected leaders. And since the captain was freely elected, he could be freely deposed at any time—and frequently was. If a captain got anything done at all, it was through persuasion, not authority. So the emigrants obeyed the captain when it suited them and disregarded him otherwise.

A word here about the wagons: They were not the heavy, boatlike Conestogas of popular lore. Conestogas were developed as heavy-duty freight wagons for the steep, rocky roads of eastern Pennsylvania. They did their job admirably on the hard roads of the East, but they were too heavy, too unwieldy for the soft ground of the plains. Most emigrants used variants of the standard flat-bottomed farm wagon, about ten feet long and three and a half feet wide. They were nicknamed "prairie schooners" by some fanciful emigrant who saw the white tops of a far-off wagon column moving over the green prairie with its billowing dips and rises, and likened them to a fleet of white-sailed ships at sea.

The trail to California ran west from Independence for about forty miles, through the country of the transplanted Shawnee Indians, then turned northwest, crossing Turkey Creek, Mound Creek, and Wakarusa Creek, and following the Kansas River for several days. The first few weeks on the trail were like an extended picnic. The children ran freely through the groves near the encampments, picking wild berries. People made new friends among their fellow travelers. Tamsen Donner and others like her collected wildflowers that amazed them with their beauty and rich scents. The men went hunting and brought back lots of fresh meat; a little group found a bee tree and returned laden with honeycomb. One of the wives discovered patches of wild peas and made an excellent pickle of them.

Reed rode off every day on his beautiful gray racing mare Glaucus, to explore the surrounding country. Virginia rode beside him on Billy, her cream-colored pony, the envy of all the other children in the wagon company. Mrs. Reed, however, preferred to stay inside the comfortable family wagon. Reading and chatting with her littlest children, she could almost forget she was actually crossing the plains.

The trail now crossed the Kansas River, also called the Kaw. Here the wagons were ferried across by Kansas Indians whose village stood nearby. These Indians were wretchedly poor—their country had little game to hunt, and they did not seem to care much for farming either. Travelers believed that they lived mostly by begging and by filching goods from the passing wagons. Reed and Virginia explored the village, and Virginia later wrote back to a cousin in Springfield that "paw counted 20050 Indians." That was Virginia's way of writing 250.

A few more days brought them to the banks of the Big Blue River, which flows into the Kansas from the north. Heavy rains had flooded the river and made it impossible to cross. The whole company was forced to wait four days in a heavy downpour, which did not improve their dispositions.

As soon as the wagons halted, Grandma Keyes's health failed completely. She died on May 29 and was buried under a fine oak tree on the banks of the Big Blue. A big cottonwood tree was cut down to make planks for her coffin, and John Denton, the English gunsmith, carved a headstone. The Reverend Mr. Cornwall, a minister traveling with the company, conducted the funeral service, and the homemade coffin was lowered into the rich, black prairie soil. The young men covered it with sod and blanketed it with wildflowers.

By now the rain had stopped, and the next day the river was low enough to cross. But the Big Blue was still too deep to ford, and the men had to spend half the day cutting down big cottonwood trees to make a raft to ferry the wagons across. The raft consisted of two twenty-five-foot trunks, hollowed lengthwise to make a track for the wagon wheels. Cross timbers lashed to the trunks kept them the proper distance apart. The emigrants dubbed the crude craft *The Blue River Rover* and slowly hauled it back and forth across the current, with a rope at each end. But it took some time to get the knack of getting the wagons safely on and off the raft, and by darkness only nine wagons had made the crossing.

The following day, May 31, was a Sunday. All good Christians should have been spending the day in prayer and contemplation. The emigrants, however, devoted the Lord's Day to ferrying the rest of the wagons across the river. The oxen and horses were swum over, which they always balked at. The pious Mr. Thornton was shocked that his fellow travelers would desecrate the Sabbath by worldly labor—but he made sure that he got across the river himself.

A heavy rain began to fall again. Two ox-drivers quarreled on the riverbank and traded punches, then went for each other with their knives. Other emigrants, who had been watching the diverting incident, pulled the two men apart before serious damage was done. But this violence was a sign that something ugly was happening to the company. The spirit of goodwill, of cooperation, of loyalty to each other was eroding. From now on quarrels would become ever more frequent as people's tempers wore thin under the daily frictions and frustrations of crossing the plains.

The company began to split up into smaller groups, and not only because of quarrels. Those who had faster ox-teams pulled ahead of their slower-moving companions, often to be delayed themselves by some mishap like a strayed ox or an overturned wagon. Families passed and repassed each other dozens of times, sometimes camping together and sometimes with strangers.

Northward and westward the trail ran on beside the Little Blue River into what is now Nebraska, then across forty miles of prairie and a ridge of sandhills to the Platte River. Along the way it crossed many creeks. This was always a great bother, for the prairie creeks had high, steep banks, and it was difficult to get the wagons safely down them and back up on the far side. Some emigrant parties took the trouble to dig gently sloping ramps to and from the water. Others didn't want to take the time, but ended up taking at least as long while their wagons were inched down to the water with ropes and double teams of oxen strained to pull them up on the far side.

There were, of course, no bridges, nor was there enough timber to build them. Getting the wagons down the banks was only part of the trouble. Once at the water's edge, your team might balk and have to be forced in with yells, curses, and whip blows. As you groped your way across the streambed, you hoped that you wouldn't encounter a soft spot in which the wagon would stick or a pothole that would upset the wagon. When a wagon turned over in the water, it had to be unloaded completely so that you could right it with the help of other emigrants. Meanwhile, your load, which was thoroughly soaked, had to be carried to the far bank by hand and spread out to dry.

The Platte River was in those days also called the Nebraska. The name came from an Omaha Indian word, Ni-bthaska, which means "shallow river." Platte is French for "flat." Both names are good descriptions, for in those days the Platte was broad and shallow, and much of its course still runs through a broad, flat plain, Shifting sands choked its bed, and in late summer it shrank to a trickle. (Today dams on its upper reaches have turned much of the Platte into quiet, man-made lakes and stabilized its seasonal flow, but the emigrants who faced the river the way Nature made it called it a mile wide and an inch deep.) Reaching the Platte, 315 miles by trail from Independence, meant that you had completed the first stage of the journey. From now on you would be traveling through a new kind of country, a land of short grass, of sagebrush and cactus and alkali, and of ever-increasing aridity. If the wide-open, sweeping tall-grass prairies of eastern Kansas and Nebraska had seemed strange to folks used to the woods of Illinois and Missouri and the East, the country beyond the Platte would be even stranger and more difficult to cope with.

CHAPTER 4

Adventures in Buffalo Country

We saw this day a multitude of bison. . . . The dark, rolling masses, even in the distance, made a low, dull, rumbling sound, like an approaching earthquake. . . . Bison constitute the poetry and Indians the romance of a life upon these vast prairies.

—Jessy Quinn Thornton, *Oregon and California in 1848*

The Platte not only signaled the end of the first part of the journey; it also marked the beginning of buffalo country. Although the Indians complained to white men that the buffalo were getting scarce, they still numbered in the millions, and emigrant companies frequently encountered large herds. The wagon trail followed the sandy bottomland between the river on the north and the sandhills on the south, a level roadway up to two miles wide. Wood was now scarce, but buffalo chips—the dried excrement of the buffalo—were more than plentiful. The Indians had used them as fuel for centuries, and the emigrants found that they kindled quickly and held their heat surprisingly well. Tamsen Donner thought them as good as hickory coals.

To cook with buffalo chips, one dug a little trench in the ground, about three feet long, one foot wide, and eight inches deep, then filled it with nice, dry chips and started the fire with dry grass or weeds. The cooking vessel sat atop the trench. At every halt the children were sent out with gunnysacks to gather a fresh supply of this useful gift of the buffalo.

Despite the defection of his Oregon-bound contingent, which had been expelled for quarreling among themselves some two weeks earlier, Owl Russell got his company to the Platte in reasonably good shape, and by June 16 they were camped near the Forks of the Platte. Here the north and south branches of the Platte River join, marking another major landmark on the trail. The party stopped here for a few days to rest the teams, catch up on the laundry, and write letters.

There always seemed to be someone coming back East along the trail—trappers, disappointed settlers from Oregon, people whose business took them back to the States—and all of them were willing to carry letters as far as Independence, where they mailed them.

On this first day, Tamsen Donner wrote back to Springfield that the journey so far had been pleasant and that the Indians had not molested them. (This was in the heart of Pawnee country, and that summer the Pawnee were the most hostile and dangerous of all the tribes of the Plains.) Indeed, the Indians came frequently to visit the Donners, and that very morning a group of chiefs had dropped in at the Donner tent for breakfast. Tamsen found them very friendly.

Like others in the company, Tamsen could not get over the beauty of the prairies they had crossed in eastern Kansas and Nebraska, a rolling land of green grass and wildflowers and groves of trees along the streams. Ever practical, she noted that it would make excellent farmland.

She wrote also that she never would have believed they could have traveled so far without difficulty. This was not entirely true: Nearly seventy years later, Eliza recalled how she and her sister Georgia had nearly been crushed by the tumbling load when their wagon tipped over in a pothole. But perhaps Tamsen was simply exercising selective memory.

It was certainly not true for many of the emigrants, for diarrhea and chills and fever had plagued the company from the beginning. Bad hygiene at the campsites and greasy food undoubtedly played a role; so probably did drinking polluted water. The diarrhea would get worse as the emigrants progressed westward; the alkali-impregnated water they had to drink was a natural laxative. Even worse was the dust—black dust on the eastern prairies; white, alkaline dust from the Platte onwards. It billowed up in choking clouds, filling nose, mouth, lungs, ears, and hair. It irritated the eyes terribly, almost to the point of blindness. In his diary, Thornton reproached himself bitterly for not having bought a pair of goggles, tinted green against the glare, before he left the States. There they sold for $37\frac{1}{2}$ cents, but in the alkali country he would have given $50 for a pair. That was no trifling sum—in Independence it would have bought two yoke of oxen and a good deal of feed.

The wagons, too, had begun to show signs of stress. Their wood shrank in the dry air, and they became loose and rattly. The effects were worst on the wheels. A wooden wagon wheel was constructed of many parts, carefully fitted together and held in place by an iron tire around the rim. But the felloes (sections of the wooden wheel rim) and the spokes shrank away from the tires, and the wheels began to fall apart. For this there were two cures. One was to whittle wooden wedges and hammer them in between felloes and tires to take up the gaps, praying that they, too, would not shrink and fall out. The other, more reliable method was to jack up the wagon, remove the wheel, take off the tire, and cut a section out of it. Then the stranded emigrant built a hot fire to soften the iron, welded the cut ends of the tire together with hammer blows, and hoped he had measured accurately. If he were lucky, there was a blacksmith or wagonmaker among his fellow travelers whom he could hire to do this. Otherwise he had to do it himself, and do-it-yourselfers were just as prone to make mistakes then as now.

As the country grew rougher, wagon tongues and axles were apt to snap. Prudent emigrants carried a couple of spares slung beneath the wagon. Otherwise they had to scrounge wood to fashion a replacement, and this was not always possible. In that case, they had to abandon their wagon and rent space for their most essential belongings in someone else's.

James Reed also wrote home on June 16. Unlike Tamsen Donner, he paid no attention to the beauties of the countryside. The thing that captured his heart was the splendid hunting. His letter, to his brother-in-law, which was duly published in *The Sangamo Journal,* boasted of his success in slaughtering elk and buffalo only a short ride away from the camp.

News from the Exuberant Hunter

South Fork of the Nebraska
Ten Miles from the Crossings
Tuesday, June 16, 1846

. . . To-morrow we cross the river, and by our reckoning will be 200 miles from Fort Larimere, where we intend to stop and repair our waggon wheels; they are nearly all loose, and I am afraid we will have to stop sooner if there can be found wood suitable to heat the tire. There is no wood here, and our women and children are now out gathering "Buffalo chips" to burn in order to do the cooking. These "chips" burn well.

So far as I am concerned, my family affairs go on smoothly, and I have nothing to do but hunt, which I have done with great success. My first appearance on the wilds of the Nebraska as a hunter, was on the 12th inst., when I returned to camp with a splendid two year old Elk, the first and only one killed by the caravan as yet. I picked the Elk I killed, out of eight of the largest I ever beheld, and I do really believe there was one in the gang as large as the horse I rode. We have had two Buffalo killed. The men that killed them are considered the best buffalo hunters on the road—perfect "stars." Knowing the Glaucus could beat any horse on the Nebraska, I came to the conclusion that as far as buffalo killing was concerned, I could beat them. Accordingly yesterday I thought to try my luck. The old buffalo hunters and as many others as they would permit to be in their company, having left the camp for a hunt, Hiram Miller, myself, and two others, after due preparation, took up the line of march. Before we left, every thing in camp was talking that Mr.. so and so, had gone hunting, and we would have some choice buffalo meat. No one thought or spoke of the two Sucker hunters ["sucker" was a nick-name for Illinoians], and none but the two had asked to go with us. Going one or two miles west of the old hunters on the bluffs, and after riding about four miles, we saw a large herd of buffalo bulls. I went for choice young meat, which is the hardest to get, being fleeter and better wind—On we went towards them as cooly and calmly as the nature of the case would permit. And now, as perfectly green as I was I had to compete with old experienced hunters, and remove the stars from their brows, which was my greatest ambition, and in order too, that they might see that a Sucker had the best horse in the company, and the best and most daring horseman in the caravan. Closing upon a gang of ten or twelve bulls, the word was given, but among them there was none young enough for my taste to shoot, and upon seeing a drove on my right I dashed among them, with Craddock's pistol in hand—(a fine instrument for Buffalo hunters on the plains)—selected my victim and brought him tumbling to the ground, leaving my companions far behind. Advancing a little further, the plains appeared to be one living, moving mass of bulls, cows, and calves. The latter took my eye, and I again put spur to Glaucus and soon found myself among them, and for the time being defied by the bulls, who protected the cows and calves. Now I thought the time had arrived to make one desperate effort, which I did by reigning short up and dashing into them at right angles. With me it was an exciting time, being in the midst of a hundred head of buffalo alone, entirely out of sight of my companions. At last I succeeded in separating a calf from the drove, but soon there accompanied him three large bulls, and in a few minutes I separated two of them. Now having a bull that would weigh about 1200 lbs., and a fine large calf at full speed, I endeavored to part the calf from the bull without giving him Paddy's hint, but could not accomplish it. When I reined to the right where the calf was, the bull would immediately put himself between us. Finding I could not operate on decent terms, I gave him one of Craddock's which sent him reeling. And now for the calf without pistol being loaded. Time now was important—and I had to run up and down hill at full speed loading one of my pistols. At last I loaded and soon the chase ended.—Now I had two dead and a third mortally wounded and dying. After I had disposed of my calf I rode to a small mound a short distance off to see if Hiram and the others were in sight. I sat down, and while sitting I counted 597 buffalo within sight. After a while Miller and one of the others came up. We then got some water from a pond near by, which was thick with mud from the buffaloes tramping in it. Resting awhile the boys then wanted to kill a buffalo themselves. I pointed out to them a few old bulls about a mile distant. It was understood that I was not to join in the chase, and after accompanying the boys to the heights where I could witness the sport, they put out at full speed. They soon singled out a large bull, and I do not recollect of ever having laughed more than I did at the hunt the boys made. Their horses would chace well at a proper distance from the bull. As they approached he would come to a stand and turn for battle. The horses would then come to a halt, at a distance between the boys and the buffalo of about 40 yards. They would thus fire away at him, but to no effect. Seeing that they were getting tired of the sport and the bull again going away, I rode up and got permission to stop him if I could. I put spurs to Glaucus and after him I went at full speed. As I approached the bull turned around to the charge. Falling back and dashing toward him with a continued yell at the top of my lungs I got near enough to let drive one of my pistols. The ball took effect, having entered behind his shoulders and lodged in his lungs. I turned in my saddle as soon as I could to see if he had pursued me, as is often the case after being wounded. He was standing nearly in the place where he received the shot, bleeding at the nostrils, and in a few seconds dropped dead. I alighted and looped my bridle over one of his horns. This Glaucus objected to a little, but a few gentle words with a pat of my hand she stood quiet and smelled him until the boys came up. Their horses could not be got near him. Having rested, we commenced returning to the spot where I killed the last calf. A short distance off we saw another drove of calves. Again the chace was renewed, and soon I laid out another fine calf up on the plains. Securing as much of the meat of the calves as we could carry, we took up the line of march for the camp, leaving the balance for the wolves, which are very numerous. An hour or two's ride found us safely among our friends, the acknowledged hero of the day, and the most successful buffalo hunter on the route. Glaucus was closely examined by many to-day, and pronounced the finest nag in the caravan. Mrs. R. will accompany me in my next buffalo hunt, which is to come off in a few days. . . ."

Even while Reed was planning his hunt, tragedy had struck an-other family, in a company twenty-five miles ahead on the trail. Their nine-year-old boy had fallen beneath a wagon, and the wheels had run over his leg, breaking it both above and below the knee. It was a bad break; the bone protruded from the flesh in both places. The leg went without proper treatment for nine days, and gangrene set in. Either the leg must come off, or the boy must die.

In desperation, the boy's family sent a rider dashing back to fetch Edwin Bryant, who had studied medicine briefly before becoming a newspaperman. On this slender basis, and because he did his conscientious best for those who sought his help, Bryant's fame as a healer had spread among the emigrants both ahead and behind on the trail. But the Oregon-bound Thornton's camp lay nearer to the injured boy's, and the messenger begged him to come, convinced that anyone so well educated as lawyer Thornton must surely be able to perform surgery. Thornton rightly refused, but rode over to the other camp to offer what help he could.

What he saw there appalled him. The suffering boy with his festering limb was tied down to a packing case, and a French-Canadian drover who had once been a hospital attendant was sharpening butcher knives for the operation. Kind people had dipped into their own medicine chests and given the boy laudanum, a standard painkiller prepared from opium, but it had no effect. Thornton, with all the authority he could muster, directed the would-be surgeons to wait until Bryant arrived, which he did shortly.

Bryant quickly examined the boy and saw that he could not live. He told the mother to spare her son the agony of a useless operation and let him die in peace. But the frantic woman insisted on making the attempt.

The drover, apparently trying to save as much of the leg as possible but not knowing what he was doing, began to amputate below the knee. A bystander held camphor to the boy's nostrils to keep him from fainting—one wonders why—but this helpful person frequently neglected his duty in his eagerness to watch the operation.

With his sharp butcher's knife the drover cut into the flesh all around the injured limb. Pus gushed out, and it was clear that the leg must come off above the knee. The drover began again, tying a tourniquet around the boy's thigh so tightly that it cut into the swollen flesh. The knife once more sliced through skin and muscle; a borrowed carpenter's saw rasped through the bone. The drover tied off the arteries and began to close the wound with a flap of skin. Then the boy, who had endured his suffering bravely for an hour and a half, died.

In an incongruous aftermath, Thornton invited Bryant to dinner at his tent, where they found that Nancy Thornton had spread a white linen tablecloth on the grass and had roast antelope, stewed buffalo meat, and other delicacies in readiness. Friends dropped by, and the two men gradually recovered from the horror they had just witnessed. Then, toward nine o'clock, everyone gathered at the tent of a Mr. Lard to celebrate the wedding of his beautiful daughter Mary to Riley Septimus Mootrey.

Thornton, ever a guardian of propriety, could not find it in himself to approve of this hasty wedding on the trail. But he was relieved to note that the women were wearing their best dresses, and even the men had washed, shaved, and put on clean clothes. As a fiddler led a procession toward the bridal tent, the guests could see the faint light of torches in the distance. It was another procession, carrying the dead boy's body to a desert grave. Life and death, could mingle incongruously on the trail.

The wagons creaked onward through a country of sand and gravel, scant grass, and many rattlesnakes and lizards. On June 17 they reached the crossing of the South Platte at 2:00 P.M. Here the river was $1\frac{1}{2}$ miles wide, but the wagons had to cross the treacherous bottom at an angle, so that the real distance was 2 miles. The bottom was quicksand, and the instant a wagon stopped moving, it began to sink. Despite this difficulty, all the wagons were brought over by sunset, a feat so remarkable that it was thought worthy of general congratulation.

On they pushed, through a boring and depressing landscape of brown sagebrush, white alkali crusts, reptiles, and dust. A long drive of 22 miles without water brought them at last to the North Platte, where the exhausted oxen could drink and rest. Here the stored-up frustrations and ill temper of the company found a vent. Owl Russell was deposed by popular vote, and Lillburn Boggs was chosen as his successor. The company did allow Russell to save face by resigning on the plea that he was incapacitated by ague. All of Russell's lieutenants, of whom George Donner was one, resigned en masse. New people had their chance to lead—and to be disobeyed and blamed, in their turn, for everything that went wrong.

CHAPTER 5

A Mountain Man's Warning

The emigrant trade is a very important one to the mountain merchants and trappers. . . . In a trade, they have no consciences, taking all the "advantages;" but in a matter of hospitality or generosity they are open-handed. . . .
    —Edwin Bryant, *What I Saw in California,* p. 143

The country grew wilder and rougher as the Donners and Reeds and their chance companions proceeded up the North Platte. They entered a zone of badlands, vast clay beds in which erosion had cut deep, crisscrossing ravines. The bluffs that bordered the river valley were carved into fantastic formations such as Courthouse Rock, Chimney Rock, a tall, lone column rising from the plains and visible two or three days' journey away; and the mighty Scott's Bluffs, which bordered the valley for some twenty-eight miles. Named for an early trapper whose comrades left him there to die, Scott's Bluffs reminded the more literary members of the company of some ancient, ruined city out of *The Arabian Nights,* inspiring them to fill pages of their diaries with lushly romantic imaginings.

On June 27 the party reached Fort Laramie, built only twelve years earlier but already legendary. Here came Sioux, Crows, Cheyennes, and other Indians of the plains to trade furs and buffalo hides for the desirable goods of the white man: cloth, blankets, ribbons and decorations, mirrors, steel knives and axes, guns and powder and lead, and whiskey. Here, too, the emigrant wagon companies stopped for the repairs that by now most of the wagons needed badly.

Fort Laramie was built at an ideal location for its purpose, at the spot where Laramie Creek flows into the sand-laden North Platte. An ancient Indian trade route crossed the Oregon Trail here. More important, there was an oasis of green grass, shady cottonwood trees, and good water in the midst of an inhospitable desert. The fort, at a new site about a mile up Laramie Creek, boasted 15-foot-high walls of whitewashed adobe surrounding a hollow square about 130 feet on each side. Two blockhouses at opposite corners protected the fort, and there was a watchtower over the gate. Inside the square were living quarters, blacksmith shops, and a corral. The whole complex covered about three quarters of an acre.

The single entrance was barred by two sets of stout log gates. Indians who came to trade, and perhaps to raid, were controlled by keeping them in the long passageway between the outer and inner gates. For extra security, they were admitted only in small groups.

The company arrived at Fort Laramie at a moment of high drama. Three thousand-odd Sioux were gathered on the plain outside the fort preparing to make war on their neighbors, the Snakes and Crows. Six hundred conical lodges covered with buffalo hides made the plain look like a gigantic field covered with shocks of cornstalks. The Sioux had just concluded a spirited war dance and were intoxicated by the excitement as well as by the traders' whiskey.

Drunk or not, the Sioux were an impressive sight in their carefully tailored garments of fringed buckskin. Tall, handsome, and proportioned like classic Greek statues, they fitted the most romantic notion of what the Noble Savage should look like. In addition to their natural endowments, both sexes spent a great deal of time on clothes, makeup, and grooming. To Virginia Reed's twelve-year-old eyes, "The Sioux Indians are the pretest drest Indians thare is."

One Indian wandered about the emigrant camp showing the white men a testimonial note from none other than Lansford W. Hastings. It stated that the bearer had rescued Hastings from Sioux marauders in 1842. Some of the emigrants, anxious to stay on the good side of this powerful and warlike tribe, invited groups of Sioux to supper. They may have been somewhat put out when the Sioux devoured everything that was set before them. But that was Indian good manners, a gracious compliment to the host.

Owl Russell, suffering the pangs of rejection by his followers, got huffily drunk and made speeches to anyone who would listen, assuring them that he was still the leader of his company in everything but name. Drunken emigrants, drunken trappers, and drunken Sioux made so much noise that even his booming voice could barely be heard.

That night at Fort Laramie, Reed met an old acquaintance, the veteran mountain man Jim Clyman. In his youth Clyman had trapped beaver in the Rockies, fought Indians, and done his share of exploring the unknown West. Unlike most trappers, he had saved his money, and he moved back east to Illinois, where he tended store and bought a farm with two of his brothers. In 1832 he had served in the Black Hawk War, in Reed's company.

Clyman later moved to Wisconsin, where he did some more farming, but in the winter of 1843-44 he came down with a cough he could not shake. That summer he went to Oregon with a party of emigrants, wintered there, and journeyed down to California in 1845. Still restless, he longed once more for the East, and in April 1846 he joined Lansford W. Hastings at the latter's camp on Bear River, in the western foothills of the Sierra Nevada.

Hastings, curious about developments, had returned to California in 1845. Starting late in the summer, he reached the Sierras in December. The luck that sometimes aids the foolhardy was with him, and the snows were unusually late that year. He made it across the mountains just before the first great storm of the season, in time for Christmas dinner at Sutter's Fort.

He spent the winter planning a real-estate development on wilderness land and working up a description of an attractive but nonexistent community. The purchasers would have to clear and improve the land themselves before the community materialized, but that was of no consequence to Hastings.

Now, in the mild California spring of 1846, he was preparing to cross the mountains again and meet the expected stream of emigrants at some point before the California trail split off from the route to Oregon. There, like a modern-day Pied Piper, he would employ his artful mind and smooth tongue to persuade them to follow him back to California along his marvelous (but untried) shortcut, under his personal leadership, and purchase lots in his nonexistent town.

Hastings had welcomed the grizzled mountain man in a warm and polite fashion, said Clyman. They spent a week in drying meat and other preparations for the journey while waiting for their companions to arrive: nineteen men, three women, and three children. Hastings did not intend to travel alone.

On April 23 they started up the Sierras on horseback, with pack animals to carry their supplies and belongings. Deep snows held them up on the western flank of the Sierras, but on May 1 they crossed the summit and camped on the shore of a clear mountain lake.

The party followed the established trail down the Truckee River and up the Humboldt, a difficult but not impossible route across inhospitable deserts and steep, rugged mountains. At last they reached the point where Hastings' cutoff (which he still had not laid eyes on) joined the regular trail. In a rare fit of realism, Hastings decided to scout out the path by which he would lead the emigrants back. (Frémont himself had come this way late in 1845 and barely made it through, even without wagons to hinder him on steep slopes or narrow paths.)

They made it across the Salt Desert—barely—following the trail left by Frémont's expedition. But when they came to the canyons and ridges of the Wasatch Mountains, east of the Great Salt Lake, even Hastings had to admit the route was well-nigh impassable for wagons. He would just have to find a better one on the return trip. Clyman was appalled. After parting company with Hastings at Fort Bridger, he warned each westbound party that he met of the extreme dangers and difficulty of the Hastings route.

Now, at Fort Laramie, enjoying his first coffee in many months,

> The former [mountain men] I should estimate at from five hundred to one thousand, scattered among the Indians. . . . Adventure, romance, avarice, misanthropy, and sometimes social outlawry, have their influence in enticing or driving these persons into this savage wilderness. . . . They conform to savage customs, and from their superior intelligence have much influence over the Indians, and frequently direct their movements and policy in war and peace. [Edwin Bryant, *What I Saw in California,* p. 99]

he talked late into the night with his old messmate James Reed and other interested persons who wanted to hear about the best route to California.

The regular trail, as they knew, crossed the Rocky Mountains, turned southwest to Fort Bridger (in present-day southwestern Wyoming), then zigged sharply northwest to Fort Hall (near present-day Pocatello, Idaho), following the water and grass at the foot of a mountain range. At Fort Hall it zagged southwest again, passing northwest of Great Salt Lake and eventually striking the Humboldt River. It was a safe trail, but long, and by now the emigrants were more than sated with travel. The great appeal of Hastings's untested cutoff was this: a relatively short leg southwest from Fort Bridger took you to the south end of Great Salt Lake. From there you could travel straight west until you struck the Humboldt, theoretically saving a good three hundred miles and three to four weeks.

At the campfire, Jim Clyman warned his listeners not to take the route on which he had come east. "Take the regular wagon track by way of Fort Hall," he said, "and never leave it. It is barely possible to get through [before the snows] if you follow it, and it may be impossible if you don't."

Reed disagreed. "There is another route," he replied, "and it is of no use to take such a roundabout course."

Clyman admitted that the Hastings route was shorter, but pointed out that the huge expanse of desert and the roughness of the mountains might make the "straight route" impracticable.

Some of the emigrants, including Boggs and Russell, believed Clyman. Reed, the Donners, and a number of others did not. Some thought him a carping malcontent. Others mistrusted him because of his shabby appearance, unshaven and dressed in buckskins stained with grease and filth from the trail. Most suspect of all, he was a trapper. Today we think of trappers as romantic heroes of the wilderness (an opinion with which most of the trappers would have agreed). But most of their contemporaries shared the opinion of James Frazier Reed: "as great a set of sharks as ever disgraced humanity, with few exceptions."

By now it was almost July, and they were not yet a third of the way to the first settlement in California; so they left behind hospitable Fort Laramie and the picturesque Sioux to push on. The Sioux had been persuaded by the manager of the fort not to go to war after all, and some of them followed the emigrant wagons for a bit on their way home. A Sioux chieftain fell in love with Virginia's cream-colored pony, Billy, with his brown mane and eyes, and tried to buy the pony and the girl from Reed. The chief, a man of some wealth, offered Indian ponies, piles of hides, and finally an old U.S. Army jacket with brass buttons. Reed declined as politely as he could.

The chief showed signs of displeasure, so Reed ordered Virginia into the family wagon, where she sulked for the rest of the day while strapping Milt Elliott rode Billy. Crowds of curious Sioux followed the slow-moving wagon and pulled aside the canvas to peek inside (perfectly good Indian etiquette). Virginia took revenge by menacing them with a spyglass.

The Fourth of July found them at Beaver Creek, a small tributary of the North Platte. Here the Oregon contingent, now reunited with the company, joined the "Californians" for a day of patriotic celebration. Owl Russell filled the air with oratory. Innumerable toasts were drunk to the United States and their glorious destiny, and the men fired off blank volleys after each toast. One young man put too much powder in his rifle and was knocked to the ground while his rifle flew through the air.

As for the Reeds, let Virginia tell the story: ". . . several of the gentlemen in Springfield gave paw a botel of licker and said it shoulden be opened till the 4 day of July and paw was to look to the east an drink it and thay was to look to the west an drink it at 12 o'clock paw treted the compiany and we all had some lemminade."

On July 11 the company reached Independence Rock, a renowned landmark. The rock, a huge granite dome, had been named by a party of trappers who had camped there over the Fourth of July more than twenty years earlier. Ever since then, travelers had written their names on the sheer sides of the rock, and now the walls were covered with signatures as high as a man could reach. They were still ninety-eight miles from South Pass, where the trail crossed the Rockies, and already the summer was half gone. Even So, Governor Boggs let his company stay over Sunday to rest and investigate the rock with its hundreds of inscriptions. The day of rest was productive, for the next day the oxen made twenty miles.

Twenty miles more over a very bad, sandy road brought them to the Sweetwater River, named by an early party of French-Canadian trappers when the mule that carried their sugar fell into the river. The Sweetwater flowed into the Platte from the west, and it would lead them to South Pass. Here on the Sweetwater they met a lone horseman traveling east. His name was Wales Bonney, and he had gone to Oregon the year before. Now he was returning to Ohio to fetch his family.

Traveling by night to avoid the Indians, Bonney hid himself and his horse in ravines by day. He had met Hastings on the trail farther west, and he carried with him a letter from the young promoter, addressed to all emigrants.

The gist of the letter was that the native California authorities had turned anti-American and were gathering an army to bar the emigrants from the promised land. (This was not true, but Hastings evidently thought it an effective appeal.) Therefore, said Hastings, all should join together in one big party for self-defense and follow his cutoff to save time and strength. He promised to meet them at Fort Bridger and guide them personally.

Near Independence Rock the Sweetwater cuts through a ridge of granite hills, forming a deep, narrow gorge called Devil's Gate. From the far side, the emigrants got their first glimpse of the snow-covered peaks of the Rockies. A few days later, the trail began the final ascent to South Pass.

Almost everyone was surprised by South Pass. They expected a steep, rocky ascent and a narrow passage between towering crags.

Instead, the trail climbed a gently rising plain, and the pass itself was a level valley almost twenty miles wide. If it had not been for the towering, blue-white peaks of the Wind River Range on either side, and the chilly winds, the travelers could not have told that they were even in the mountains.

But even the most ignorant of the emigrants knew that here they were standing on the backbone of the continent. This was the dividing ridge between the streams that flowed east into the Mississippi and those that flowed west into the Pacific Ocean. It was a solemn moment, and many of the emigrants had homesick thoughts as they paused for a last look at the waters flowing toward their old homes. Of course, it was exciting to go the last few miles to Pacific Spring, on the western slope of the Continental Divide, whose waters drained eventually to the Gulf of California. But most people found it sobering to consider how far they had come already, and how much farther they still had to go. There was something final about crossing the Continental Divide—a last link with the old, familiar world was severed.

The next few days took them over a dry, undulating plain where a number of oxen were poisoned by drinking alkali water from pools at the crossing of Dry Sandy Creek. Reed lost two oxen, Jake Donner lost two, and George Donner lost one. More oxen died the next day en route to Little Sandy Creek.

The Little Sandy was a small, unprepossessing stream that flowed in a deep gulch it had cut through the easily eroded soil of the upland. It made frequent bends, where the outer bank was high and steep, while the inner bank sloped down gradually to the streambed. Sage and bunchgrass provided a sparse cover for the ground on either side, and scanty grazing for the teams. The regular emigrant trail followed the Little Sandy down to its junction with the Big Sandy, which led in turn to the Green River, Black's Fork, and Fort Bridger. It was on Little Sandy Creek, on Sunday, July 19, that the Russell-Boggs company made their last camp together as a whole. The following day the Oregonians and many of the Californians would take the new Greenwood cutoff west to Fort Hall. This cutoff, established only the year before by the veteran mountain man Caleb Greenwood, saved perhaps a hundred miles, but it included a forty-mile, waterless desert crossing.

The Reeds, Donners, and others who had chosen the Hastings cutoff would head south to Fort Bridger. They were in high spirits, elated at the thought of what they believed to be a much better and shorter route. Except for Tamsen Donner, that is. Thornton noticed that she was uncharacteristically "sad, gloomy, and dispirited, in view of the fact, that her husband and others, could think for a moment of leaving the old road and confide in the statement of a man of whom they knew nothing, but who was probably some selfish adventurer."

There were tearful farewells as the Reed-Donner party and their followers turned left down the Little Sandy toward Fort Bridger. But both groups were in a hurry to cross the Sierras before the snows came.

> I wrote several letters to my friends among the emigrant parties in the rear, advising them <u>not</u> to take this route [the Hastings cutoff]. . . . Our situation was different from theirs, We were mounted on mules, had no families, and could afford to hazard experiments, and make explorations. They could not. [Edwin Bryant, *What I Saw in California*]

CHAPTER 6

The Donner Party—
A Roll Call

The day after our separation from the Russel party, we elected George Donner captain. From this time the company was known as "The Donner Party."
> —James Frazier Reed, in *The Pacific Rural Press* (c. 1871)

Despite their hurry to reach California, the group that had opted for Hastings's route made little progress that first day—only about five miles down the tortuous Little Sandy. The next day, a Tuesday, they stayed in camp. One reason may have been that more oxen were sick or dying from the bad water they had drunk a few days ago, but the party had other business to consider. With neither Boggs nor Russell to take charge, they had to choose another leader.

The obvious choice should have been Reed, who was intelligent, dynamic, forceful, and old enough to command respect. But Reed had antagonized too many of his companions by his aristocratic ways. Not that plain Americans did not appreciate wealth and social standing (and secretly hunger after them themselves), but the unspoken rules of the game required that the gentry had to act as if they were just plain folks, no better than anyone else. Reed could not or would not wrap himself in false humility; so the majority voted not to give the uppity Mr. Reed a chance to put on his highborn airs.

Instead, they chose George Donner, whom everyone liked and who was genuinely modest, despite his wealth. It made little difference in fact, because Reed took charge anyway, but from now on the company was known as the Donner Party.

Besides the original core of thirty souls from Springfield, the Donner Party now included these reinforcements:

Antoine (or Antonio; last name unknown), a Mexican herder who hired on at Independence.

William Eddy, coachmaker, from Belleville, Illinois, aged about twenty-eight, with his wife, Eleanor, twenty-five, and their two small children, James P., three, and Margaret, one. The best hunter and woodsman in the group, Eddy would show heroic qualities later on.

Patrick Breen, forty; his wife, Margaret (usually called Peggy), about forty; and their children: John, fourteen, Edward J., thirteen, Patrick, Jr. eleven, Simon P., nine, Peter, seven, James, four, and baby Isabella, one. Both born in Ireland, Patrick and Peggy had come to the States in about 1828 and eventually settled in Iowa, where Breen became an American citizen. At a time when most of the Irish who came to America were illiterate peasants, Patrick Breen could read, write, and express himself elegantly on occasion. He was handsome, intelligent, and a successful farmer. He was also dominated by his shrewish wife. Although not of the same social class as the Donners, he was reckoned well-to-do, for he brought with him three wagons, seven yoke of oxen, milk cows, several saddle horses, and the family watchdog, Towser.

Traveling with the Breens in his own wagon was their good friend Patrick Dolan, about forty, an Irish-born bachelor and neighbor in Iowa. Dolan had a jolly, lighthearted nature and was a bit of a comedian. He was a favorite with all the children, whom he would entertain with songs and jigs that he performed on the tailgate of a wagon.

Lavina Murphy, fifty, a widow from Tennessee who had moved to Missouri. (Recent research by scholarly Donner enthusiasts indicates that Mrs. Murphy, although she appeared to be about fifty, may actually have been thirty-seven. Nevertheless, her oldest child, Sarah, was twenty-three, which would make Mrs. Murphy fourteen at the time she gave birth to Sarah!) With her was her large family: John Landrum Murphy, fifteen, Mary M. Murphy, about thirteen, Lemuel B. Murphy, twelve, William G. Murphy, eleven, and Simon P. Murphy, ten. Also with them were two married daughters with their families: Sarah Murphy Foster, twenty-three, and her husband, William M. Foster, twenty-eight, and their little son George, four; and Harriet Murphy Pike, about twenty-one, her husband, William Pike, about twenty-five, and their daughters, Naomi L., three, and Catherine, one. The Murphy clan were ordinary, decent farm people. Mrs. Murphy was rumored to be a secret Mormon.

Lewis Keseberg, from Westphalia, Germany, about thirty-two; his pretty wife, Philippine, about ten years younger; and their children, Ada, three, and Lewis, Jr., one. Keseberg was tall, blond, and good-looking, with a military bearing. He was an excellent shot. He was also hot-tempered, overbearing, and brutal. Keseberg, who had come to the United States only two years earlier, had visited Paris frequently. He spoke German, French, and English fluently, and also a little Spanish.

Keseberg cherished a bitter grudge against Reed over an incident that had occurred way back on the Platte. As the wagon train passed a Sioux grave, Keseberg and another German had had the indecency to rob the grave and take the buffalo robes from the dead man's body. Reed, horrified by the desecration, forced Keseberg to put the stolen robes back in place and bawled him out for putting the whole company in danger by risking the anger of the Sioux. He punished Keseberg by temporarily banishing him from their section. (This incident is disputed by revisionists.) Keseberg also hated Reed for threatening to punish him the next time he was caught beating his wife, an activity to which he seemed much addicted.

Traveling with Keseberg was an elderly Belgian named Hardkoop, whose first name is not recorded. Hardkoop, about sixty, was originally from Antwerp but had come to Cincinnati and done well in the cutlery business. He had bought a farm, but wanderlust had seized him and he was on his way to see California. He planned, on his return, to sell the farm and spend the rest of his life with his son and daughter in Antwerp.

"Dutch Charley" Burger (real name Karl), thirty, seems to have been a teamster for Keseberg. He was from Germany.

Joseph Reinhardt, about thirty, and Augustus Spitzer, about the same age, both from Germany, were partners (so the historians believe). Such arrangements were fairly common. Two or more single men who could not afford the journey on their own would pool their resources to buy a wagon, teams, and supplies.

Mr. Wolfinger (first name unknown), probably about thirty, and his wife, Doris, probably the same age, both from Germany. The Wolfingers were believed to be wealthy, and Mrs. Wolfinger aroused the envy of some of the other women by her habit of wearing fine clothes and quantities of jewelry.

The George Donners had two passengers they had picked up en route. One was a pathetic young man, Luke Halloran, about twenty-five, who had joined them at the Little Sandy. Halloran hailed from St. Joseph, Missouri, and was dying of tuberculosis. He was headed for California in a desperate effort to recover his health. His horse had broken down, and the family that had been carrying his belongings in their wagon refused to take him farther. Tamsen and George took pity on the dying young man and made room for him in their wagon.

The other was Charles T. Stanton, a bachelor of about thirty-five. Originally from Syracuse, New York, he had moved to Chicago, and for a time had prospered as a merchant. However, the severe depression of 1844 had ruined his business. Charley Stanton was small but wiry and tough. He had taught himself botany and geology, about which he knew a good deal. He was naturally drawn to the better-educated members of the company, the Donners and Reeds. It is not known just when or where he joined the Donners, but he was with them now for better or for worse.

"Fort Bridger," as it is called, is a small trading-post, established and now occupied by Messrs. Bridger and Vasquez. The buildings are two or three miserable log-cabins—rudely constructed, and bearing but a faint resemblance to habitable houses. Its position is...about two miles south of the point where the old wagon trail, via Fort Hall, makes an angle, and takes a northwesterly course. [Edwin Bryant]

Jim Bridger, the founder and proprietor of Fort Bridger, was a mountain man, and one of the greatest. The mountain men were trappers of a very special breed. They lived the year round in the Rockies and other ranges of the West, trapping beaver for their rich, lustrous fur.

A mountain man's life was harsh and lonely. He spent many hours waist-deep in icy mountain lakes and streams setting his traps or emptying them of the catch. Many a mountain man developed rheumatism from this constant exposure. But a mountain man trained himself to endure every discomfort.

He had to be constantly on guard against danger from wild animals and unfriendly Indians, always on the alert for any sight or sound that might spell danger. A clump of grass that bent in the wrong direction, a bird call that seemed out of place, strange scratches on a tree trunk . . . all these and more he must be continually aware of as he went about his work. A moment's lapse of attention might mean death. The death rate was high among mountain men.

The mountain men shared the average white American's bigotry against Indians, yet they enjoyed living like Indians. Almost all of them came sooner or later to admire a particular tribe and identify with it. Some went through adoption ceremonies and became full-fledged members of "their" tribe. Many more simply took Indian wives.

To survive among the Indians—even friendly ones—a mountain man had to master every wilderness skill: reading trail signs, finding his direction, hunting, fishing, hand-to-hand combat with knife or whatever other weapon came to hand, stealing horses, surviving a mountain blizzard. A successful mountain man (and that means one who survived) learned these things even better than the Indians.

Many of the mountain men were thugs who would have been jailed or hanged if they had stayed at home among the whites. In the mountains, their violence and ruthlessness served them well. But not all were of the criminal type. Some were eccentrics who reveled in being alone. Others hated the drudgery of farm life or the constricting rules of nineteenth-century respectable behavior. And there were some who loved the romance and adventure of the trapper's life. One thing they all had in common: Each man was completely his own master.

The mountain men roved far and wide in search of furs, and in their rovings they explored much of the West. Jim Bridger, for instance, discovered Great Salt Lake by floating down Bear River in a boat of animal hides. (He did it to settle a bet on whether the Bear River emptied into the Atlantic or the Pacific.) And the mountain men pioneered the trails that the emigrants followed.

There were never very many mountain men—probably between five hundred and a thousand at their height. Their reign began in 1823, when the first trappers went up the Missouri to live in the mountains. It waned in the late 1830s, when the beaver were trapped out almost everywhere and the dictators of fashion in far-off Paris tired of hats made of beaver fur (the chief and almost only use of beaver) and turned instead to top hats made of silk. All Europe and America followed suit, and all at once there was no more market for beaver. End of a profession.

Some of the mountain men stayed on with the Indians. Others became scouts for explorers like Frémont or guides for emigrants. Most drifted back to the settlements, where they lived by telling highly romanticized, gory tales of their exploits at the local saloon in exchange for drinks and food.

Jim Bridger did none of these things. He had saved his money and gone into business himself as a fur trader, together with a couple of other ex-trappers. When the bottom fell out of the fur market, he turned to other ventures. In 1843 he and a partner, Louis Vasquez, built a "fort" on the Oregon Trail where they sold supplies to emigrants at high prices and repaired the travel-battered wagons. They also sold oxen, horses, and mules to replace worn-out animals.

Fort Bridger lay in a beautiful mountain meadow on Black's Fork of the Green River, in what is now the southwestern corner of Wyoming. In 1846 the land was theoretically part of Oregon; in actuality it was Shoshone territory. At the fort the snow-fed stream divided into several channels that ran through the meadow. The water was clear and pure and icy-cold, and full of big trout. The fort itself was only two large, ill-kept log cabins at either end of a palisaded corral, but it was always a welcome sight to trail-weary emigrants.

The Donner Party pulled into Fort Bridger on July 27 after a long day's drive of eighteen miles. To their dismay, Hastings was not waiting for them there. He had gone ahead with a party of eighty-six wagons, since the season was late and few more clients were expected. But he had left directions with Bridger and Vasquez for any latecomers who might wish to join his party. They should follow his party's wagon tracks, he said, and catch up with him along the way.

The men of the Donner Party questioned the two ex-mountain men anxiously about the Hastings route. Bridger and Vasquez assured them that Hastings's new trail would save three or four hundred miles of travel to California. It was level and firm most of the way, they averred, easy going, with plenty of grass and water. True, there was one stretch of desert to negotiate, but it was only forty miles, no more than the folks who took Greenwood's cutoff to Fort Hall had to cross.

This was an outright lie, for Bridger and Vasquez knew better. But they wanted to encourage emigrants to use the Hastings route, because the Greenwood cutoff to Fort Hall was diverting most of the traffic away from Fort Bridger. Hastings's cutoff, however, went by way of Fort Bridger, which was also the last supply post on the trail. So it was very much to their advantage to play Hastings's game, and they played it to the hilt.

Reed's friend Edwin Bryant, the journalist, had tired of the slow pace of a wagon company and left it at Fort Laramie. He went ahead on muleback with nine friends, intending to take the gamble of Hastings's desert route. At Fort Bridger Bryant had talked with Joe Walker, another renowned mountain man, on his way east with a herd of horses from California. Walker had guided Frémont across the Salt Lake Desert in 1845—the very route that Hastings proposed to follow—and he knew how difficult and dangerous it was. He warned Bryant in the sternest manner against attempting it. (Joe Walker also ran into the Donner Party somewhere east of Fort Bridger, but they rejected his warning.)

Bryant and his friends decided to take the risk, since they had no families, were not encumbered by wagons, and were looking for adventure. But Bryant left letters at Fort Bridger for Reed and several others, warning them against the Hastings cutoff and urging them to go by way of Fort Hall. Bridger and Vasquez never delivered these letters.

The Donner Party stayed at Fort Bridger for three days, resting the tired oxen and repairing the wagons, which had been badly shaken on the trail from Fort Laramie. Reed wrote an enthusiastic letter to *The Sangamo Journal* back in Springfield, praising Bridger and Vasquez as "two very excellent and accommodating gentlemen."

He also wrote optimistically, "We are now only 100 miles from the Great Salt Lake by the new route,—in all 250 miles from California [Reed's geography was far off the mark on this point]; while by way of Fort Hall it is 650 or 700 miles—making a great saving in favor of jaded oxen and dust. On the new route we will not have dust, as there are but 60 wagons ahead of us. The rest of the Californians went the long route, feeling afraid of Hastings' Cut-off. . . . Mr. Bridger informs me that the route we design to take, is a fine level road, with a plenty of water and grass, with the exception before stated. . . ."

A few more people joined the party at Fort Bridger. One was a young driver hired by George Donner to replace Hiram Miller, who had gone off adventuring on muleback with Bryant. The young man, Jean-Baptiste Trudeau, twenty-three, came from New Mexico. The son of a French-Canadian trapper and a Mexican mother, he claimed to know the desert and the Indians well. The emigrants usually called him Bateese, having trouble with his French name, and they wrote his last name as "Trubode." Jean-Baptiste probably couldn't write it at all.

The others were the McCutchen family of Missouri. William McCutchen, about thirty, was a giant of a man, six-foot-six and massively built. Although he had little education, he was an ardent Shakespeare enthusiast, and when angry he larded his conversation with powerful Shakespearean epithets. With him were his wife, Amanda, about twenty-four, and their baby daughter, Harriet, one year old. The McCutchens had apparently been stranded by a broken-down wagon. Somehow they were shoehorned into the already crowded wagons of one of the families in the Donner Party. (No one bothered to write down which one, so we don't know who helped out the stranded McCutchens.)

The two very excellent and accommodating gentlemen, Bridger and Vasquez, told Reed that he was about seven hundred miles from

Sutter's Fort and that the party should cover the distance in seven weeks. It was now the end of July; seven weeks would see them at Sutter's toward the end of October. Time was running a little short, and the emigrants felt a new sense of urgency as they left Fort Bridger on July 31.

The trail now led them over numerous high, steep ridges, and Bridger's "fine level road" turned out to be very rough as it crossed the Wyoming badlands. Even on the level stretches the ground was full of bumps and hollows that made it about as smooth as a badly potholed modern city street. (However, this had been true all the way across the plains and was nothing new.) Still, there was plenty of water and grass for the stock, and the wagons made better than average distances each day.

Even while pushing for distance, the travelers had time to marvel at the natural wonders they passed: soda springs where naturally carbonated water bubbled from the earth, iron-bearing springs that colored the earth around them rusty-red, and grotesquely eroded formations of rock and clay that jutted from the ground or leered from the tops of bluffs like gargoyles.

They went down narrow ravines and along hillsides so steep that it was a wonder the wagons did not tip over. On some downgrades the wagon brakes were not strong enough to hold the wagons back, so the travelers had to chain the rear wheels to keep them from turning. Otherwise the heavily loaded wagons, gaining momentum, would have rolled down onto the ox teams. They were entering the Wasatch, one of the more rugged mountain ranges of North America.

On August 4 they crossed still another ridge and came to a creek that flowed westward into a deep, narrow canyon with sheer, rocky walls. Awesome cliffs of red sandstone flanked its entrance. Passing between these towering portals, the party followed the canyon to another stream, this one flowing northwest. The information they had gleaned from guidebooks, mountain men, and trading-post gossip told them that this must be the Red Fork of the Weber River, which would lead them to Great Salt Lake. They were on course, and everything was, to all appearances, fine.

The tracks left by Hastings' party followed the stream for about four miles and then crossed it. But something they found at the crossing made the Donner Party stop short. It was a letter from Hastings, stuck prominently in the top of a sage bush by the trailside. The man who claimed to have led an emigrant party to Oregon in 1842 had run into trouble in the canyons of the Weber. His letter said simply that the road was very bad and he feared he might not be able to get his wagons through. He advised anyone coming after him to make camp and send a messenger ahead to catch up with him. Hastings would then return and guide them through the mountains by a shorter and better route.

Even Reed's faith in Hastings must have been shaken by this news. But the emigrants had no choice. They had come too far to turn back to the old trail to Fort Hall. Time was too short—they could not spare the extra weeks.

CHAPTER 7
Lost in the Wasatch

At times we had to turn the wheels by their spokes; then we were forced to hold them back again with all our might so that the wagon would not rush too fast upon a lower-lying rock and be dashed to pieces.
—Heinrich Lienhard, describing the passage down the
Weber River Canyon with Hastings's party in 1846

The situation was alarming. Hastings, the guide on whom they now depended, had disappeared once more. Not only that, he now disavowed the very trail he had recommended with such authority. What sort of guide was Hastings, anyway? How far could one trust such a man?

One thing was clear: Something had to be done immediately. The company went into a hurried conference and decided to send a scouting party after Hastings. Three men volunteered to go: Reed, McCutchen, and wiry little Charley Stanton. Horses were saddled, rations were hastily packed, and the men rode off to track down the elusive Hastings, who never seemed to be there when he was needed.

Four days passed with no sign of the three scouts. The waiting party began to worry that the men had been waylaid and killed by Indians. They had other worries, too. Already there was snow on the high peaks of the Wasatch, and it seemed to be creeping lower. Some of the families discovered that their supplies were running low.

They waited. . . .

On the evening of the fourth day, August 10, Reed reappeared, alone and on a strange horse. He was exhausted and worried. His own horse had given out, he explained, and he had borrowed this one from someone in Hastings's company. McCutchen's and Stanton's horses had also given out, so they were staying with Hastings's group on the shore of Great Salt Lake while their horses recovered.

Then Reed delivered his report about his encounter with Hastings. It was a horrifying tale he brought back. The route down the Weber River traversed not one but two long canyons, choked with brush and boulders of all sizes. The men of Hastings's party had been forced to hack their way through tangled, stubborn thickets of alder and poplar and heave massive rocks out of the way simply to clear a path. Sometimes the boulders were too massive to move, and there was not room to get a wagon around them. So Hastings's men had sweated and cursed and built flimsy ramps of brush and smaller rocks to get over the top. The riverbed shifted frequently from one wall of the canyon to the other, with the usable bank always on the far side; so the path crossed the river many times. For a week Hastings's party had averaged only a mile and a half a day.

Here and there the riverbank disappeared entirely, and the men had to take the wagons right down the streambed, a jolting journey over slippery boulders, with tricky holes and turbulent rapids. Fortunately the water was only a few feet deep, but the current was so strong that the wagon wheels had to be locked to brake them, just as on the steepest mountain grades. In some places the obstacles were just plain impassable, and the men had to take the wagons right over the mountain spurs, up slopes so steep that an ox in harness could not keep his feet. But the desperate emigrants found a solution. Atop the worst slopes they rigged a homemade windlass and winched the wagons up one by one. The oxen and humans had to scramble up as best they could.

♦

[T]he bluffs of this ravin [ravine] are formed of red rock made of smoothe water washe[d] pebbles and . . . are verry high and perpendicular and in many places hanging over[.] the narrow vally is completely Strewn over with the boulder which have fallen from time to time from the cliffs above. [Diary of James Clyman, June 4, 1846]

Somehow Hastings's wagons got through without major mishap, except for one wagon that slipped and fell, team and all, seventy-five feet to the bottom of the canyon. The wagons came through in small groups, while Hastings dashed importantly back and forth among them on his horse, offering false inspiration and empty advice. (These were not Reed's words, but they are clear from the records left by members of Hastings's party.) At last they reached level ground and stopped to rest by a huge black rock near the south shore of Great Salt Lake.

Here Reed and his companions had caught up with Hastings. And Hastings, once more reneging on his promise, told Reed that he could not possibly come back with him and guide the Donner Party to the lake. He had to pilot his sixty-six (now sixty-five) wagons across the Salt Desert and on to the Sierras before snow blocked the way.

However, he did agree to ride back part of the way with Reed, as far as the edge of the mountains. There the two men climbed to the top of a high peak and Hastings pointed out, in a nonchalant, general sort of way, a route back to the Donner Party's camp on the Red Fork of the Weber. This, said Hastings, was the way over which Reed should lead the Donner Party to the fertile valley of the Great Salt Lake.

Had the land been flat, Hastings's new shortcut would have been a good idea. The route down the Weber made a long, tortuous loop like a horseshoe that someone had tried to twist into a corkscrew. His latest suggestion cut across the base of the horseshoe, saving a fair number of miles. But the country was in fact so ruggedly mountainous that the going was actually rougher than the way down the narrow, boulder-choked canyons of the Weber.

Reed rode back across the mountains on his borrowed horse, blazing his route on the runty trees that dotted the mountainsides. He was actually following the same path that Hastings and Clyman had taken when they rode east on muleback that spring. However, Hastings had not bothered to tell Reed that they had taken this route because they had lost Frémont's trail and had to bushwhack, partly guided by an old Indian trail. In so doing, Hastings had missed the canyons of the Weber and so had never seen them until he confidently led his party of sixty-six wagons into them.

That night the Donner Party held another emergency council. Reed laid out the pros and cons of each route as well as he could. He told them that even though Hastings's party had cleared a road of sorts through the river canyons, he doubted that the Donner Party could get through without losing some of their own wagons. On the other hand, he pointed out, the mountain trail he had taken back was also difficult, and they would have to clear a whole new road.

In his own opinion, he said, they would do better to go across the mountains, in spite of the labor this would cost them. The absent McCutchen and Stanton had agreed, he said. The company argued it out and ended by voting unanimously to follow Reed's suggestion.

By morning Stanton and McCutchen still had not come in, but there was no time to lose. The party started off without them, assuming they would find each other along the trail. They splashed across the Weber, followed Hastings's wheel tracks beside the stream for about half a mile, and turned sharp left up a little creek into the mountains. The backbreaking, excruciatingly frustrating work of clearing a road began immediately.

With ax and pick and shovel, the men set to work. But progress was slow, for they were short of manpower. Stanton and the giant McCutchen were missing. Uncle George and Uncle Jake and the old Belgian, Hardkoop, could not work as fast as the younger men. The German men were unused to this kind of labor and probably wasted a good deal of motion and energy. Luke Halloran, the invalid, was too sick to work at all.

Two days of hard work took them over a steep divide and down to a stream that trappers had named Bossman Creek. Coming down the far side of the divide was even worse than going up, for the only possible route went along the slope, and the wagons, top-heavy with their loads, constantly threatened to tip over.

Bossman Creek's real name was Beauchemin, probably the name of a French-Canadian trapper. It translates as "beautiful road," but the canyon of the Bossman was anything but that. The floor was choked with a thick jungle of aspen and willow, laced together with tough, thorny bramble vines. Faced with this, the party made camp after having traveled a total of two miles. It was August 12.

The next morning the men again attacked the tangled, thorn-studded thickets. Grueling work gained them four miles in two days. Morale began to fail. Even farmers were not used to such strenuous work with so little rest. There were endless trees to fell and drag out of the way, and endless boulders and dirt to dig and pry and heave aside. Hands blistered, backs ached, and tempers grew raw. And at the end of each miserable day there were still all the regular chores of the camp waiting to be done.

Men grumbled, slowed down, and quit work early. Reed, driving himself at a furious pace, tried to persuade the others to work harder. Instead they talked back to him and complained that it was his fault that they were in this fix, conveniently forgetting that no one had forced them to follow Reed down the Hastings cutoff in the first place.

Incredibly, on the third day three wagons clattered down the newly cleared road into their camp. They carried the Graves clan, thirteen strong, from Lacon, Illinois.[1] The head of the family was Franklin Ward Graves, fifty-seven. The scant biographical information available depicts him as a big man, good-natured, hospitable, and kind. For some reason he was known as "Uncle Billy."

Uncle Billy came from Vermont and had settled in Illinois when he was forty-two. He served as a drum major of infantry in the Black Hawk War and later cleared a sizable farm out of the woods on the rich bottomlands of the Illinois River. Counting uncleared land, he owned five hundred acres. But he was a backwoodsman at heart, more hunter than farmer, and he was uncomfortable with civilized ways. In fact, he lived as much like an Indian as possible. In summer he shed shoes, hat, and coat. This rather shocked his contemporaries, for whom these items were emblems of respectability.

His wife, tall, thin Elizabeth Graves, was forty-seven years old. She wore a blue calico dress and an old sunbonnet; like her husband, she went barefoot. Every day, weather permitting, she crossed the river in a little canoe and sold honey, wild fruits, and homemade soap to the villagers of Lacon.

With them were their numerous children. The oldest, twenty-two-year-old Sarah, was newly married to a young farmer named Jay Fosdick, twenty-three. Then came the beautiful Mary Ann, twenty, William C., eighteen, Eleanor, fifteen, Lavina, thirteen, Nancy, nine, Jonathan, seven, Franklin Ward, Jr., five, and Elizabeth, Jr., one. Sarah and Jay Fosdick were with them only by a fluke. Sarah had planned to stay home and wed Jay in the fall. But at the last minute she changed her mind; the young people were hastily married and joined the family caravan. The Graveses also had an ox-driver, twenty-five-year-old John Snyder, who somewhere along the trail became engaged to Mary Graves.

Uncle Billy had grown restless on his five hundred acres and longed to explore the Pacific country. So when a buyer for his farm turned up in the spring of 1846, he sold it gladly for $1,500. The payment was mostly in silver half dollars, which Uncle Billy hid cunningly in holes that he bored in thick cleats that he nailed to the floor of his wagon.

The Graves family had apparently traveled much of the way with a company that left Independence ahead of the Donners. But along the Platte the dreaded Pawnee swooped down on the herd and made off with more than a hundred horses and oxen. Some of the emigrants lost heart right then and turned back to the States. The others kept on, splitting into smaller groups. Four of the men went out with no weapons but their long blacksnake whips to recover their animals from the Pawnee. Two of them were killed. Uncle Billy pushed on undeterred, and at Fort Laramie went on solo with his family. At Fort Bridger he heard about the Donner Party and pushed ahead to join them on the Hastings cutoff.

The newcomers were gladly welcomed and promptly put to work hacking a path through the thickets. Even with these reinforcements, it took six days to clear a track along the Bossman, up a side canyon that they christened Reed's Gap, and over the highest mountain they had crossed yet. The wagons remained in camp, while the men walked or rode each morning to the work site. Two bad swamps held them up, and on the mountainside the trees were bigger (thus taking more labor to cut and dispose of) than those down in the canyons.

At last the task was completed, and the wagons lumbered ahead. The road could be called a road only by courtesy. The men, bone-tired and working against time, left stumps sticking up from the ground and leveled only the worst patches of road. The wagons had to steer carefully around stumps and boulders. The road curved back and forth, crossing the creek innumerable times.

It was a tight squeeze through the thicket-choked canyon bottoms. The men had cleared a path only wide enough for the wagon wheels. In their hurry they left the branches that hung over the path on both sides, and these nearly ripped the canvas tops from the wagons. How Reed's oversized palace car got through at all is to be wondered at. One of his other wagons tipped over, but they got it on its wheels again.

A grueling climb, by now an everyday experience, brought the weary travelers to the top of the mountain. From here they could see the Salt Lake Plains, and the sight gave their spirits a lift. Perhaps they would extricate themselves from these never-ending canyons after all! With renewed hope, they proceeded down, crossing a steep little ravine that the road crew had filled with brush and rocks. At the day's end they rested in a pleasant little valley with fine water and good grass, and the half-starved oxen had their first decent pasture in two weeks.

Reed wrote in his diary that the mountain was "a natural easey pass with a little more work." His standards of travel must have changed considerably since he left Springfield. His optimism seems even stranger in light of the fact that one of his wagons broke an axletree on the same "natural easey pass."

The next day, August 19, brought mingled good and bad news. A search party found Stanton and McCutchen and brought them in. The two men had lost the trail and wandered aimlessly in the maze of canyons and ridges. When located, they were near starvation and were about to resort to slaughtering and eating their horses, a truly last-ditch expedient. The bad news was that still another mountain ridge lay between the camp and the level plain of Great Salt Lake. This revelation caused consternation among the emigrants. But they could not go back; with sinking hearts they must go ahead.

Stanton, McCutchen, and a few others went off to search out a route. The easiest way they could find still cost the harried party at least two more days' labor at hacking and prying. (This according to Reed's diary. Other sources say five days.)

Up and over the mountain the wagons groaned, then down into still another canyon with a little creek flowing through it. The end of the canyon was choked with the usual willow brush. Another quarter-mile or less of ax work would have taken the wagons out onto the open Salt Lake plain. But even this short distance was more than the males of the Donner Party could face, for by now they loathed the work of clearing with near-hysteric intensity. Instead, they muscled the wagons up the canyon slope and down the other side. The canyon wall at that spot is a high, very steep spur of the mountain, enough to challenge the endurance of a well-nourished modern hiker in good physical shape. It took almost every available yoke of oxen hitched to each wagon in turn to get the wagons up and over. And there were twenty-three wagons to move. It says much about the party's state of mind that they preferred this herculean effort to the alternative of a few hours' more brush-clearing. Nevertheless, on Friday, August 21, they camped at last on level ground.

Another three days' plodding brought them to the tracks of the party that Hastings had taken down the "impassable" canyon. The weary and discontented emigrants made camp by a brackish spring. From the time they had found Hastings's note in the bush on the Weber, it had taken them eighteen days to travel thirty-nine miles (the total of Reed's daily estimates).

The Salt Lake plain was easy going, a pleasant change from what they had just been through. The farmers in the party noted approvingly the good soil, lush grass, and plentiful water. The dreaded dry drive across the desert still lay ahead of them.

On August 25 the company made camp by some slightly brackish springs that Reed called the Lower Wells. One wagon, however, did not come in until eight that evening. Luke Halloran, the frail consumptive, was dying, and George Donner had stopped his wagon to make the young man's last moments as comfortable as possible. He died at about four that afternoon, with his head in Tamsen's lap. In gratitude, Halloran left all he owned to the family that had befriended him: his horse, bridle, and saddle, and an old trunk with its contents. The trunk was opened, and to everyone's surprise it contained $1,500 in gold coins and the full regalia of a Master Mason. The young invalid had guarded his secrets well.

Boards were donated to make a coffin, and the next day the company moved two miles to a better campsite, where there were more springs (Reed noted that one of them had "delightful water being entirely fresh"). Here the Masons in the group conducted a funeral service according to the rites of their order. Halloran was laid to rest in the marshy ground near the grave of a man from Hastings's party.

CHAPTER NOTE

1. Revisionists have calculated that the Graves contingent caught up with the Donner-Reed party at the eastern flank of the Wasatch, as they were waiting for Reed and his two companions to return from their attempt to reach Hastings.

CHAPTER 8
The Dreadful Dry Drive

. . . We had a view of the desert plain before us, which as far as the eye could penetrate, was of a snowy whiteness, and resembled a scene of wintry frosts and icy desolation. Not a shrub or object of any kind rose above the surface for the eye to rest upon.
—Edwin Bryant, *What I Saw in California*

Out of respect for the dead, and perhaps also to take a much needed rest, the party did not travel that day. On August 27 they were on their way again, following the level expanse of an ancient beach that had been formed centuries ago, when the Great Salt Lake was much larger. Level the landscape might have been, but in other respects it was hardly cheering. A long, hard drive took them northwest around the foot of a mountain range through dry, barren plains dotted with sage and an occasional stunted tree. Jackrabbits, lizards, and ants were the only visible inhabitants of this desolate area. They passed two or three springs from which little streams flowed toward the lake, but the water was so salty that neither people nor animals could drink it.

Rounding the mountains, Hastings's tracks perversely doubled back sharply and headed almost due south. Where in the world was that fool Hastings leading them? At day's end they camped by a group of brackish wells. "Miserable water," Reed noted, underlining the words for emphasis.

The disheartened emigrants were glad to leave this campsite, but the next day brought them only more of the same drought and dreariness as they trudged south on the trail of the unpredictable Hastings. On their left the barren, jagged crest of the nameless mountain range loomed inhospitably above them; on the right an equally uninviting valley, its floor splotched with large salt incrustations, stretched off to yet another desert range.

Evening brought a welcome surprise: fresh, clear springs surrounded by plentiful grass. Here the Donner Party spent the next day filling the water casks, stocking up on firewood (the bountiful buffalo-chip country was far behind, but there were scattered trees on the hillsides), and cutting grass to sustain the oxen on the long dry drive that loomed ahead of them.

Once they had crossed the mountain ridge to their west, the desert crossing would begin. Hastings had said it could be done in a day and a night, but by now they had learned to put little faith in anything he said. Suddenly someone caught sight of a board lying on the ground, with tattered scraps of paper clinging to its surface. More scraps of paper lay on the ground nearby. The emigrants could make out traces of writing, but they could not decipher the jumbled fragments. Obviously someone had tried to leave a message, but either birds had pecked it to pieces or Indians had destroyed it out of malice.

While the bewildered emigrants tried to puzzle out the mystery, Tamsen, who loved nothing better than having a problem to solve, came to the rescue. Kneeling on the ground by the board, she began to pick up the nearest pieces of paper, fitting them together like pieces of a puzzle. Others saw what she was doing and joined in. At last a message began to emerge, in a hand they recognized as Hastings's. The message was brief and fragmentary, but devastating. It said: "2 days . . . 2 nights . . . hard driving . . . cross desert . . . water."

The men and women tried to figure out what the cryptic message could mean in terms of miles. If forty miles required a day, a night, and another day, what could two days and two nights measure? Fifty miles? More?

They left at daybreak the next morning with many apprehensions. It was now August 30, late in the season, and they knew that the worst parts of the California Trail still lay ahead.

From the springs the trail led west over twelve miles of dry sagebrush country to the slopes of the mountain range that stretched across their path as far as they could see. They stopped at another brackish spring; Reed noted afterward: "ought to be avoided water not good for cattle. Emigrants should keep on the edge of the lake and avoid the mountain entirely here commenced the long drive through the Salt dessert."

After leaving the brackish spring, the party followed Hastings's trail up a rocky, thousand-foot ridge, an effort that probably took them most of the day. From the top they could see the vast, white desolation of the Salt Lake Desert stretching before them. The weary emigrants descended the mountain with the last daylight and probably stopped for an hour or two at the base to rest the oxen.

They crossed another barren valley and a low, volcanic ridge before they came to the salt desert proper. In the light that the desert moon and stars afforded, the country ahead of them looked like a wildly tossing sea full of whitecaps. It was, as they soon found out, a series of sand dunes alternating with soft, powdery level stretches where the animals' hooves and the wheels of the wagons sank inches deep. (Bryant, coming this way in August, found his mules sinking knee-deep, and sometimes up to their bellies.) It was hard going, as anyone who has tried to run along a soft, sandy beach knows, and it was made worse by the dust that rose around them like a choking fog and by the intense heat of the desert sun after it rose.

It was on this dreadful stretch that the Donner Party lost its last semblance of unity. Already, back in the Wasatch, the emigrants had begun to resent and distrust each other. Now, in the desert, the wagon train literally disintegrated as the speedier wagons pulled ahead and left their slower companions behind. It was each family for itself.

Soon the wagons were stretched out over a space of two miles or more. William Eddy, with his light wagon, was in the lead, the others spaced out behind him according to weight or the driver's wish to save his team's strength. The heavy wagons of the Donners and Reeds brought up the rear.

The dune region eventually gave way to salt flats. Not even a solitary sage bush or cactus broke the fearful monotony of the dazzling white expanse. Isolated peaks rising in the distance provided the only variety. Not a living creature was to be seen or heard. The only sounds were those of the wagons, the animals, and the people themselves. One can imagine they didn't have much to say.

In the salt desert the atmosphere and the light began to play strange tricks, and the emigrants began to see mirages. Eddy glanced across the plain and discovered twenty men in single file marching along beside him, a little distance away. They were all walking in the same direction as himself, and they marched in step with a precision that an army drillmaster would have envied. Every movement of their bodies was in unison. When Eddy stopped to take a better look, the mysterious men stopped, too. He peered at their faces and found that they looked just like him. Their clothes all matched his, too. When Eddy made a movement, the twenty men copied it simultaneously. If he took a step ahead, so did they, and they all stopped abruptly when he stopped. Eddy realized that the men were a bizarre reflection of his own image, multiplied twenty times. Others in the party saw lakes and fields; once they saw a mirage of their own wagon train in the distance and cried out in joy, thinking it was Hastings, come back to rescue them.

At first the salt crust that covered the flat plain was hard and firm. Then, to their dismay, it became soft and mushy. Contrary to any reasonable expectation, the ground beneath this crust of salt, in this bone-dry desert, was soaked with water!

Charley Stanton, the self-taught geology buff, could have explained to them that this groundwater was exactly what produced the crust of salt. Seeping along through the porous soil from some far-off source, it became saturated with minerals. It rose to the surface by capillary action, evaporated swiftly under the scorching heat of the sun, and left its load of salt and alkali behind. But there is no record that anyone took the trouble to ask him.

Ox hooves and wagon wheels soon broke through the weakened crust and sank into the soft, oozy mud beneath. At times the wagons were hub-deep in the soft, clinging slime. The added resistance and the treacherous footing slowed the weakened teams to a painful crawl.

The wagons could no longer follow each other in single file. They had to fan out widely so that each could travel on as much unbroken crust as possible, or at least avoid mud that had been churned up by another wagon. Back on the grassy prairies, fanning out was normal. Here on the salt flats the extra motion took a heavy toll of time and strength, but it was unavoidable.

The evening of the third day came, bringing relief from the day's heat. The emigrants pushed doggedly on, stopping only for brief rests. The last wagons—the heavy vehicles of the Donners and Reeds— were still far out on the salt flats, miles from the mountains where they expected to find water. The supply, perhaps enough for half that distance, was dangerously low. It was clear to the leaders that they and their families faced death from thirst if they could not find water soon. The flagging oxen obviously could not pull much farther without water. Reed volunteered to ride ahead and search for a spring.

Before he left, Reed gave his teamsters orders to drive the oxen until they could no longer budge the wagons, then unyoke the exhausted beasts and drive them slowly along the trail to water. Peering through the glare, he could see that the trail turned sharply left, detoured around an isolated rock pinnacle, and headed for a green-clad mountain range. Where there was green, common sense said there had to be water.

Reed swung up on a horse and set off. He soon caught up with the other wagons and found their families in as much distress as his own. Some of the men had unyoked their oxen and were driving them ahead in search of water. Others stubbornly tried to get their wagons as far as possible before the oxen collapsed. Exhausted oxen lay here and there on the ground, unable to move.

Leaving the wagons behind, Reed soon reached the mountains. With dismay he saw that the inviting green mantle was neither grass nor trees. It was the spiny green branches of greasewood, a hardy desert shrub. Not a spring, not even a seepage, could be found.

Reed found a rocky pass and rode across the ridge. From the summit he saw not grass nor firm ground, but another wide stretch of salt flats, perhaps twelve miles in extent, that separated him from the mountains that marked the end of the Great Salt Desert. He knew that his hard-pressed horse could never make it back to his wagon without a drink. His only choice was to push on.

The tired horse made poor time. It was evening before Reed came up to the spring at the foot of Pilot Peak, just east of the present-day Utah-Nevada line. He passed William Eddy's wagon, temporarily abandoned, and found Eddy himself at the spring with his oxen. Eddy had reached the spring at ten o'clock in the morning and taken the rest of the day to rest himself and his animals. And Eddy was not a lazy man.

A few other emigrants were there with their oxen. Reed stayed only an hour, then started back in the early darkness with Eddy. Eddy was carrying a bucket of water for one of his own oxen that had given out along the way. Reed himself had no bucket with him, and could not possibly have carried it back on horseback the twenty or more miles to his wagon in any case. All he could take back was the news that there was water ahead.

By the light of the desert moon, Reed saw some of the women and children trudging toward the spring. Other families, feeling safer in the familiar shelter of their wagons, waited anxiously for the men to come back. He heard men cursing Hastings as they awkwardly tried to drive their oxen and carry water pails at the same time.

About eleven o'clock Reed encountered Milt Elliott and James Smith driving his own oxen and horses to water. He cautioned them to keep the animals on the trail, "for as soon as they would scent the water they would break for it."

Along the trail Reed passed others from the rear wagons. There was Uncle Jake Donner with his oxen, and there was Uncle George. Reed's weary horse carried him past the Donner wagons, looming in the desert night. He rode on, and just before daybreak reached his own wagons, only a couple of miles beyond the spot where he had left them. His teamsters had not obeyed their orders to push the oxen to the limit, but had unyoked the poor beasts as soon as they began to falter and driven them to water. This was a humane act and under normal circumstances a prudent one. But it left Reed's wagon sitting far out in the desert and had disastrous consequences for the Reeds.

The five family dogs—Barney, Tracker, Tyler, Trailer, and little Cash, the children's pet—greeted him at the wagons. Margaret and the children were safe, guarded by Baylis Williams, the handyman, and Walter Herron, the teamster.

Herron took the horse and led it toward the distant spring while the others waited. It was a long wait in the palatial Reed wagon, under the broiling desert sun. Noon came, and still there was no sign of faithful Milt returning with the revived oxen. The water was almost finished. At sundown the family set off on foot.

It was a desperate gamble, this march of twenty-odd miles. The three older children could walk on their own, but Reed had to carry three-year-old Tommy in his arms. Margaret Reed was an invalid, and it was touch and go whether she could last out the journey.

After a while the children became exhausted, and Reed spread a blanket on the ground for them to lie on. He covered them with shawls against the chill of the desert night, but a "cold hurricane" soon began to blow, and the pathetically complaining children became dangerously chilled. Reed commanded the five dogs to lie down around the children while he and Mrs. Reed sat with their backs to the wind to form a living windbreak. The warmth of the dogs' bodies soon revived the children.

Suddenly the dogs leaped up, barking in alarm, and dashed at some unknown danger. Out of the dark charged a young steer, crazed by thirst and heading straight for the family group! Reed drew his pistol while the dogs, barking frantically, nipped at the steer's legs. At the last moment it swerved aside, narrowly missing the huddled family. Reed recognized it as one of his own steers and involuntarily cried out that it was mad. Margaret and the children leaped to their feet and fled, scattering like frightened quail. "It was some minutes before I could quiet camp." Reed wrote later with a good deal of understatement, "there was no more complaining of being tired or sleepy the balance of the night."

On they marched for another ten miles, with fear giving the children energy. At daybreak they reached the wagons of Jacob Donner, where Aunt Betsy and the children were asleep. We can assume that the barking of the two families' dogs woke them, and Reed finally learned what had happened to his livestock.

Not only had his teamsters failed to take the wagons as far as possible, they also had lost nine yoke of oxen, almost all he had. On the way to the spring a worn-out horse had lain down. While the men tried to get it up, the oxen, momentarily unguarded, had apparently scented water and dashed off. The men were still out looking for them. Had the oxen been driven to the point of exhaustion, as Reed had ordered, they might not have had the strength to bolt.

The Reeds still had with them a little water, a few crackers, and chunks of loaf sugar to suck on when they felt thirsty. Reed was all set to press on to the spring to see what could be done about his missing oxen. But Aunt Betsy Donner insisted that Margaret Reed and the children ride with her in her wagon because they were so tired. Reed accepted the offer thankfully and strode off, while Aunt Betsy made a fire and prepared breakfast for her guests: bacon with milk gravy, salt-rising bread, and, for Mrs. Reed, a good cup of tea.

Along the trail, men and boys were already returning from the spring with their teams. Jake Donner was among them; he told Reed that he had reached the spring at two in the morning. Yes, he would be glad to give a ride to the Reed family.

That evening Uncle Jake's wagons rolled up to the spring. Everyone, if not their wagons, was in from the desert. They had traveled more than eighty miles without water, and it had taken them six days! The date was now September 4. According to Hastings's *Emigrant's Guide,* they should be approaching the Sierras by now.

Reed was not the only one who had lost cattle. Men and boys rode out on the tired horses, scouring the desert and the nearby mountains for the strays. But after three or four days of searching there were still thirty-six oxen missing, half of them belonging to Reed. If they didn't turn up, Reed would somehow have to get his three heavy wagons to California with the power of one ox and one cow.

One day two Indians came into the camp and indicated by signs that they knew where the cattle were. But most of the men were away, and the women were nervous about the Indians, who they feared were spies. They did not encourage them with the customary gifts of food, and the Indians went away.

Almost as soon as they had reached the spring and given their animals a drink, the men of the Donner Party had begun going back into the salt desert to retrieve the wagons they had abandoned; among other things, these wagons carried the vital food supplies.

Reed's wagons, however, lay the farthest out of all. On Sunday, September 6, Reed abandoned his fruitless pursuit of his missing teams and rode out to fetch his wagons in. Some of the other men rode with him. They took horses and mules for draft animals this time instead of the slow-moving oxen.

Reed by now realized that he had no real chance of recovering his oxen, and he decided to abandon two of his wagons, transferring the most essential portions of their loads to his once-magnificent "palace car." There was no point in dragging all three wagons back to the spring to do this. Reed simply loaded the food, clothing, and bedding into the family wagon and left the rest. However, he did not want to leave his valuable goods out in the open for the Indians to pilfer, and he insisted on caching them—next year he might return and get them. The other men did not begrudge Reed the time to do this, for they all appreciated the value of property. They even helped him.

The approved method of making a cache was to dig a large, deep hole, remove the wheels from the wagon, and lower the wagon bed into the hole. The goods were packed into the wagon bed and covered with tarpaulins or whatever else would keep the dirt off them, and the excavated earth was shoveled back and leveled off. The final step was to drive one's teams back and forth over the spot until all traces of the hole were obliterated in the general mess of hoofprints.

But here in the salt flats there was water just a few inches down, so a hole was not practical. Instead, they laid one wagon bed on the ground, piled the goods into it, and heaped dirt over the whole collection. It was a big mound; there was not a chance that the Indians would not see it, and they would almost certainly dig into it and pilfer it. But at least the men could feel that they had made the attempt. Reed rode back to the spring—twenty-eight miles—and the wagons came in the next morning. George Donner and Keseberg had also had to abandon wagons, one each.

The next couple of days were occupied in repairing the wagons and resting the oxen. Of his once large herd Reed now had left one mismatched yoke—an ox and a milk cow. He managed to borrow a spare ox from Patrick Breen and another from Uncle Billy Graves, against a promise of future payment. This added up to two yoke, but the oversized family wagon needed four yoke, even with a normal load. Two yoke of tired, underfed animals would never be able to move it with its present overload of food supplies.

Once more Reed had to turn to his none-too-friendly traveling companions and ask if he could parcel out his load among the other wagons. The other families refused to carry the food unless they could have a share for themselves. It was a hard bargain, but Reed had no choice but to accept the terms, and he had to admit that some of the other families needed the food badly.

With one stroke—the loss of their oxen—the Reeds had been reduced from wealth to near-poverty. Their valuable goods were abandoned in the desert, and they were now dependent on the tenuous goodwill of their companions to get through the rest of the journey.

At three in the morning William Eddy climbed the flank of Pilot Peak and witnessed a magnificent sunrise. It was the only magnificent thing about that day's journey. The wagons were in dreadful shape, and it was anyone's guess how much longer they would last. The oxen's bones showed through their dull, unhealthy-looking hides. The people were tired and in extremely low spirits. Two of the men were not even there—Milt Elliott and young William Graves were still out in the desert, hunting the lost oxen. No matter, they'd meet the men somewhere along the trail.

As the party plodded along the feet of the mountains the capricious desert weather presented them with yet another shock: a snowstorm. Consternation was the response. What would they have to face in the Sierras if they had snow already down here in the desert?

While they pondered the depressing possibilities that awaited them, in midafternoon they met Milt Elliott and young William Graves. The two had no oxen with them, but they had news. The party was not far from a spring where they could camp, but after that they faced a dry drive of forty miles. The two men had probably found a note sent back by Hastings, who for once in his life was telling the truth.

They camped early to rest for the long drive and left at dawn the next morning. Hastings's trail led them about ten miles through an easy mountain pass and continued west across a wasteland of sagebrush. They traveled all day and night, stopping only to rest the oxen, feed them a bit of hay they had cut at the last pasture, and give them a tiny ration of water. At four the next morning they reached a temporary haven, a valley with good water and grass. They had traveled thirty-five miles. (Reed made it twenty-three miles in his logbook, but he often underestimated distances.) Along the way they had suffered more losses—some of the cattle had died, and the surviving ones were in very bad shape. They had to be given twenty-four hours' rest.

CHAPTER 9

Blood on the Humboldt

At this point in our journey we were compelled to double our teams in order to ascend a steep, sandy hill. Milton Elliott, who was driving our wagon, and John Snyder, who was driving one of Mr. Graves's, became involved in a quarrel over the management of their oxen.
—Virginia Reed Murphy, *"Across the Plains in the Donner Party (1846),"* The Century Magazine, July 1891

The Donner Party now faced a terrible dilemma. If they tried to get some speed out of their worn-out oxen, the beasts would drop dead in their tracks. If they spared the animals, they would never reach the Sierras before snow blocked the pass. In a spasm of desperation, they took a vote and decided to risk sending someone across the mountains to Sutter's Fort, the first outpost of civilization in California, to fetch help. They agreed it had better be two men for safety against Indians and accident. It was a dangerous gamble, for any diminution of the party's strength was risky. It was not even sure that the men would get through. But if they did, it might make the difference between life and death. And Sutter was already legendary for the generous help he gave to stranded Americans.

John Augustus Sutter, lord of Sutter's Fort and a vast domain of land, was one of the strangest figures to strut across the stage of California's history. The simile is deliberately chosen, for Sutter was nothing if not a man acting a part.

The Lord of New Helvetia

Sutter was born in 1803 in southwestern Germany, where his father managed a paper mill. As if Fate had chosen to mark him as an exile at birth, his parents were not German, but Swiss. Returning to Switzerland as a youth, he finished his schooling, married, and went into business. He failed twice, once as a cloth merchant and then in the stationery trade. Disgraced, Sutter fled his homeland in secrecy to escape his creditors, leaving his wife and children behind to be supported by her wealthy relatives.

Somehow, Sutter made his way to America, where the failed businessman fashioned a new and romantic identity for himself. Too humbly born to have become an officer (a dignity that the Swiss reserved for the aristocracy and the richer commoners), he now presented himself as Captain John Augustus Sutter, lately of the famed Swiss Guards of King Charles X of France, and a worthy veteran of several European campaigns. In truth, Sutter had no military experience beyond a few years' part-time service in the Swiss militia.

Sutter was, in fact, as big a liar as Hastings and an even more talented con man, although, to be fair, he was handicapped by a certain basic kindliness and generosity that Hastings, for all his charm, seemed to lack. These qualities did not, however, prevent Sutter from swindling his fellow Swiss and German immigrants with disastrous business schemes and loans that he never repaid.

Having earned an untrustworthy reputation in the East, Sutter drifted west to the Missouri border and made a couple of trips to Santa Fe (then Mexican) as a trader. In 1838 new horizons beckoned him, and he joined a party of traders and missionaries bound for Oregon. From there he went on a roundabout journey by sea to Alaska and Hawaii. The next year he popped up in California and at last came truly into his own.

California belonged to Mexico, and Mexico was a Catholic nation where only the Catholic religion was tolerated. Mexican law required that all settlers become Roman Catholics if they were not so already. Sutter was the grandson of a Protestant minister and had been brought up in a strict Protestant household. But it bothered him not at all to go over to the enemy faith—perhaps he did it gladly as a kind of late rebellion against his stern parents.

Sutter may not even have bothered with the formalities of conversion, but simply told the Mexican authorities that he was a Catholic already. In any case, he soon talked the governor-general into granting him a huge tract of wild country at the junction of the American and Sacramento Rivers—nearly forty-nine thousand acres in extent—on condition that he develop it. Mexico was making a belated effort to fill up this neglected province with loyal settlers before the Americans swarmed in and took it over by force, as they had in Texas.

Sutter named his domain New Helvetia, from the Latin name for Switzerland, and ruled it like an independent nation. He taught the local Indians how to herd cattle and sheep and raise crops. Fraudulent as his military claims were, he even organized a well-drilled Indian battalion. He built a substantial fort near the junction of the two rivers; the city of Sacramento stands there today.

Americans knew of Sutter because of his generous hospitality to emigrants from the States, and Sutter's Fort was where they headed when they came down from the Sierras, tired and travel-worn. Sutter's generosity was amply repaid, for his shops at the Fort did a brisk business in liquor and other essentials.

The Donner Party were so disoriented by their hardships in the desert that they could not be certain of how far they were from Sutter's (actually they had six hundred miles still to go—fifty days' worth of travel if the oxen held out). Two men volunteered to make the dash for help: the muscular giant William McCutchen and the wiry little bachelor Charles Stanton. Some of the party may have had their doubts whether the two men would really return once they were safe and comfortable in California. But McCutchen was leaving a wife and child with the company, and he didn't seem the sort to abandon them. Stanton, although a bachelor with no family ties among the

Donner Party, struck everyone as a man who would keep his word. The two-man mission set off without delay, big McCutchen on a horse and the little bachelor on a mule that McCutchen had loaned him.

In the meantime, Reed had come reluctantly to the conclusion that he could go no farther with his big wagon and only half the number of oxen he needed to pull it. He buried most of what little property he had not been forced to jettison already. Then William Eddy stepped forward with a proposal: He would team up with Reed, letting Reed use his oxen in return for sharing the big wagon with Eddy. Eddy in turn would lend his own rickety, but still rolling, wagon to William Pike of the Murphy clan. After some dickering, the deal was consummated, and the company used up the rest of the day in camp redistributing the loads.

The next few days gave them easier traveling. On September 13, a Sunday, a pull of thirteen miles or so brought them to a spring-fed meadow where warm water bubbled from the ground—they were entering a region of numerous warm springs. It was a pleasant resting spot, yet the next day Reed confided to his diary: "Left the . . . Mad-Woman camp, as all the women in camp were mad with anger." He discreetly did not set down the reason for this outburst of rage, but it may well have begun as a personal quarrel that spread until everyone was involved. Certainly every adult in the party now had an ample store of frustration and anger to vent.

Despite the delicate emotional climate, the party made good progress the next day and camped at the eastern foot of a mountain range by a pair of mineral springs that had formed high, conical mounds with their deposits. It was a phenomenon that under normal circumstances they would have marveled at. The weary, tense emigrants noticed another puzzling phenomenon as they crossed this stretch of strange country: The springs were always on the eastern flank of a mountain, never on the west. But they had no more dry drives for a while.

Following the wheel marks of Hastings's wagons, they crossed a wide basin bordered by low mountains and camped in a beautiful, well-watered valley that Reed dubbed Mineral Valley. (Later, Mormon prospectors found handsome red stones there and named it Ruby Valley. The stones turned out to be garnets, but the name stuck.) To the west the way was blocked by the high, rugged range of the Ruby Mountains, and Hastings's tracks turned abruptly south. Typically, Hastings had missed the trail on which he had come east with Jim Clyman. The Ruby Range stretches roughly north and south for about eighty miles; Hastings, navigating by slipshod guesswork, had managed to strike the mountain barrier almost smack in the middle.

The Donner Party went down the valley in easy stages, looking hopefully but vainly for a break in the steep mountain wall that barred their way. But there were compensations for their disappointment. The valley and the mountain slopes were full of game, and the men took a day off to go hunting. Fresh pronghorn antelope and bighorn sheep provided a welcome change from their dwindling and monotonous rations of bacon, bread, dried beans, and heavily salted pork.

One day a large band of Indians visited the campsite. They behaved as if they had never seen a white person before. They seemed curious and friendly. But the next day two of George Donner's horses were missing.

The party was now in Digger Indian country. "Digger" was not the name of a tribe; it described an impoverished way of life. The Diggers were fragments of various Great Basin tribes and subtribes: Shoshone, Ute, Paiute, Gosiute, Washoe, Mono, Bannock. Pushed out of the more desirable parts of the Great Basin by their stronger relatives, they wandered the desert in small, scattered bands, living mainly on edible roots and bulbs that they dug from the ground with sticks; hence the name Digger. This diet was supplemented by insects, grubs, burrowing animals, and jackrabbits. In season, there were wild berries, spawning fish from the few desert rivers, and migrating waterfowl. Once in a while the Diggers were lucky and caught a pronghorn or a deer. For the most part they lived in wretched, hand-to-mouth poverty without even proper shelter. Instead of snug lodges of earth or logs or tipis of buffalo hide, they sheltered in piles of brush heaped around a rudimentary framework of willow boughs.

The Diggers were generally unwarlike. The stronger tribes despised and persecuted them. So did the few whites who had met them. Mountain men sometimes shot the Diggers for sport. Had they been less brutal, the Diggers might well have helped the Donner Party. Instead, they took the opportunity for vengeance.

There was no time to search for the missing horses, even though one of them was Uncle George's favorite. The party dared not lose any more time, and once more they followed the inexplicable southbound trail left by Hastings. At last, on the fifth day (September 21), a pass opened up on their right. It took them four miles across the mountain range and out into a waste of sagebrush and greasewood, where they luckily found a creek to camp by.

The trail turned north again, following the western flank of the Ruby Mountains. Hastings, ignorant of the country he was traversing, was trying to get back on his original track to the Humboldt River. The anxious members of the Donner Party, of course, could not know this. The long and apparently pointless detour made them think that Hastings had lost his mind. But they were as lost as Hastings, and his wagon tracks were the only guide they had. Fortunately, his trail ran along a north-flowing creek, so at least they had water near at hand. But the psychological strain was getting near the bursting point.

A few days later (September 24, by Reed's logbook), they camped at the head of a canyon that led to the Humboldt River, where they would rejoin the regular emigrant trail to California. Many Indians, stark naked, came to gape at the white strangers with their peculiar animals and houses on wheels. These Indians were timorous and did not venture into the camp.

The next morning, the party followed a winding path down the canyon. "We made sixteen miles 16 for six miles," wrote Reed, "a very rough cannon a perfect snake trail." He meant that they had traveled sixteen miles to make six miles of actual progress.

After negotiating this obstacle course, the weary party camped at the last level, dry spot that was large enough to hold all the wagons. The following evening saw them camped on the south bank of the Humboldt, where the creek they had been following joined it. At last they were back on the established trail!

Their joy and relief may have been damped somewhat by the sight of the river. Fed by melting snows in the mountains, the Humboldt was a roaring torrent in the spring. But this late in the autumn it was only a sluggish trickle between stagnant pools, and dry in some places. The water was warm and tasted of rotten eggs.

Adding to their disappointment, some Indians came into camp and told them by signs that they were still about two hundred miles (or the equivalent in days of travel) from the Humboldt Sink, where the river disappears into a rancid swamp in a desert valley. The Humboldt follows a very winding course through the desert, and the trail crossed the river frequently to shortcut its big bends and squiggly meanders. Runty willows and bushes lined the riverbanks, and grass grew in the relatively moist zone above them. Beyond that there was nothing but thinly scattered greasewood and brush on either side. It was monotonous going.

Most of the grass along this stretch was gone, eaten by the teams of the earlier emigrant parties, which had taken the regular trail by way of Fort Hall and passed down the Humboldt weeks before. The little grass that was left was dried up and held little sustenance for the animals. Because of the scarcity of forage, the Donner brothers, whose oxen were in somewhat better condition than those of the other families, went ahead. The others formed a slower-moving rear section. The group was lagging badly now. Even Hastings's party was a good two weeks ahead of them.

Two days down the Humboldt, a Digger Indian of the Paiute tribe visited the rear section of the party. He spoke a little English, which he had learned from other emigrant companies. Later that day a second Indian joined them. This one knew some ox-driving commands. "Gee! Whoa! Huoy!" the Indian shouted happily. These words, plus a few profanities, indicated that he had indeed been with ox-drivers. The emigrants, thinking of Robinson Crusoe, named this Indian "Thursday" for the day on which they met him. (Actually it was a Friday—they had lost track of time.)

The Paiutes, the Digger tribe that inhabited the Humboldt Valley, had no love for whites. It was their people who had been massacred by mountain men, and they craved revenge for their slaughtered kin. The Donner Party, ignorant of the atrocities, invited the two Indians to stay overnight.

The party crossed a ridge and camped at a spring halfway down the far side, their Indian friends with them. Someone was careless with a campfire, and the flames spread to the dry brush. All hands turned out to battle the blaze, which was extinguished with the aid of the Diggers after threatening three of the tinder-dry wagons. The grateful emigrants fed the Indians a good meal, but in the morning they were gone. So were two oxen and an expensive shirt, all belonging to Uncle Billy Graves.

Two nights later the Diggers stole a fine mare from Uncle Billy. When William Eddy went out the next morning to hunt for pronghorn, lurking Digger bowmen sniped at him with arrows and drove him back to the safety of camp. The Diggers' bows were weak, but it was rumored that they used poisoned arrows.

September slid into October almost unnoticed in the parade of weary days. But it was fall now, and the days were shorter, the nights colder. In the mornings there was a thin layer of ice in the water in the buckets, and sometimes the ground was frozen. The emigrants, driven by worry, pushed their tired oxen hard. They were slowly—oh, so slowly—beginning to catch up with Hastings. But the effort told on everyone, and hostility was the prevailing mood.

The general resentment found a focus on James Frazier Reed. The sullen, angry emigrants blamed the "proud aristocrat" for having led them into their disaster by insisting on following Hastings.

The festering conflict burst into bloodshed after a noon halt. The trail, for some reason, left the river and ascended a long, steep hill of sand, strewn with rocks near its top. Reed's section of the wagon train had stopped at the foot of the hill for their midday break; the trouble began when the wagons got under way again.

The hill was a difficult pull at best, and even more of an irritation now that everyone's temper was rubbed raw. With the steep grade and the soft footing, the oxen had to be double-teamed, one more annoyance on top of everything else. With the help of the extra teams, two of Uncle Billy Graves's wagons were hauled to the top without incident. But his last one was driven by headstrong young John Snyder, the teamster who was to wed Mary Graves. Snyder foolishly chose this moment to demonstrate his manly independence. Spurning the other men's offers to lend him their teams, he swore he would get his wagon up without help from anybody.

Snyder cracked his whip, and the gaunt, tired oxen strained forward. They made very slow headway. Next in line was Milt Elliott, driving the palatial wagon that the Reeds now shared with the Eddy family. Milt had borrowed a yoke of oxen from William Pike and hitched them on for the uphill pull. He grew impatient with Snyder's slow progress and started up, intending to pass Snyder on the hill. He failed to swing wide enough, and his lead oxen became entangled with Snyder's team, bringing everything to a stop.

Snyder cursed Milt, and Milt cursed him back. At this, Snyder flew into a violent rage and began beating Milt's oxen over the head with the heavy handle of his whip. Reed, who had been off hunting antelope, rode back just in time to see this ugly development. He jumped off his horse and ran to stop the infuriated Snyder. It was not only wrong to abuse the poor animals so, he told the young teamster, it was downright dangerous, for the party needed every ox it still possessed. Snyder then turned viciously on Reed, threatening to whip him, too. Reed, summoning all his diplomacy, curbed his own hot temper and replied that they should first get the wagons up the hill and then settle the quarrel.

This conciliatory approach only roused the bully in Snyder. His words and gestures became increasingly menacing, and Reed drew his hunting knife to warn the young teamster off. At this, Snyder, completely out of control, struck Reed a terrible blow on the head with his clublike whip handle, gashing his scalp severely. As Reed stood stunned by the unexpected blow, his wife rushed in to separate the two men. Snyder, in a murderous rage, dealt her a brutal blow to the head. At this, the injured Reed sprang to his wife's defense and stabbed Snyder just below the collarbone with such force that he cut through a rib and penetrated the teamster's left lung.

The crazed Snyder managed to inflict two more vicious blows to Reed's head, the last one bringing Reed to his knees, before he turned away, staggering.

Young Billy Graves caught Snyder in his arms and helped him up the hill for a few steps, then eased the wounded man to the ground. Patrick Breen, who had watched the brief melee aghast, hurried over to help. "Uncle Patrick, I am dead," whispered Snyder, and within a few minutes he expired. According to some accounts, he confessed just before he died that he had been in the wrong. If so, his confession fell on deaf ears, for the rest of the company blamed Reed.

Reed himself was horror-struck by what had happened. With blood from his wounds still running down his face and shoulders, he threw the fatal knife into the river. He had been fond of young Snyder, and he was not a killer by nature. But now he must face the vengeance of his hostile companions in the wagon company.

The company went into camp at once, with Reed's wagon segregated from the others as if it, too, were tainted with guilt. No one offered to help the badly injured Reed. His wife, herself injured and in shock, could not help him. Only twelve-year-old Virginia had the presence of mind and self-control to wash off the blood, clip the hair away from her father's wounds, and bandage him. (Reed bore the scars of Snyder's attack until his death.)

In anguished terms, Reed expressed his contrition and offered boards from his own wagon to make a coffin for Snyder. The offer only inflamed the company's ugly feelings, as if the high-and-mighty rich man were trying to buy his way out of trouble.

Snyder had been a favorite among the company for his exuberant personality, while Reed was generally disliked for being an "aristocrat." True, he did have a proud and dominating personality, with gentrified tastes and mannerisms. He had also begun the journey with an outfit that was far more costly and luxurious than those of the rest of the party. Unforgivably, he had a slew of hired hands to do the camp chores for him. He had a blooded racehorse and liked to show off its speed, while Virginia had a handsome pony all her own, on which she used to ride after her father on hunting trips instead of staying with the wagon and helping with the chores like the other girls her age. All these things were now held against him as items in his guilt by his envious fellow travelers. And Reed's old friends the Donners, who would have stood by him, were many miles ahead on the trail.

The men of the company held a kangaroo court at which they would not even let Reed appear in his own defense. While Reed sat in isolation in his wagon, one man after another accused him of murder. They wrote statements to use against Reed when they brought him to trial in California at journey's end. But this was not enough for some of the more vengeful members of the party, in particular

Lewis Keseberg, who had hated Reed ever since the grave-robbing incident on the Platte. The Graves family, too, craved vengeance for the death of the young man who had been almost one of them.

That evening Keseberg took an ox yoke and propped up his wagon tongue with it. Everyone had been on the trail long enough to know that this was how evildoers were hanged in a wagon train. But Reed was not entirely without friends. Milt Elliott and William Eddy stood by him in the crisis.

The three men snatched up their weapons and faced the threatening crowd. Reed had a six-shooter, two double-barreled pistols, and a rifle, while Milt had a rifle and a double-barreled shotgun. Eddy was armed with two six-shooters, two double-barreled pistols, and a rifle. At this concentration of firepower, the would-be lynchers hung back.

For a while the two sides stood glaring at each other, waiting tensely for someone to make the first move. At last, Eddy broke the stalemate with a proposal: Reed should leave the company the next morning and ride ahead to California.

At first, Reed refused to go. He felt the sentence was unjust—he had, after all, acted in defense of himself and his wife—and he feared to leave his family unprotected among his enemies. But Mrs. Reed and the children, fearing for his safety if he stayed, begged him to leave, and the other emigrants promised to look after them. Besides, Mrs. Reed pointed out, it would be best for everybody if he went ahead to California and came back with provisions in case McCutchen and Stanton did not get through. At this, Reed agreed.

CHAPTER 10

Perilous Journeys and Dastardly Doings

. . . the occurrence produced much feeling against him [Reed].
—Jessy Quinn Thornton, *Oregon and California in 1848*

They buried Snyder by the trailside the next morning. No one had made a coffin for him, despite Reed's offer of boards. Perhaps the spirit of self-righteous vengefulness was still too strong for anyone to accept Reed's gesture of conciliation; perhaps the men were simply too exhausted, emotionally and physically. Instead, they wrapped the young teamster's body in a piece of cloth and lowered it into the grave with a board beneath it and one on top to discourage scavengers from digging it up.

As soon as the grave was covered, Reed, his head swathed in bloody bandages, mounted his fast mare Glaucus and rode sadly off into exile. His vindictive companions refused to let him take a weapon, which in hostile Indian country was almost a death sentence in itself. True, he could get a gun from his friends the Donners when he caught up with them, but until then he would be a helpless target for the Diggers. But someone, either Virginia and Elliott, or perhaps William Eddy, managed to sneak ahead of the wagons and smuggle a gun to him that night.

Three days of hard riding brought Reed to the Donner wagons, where he got a night's rest among friends. He left after breakfast the next morning, but no longer in lone disgrace. His ex-teamster Walter Herron volunteered to go with him on his perilous trip. Herron had no horse, but that made no difference, as Reed's tired mare could no longer travel very far at a pace faster than a walk. If Herron got tired or footsore, Reed said, he could take a turn riding.

The two men had only a few days' rations with them—all the kindly Donners could spare—but there were flocks of migrating waterfowl all along the Humboldt now, and they reckoned that they could survive by hunting.

Meanwhile, the demoralized majority of the company proceeded grimly along the Humboldt. Whatever group spirit they had possessed at the beginning of the Hastings cutoff had long since evaporated in the canyons of the Wasatch and the hellish drive through the Salt Desert. They were no longer a disciplined entity. They were not even a friendly collection of people who happened to be traveling in the same direction. These emigrants were now sick to death of each other. As long as Reed had been with them, all their resentments could be concentrated on him. But now he was gone, and they had only each other to loathe. They were an uneasy cohort of mutual enemies who clustered together only out of the bitterest necessity.

Two days down the trail from the scene of Snyder's death, they found a trailside note from Reed. He told them that a party ahead of them had been attacked by the Diggers and that an emigrant had been killed. Since Eddy and Pike, out hunting that morning, had been shot at repeatedly by Indians lying in ambush, the party's nerves were doubly set on edge.

Then someone noticed that the old Belgian, Hardkoop, was missing. For the past few days the old man, his strength exhausted, had been riding in Keseberg's wagon, no longer able to keep up on foot. They asked Keseberg what had happened; he replied blandly that he had no idea. One of the men—the chronicles don't say who—set out to look for Hardkoop and found him collapsed beside the trail five miles back. Hardkoop told his rescuer that Keseberg had put him out of the wagon to die. Somehow, the man got Hardkoop back to camp, probably riding double on the weary horse.

The next morning William Eddy found that his ill-assorted team was too weak to pull the ponderous Reed family wagon. The luxurious vehicle, planned with such care and built at such great expense, must be abandoned. Eddy managed to procure a light wagon from Graves, probably at a stiff rent, and the Reeds shifted their few remaining possessions to this humbler conveyance.

Eddy could not find room for all his own goods in the wagon and had to cache some of them. This delayed him so that he could not start out until after the other wagons had all left. No one, of course, offered to help him. By now it was every man for himself.

After half an hour on the trail Eddy discovered Hardkoop, once more heartlessly abandoned by Keseberg. The old man begged Eddy to let him ride in his wagon. He was not only old, he pleaded, but also sick and worn out by the hardships he had suffered on the trail. He could go no farther on foot.

At this point Eddy was trying to get his wagon through a particularly difficult stretch of deep, soft sand, and he didn't want to risk adding even the slight weight of the half-starved old Belgian to the load of his exhausted team. He promised to take Hardkoop into the wagon as soon as he got past the sand, if Hardkoop could get that far on his own. Lost in his own problems, Eddy forgot about Hardkoop.

That evening in camp someone again remarked that Hardkoop was not there. Some of the boys, who had brought up the rear with the few remaining loose cattle, said they had seen the old man sitting under a large clump of sagebrush, completely given out. His shoeless feet had swollen until the skin had burst.

Eddy had the first shift on guard duty that night, and he built a big bonfire to guide Hardkoop in case he revived enough to travel. Milt Elliott stood the second watch, and he kept the fire going. The night was very cold.

In the morning, there was still no sign of Hardkoop. Mrs. Reed, Eddy, and Milt Elliott pleaded with Keseberg to go back for him, but Keseberg contemptuously refused. The Breens and Graveses still had saddle horses, and the three pleaders now turned to them. Patrick Breen also refused to help. He could not possibly spare a horse for such an errand, he said, and Hardkoop would just have to die. As for Uncle Billy Graves, that self-reliant frontiersman snapped that he would not kill one of his horses to save Hardkoop's life and angrily told them not to bother him any more about that old man.

Eddy, Pike, and Elliott then offered to go back on foot and carry Hardkoop to the wagons. The other emigrants refused to wait for them. To travel in such a small group with the Diggers lying in ambush would probably be fatal, so the three decent men gave up their effort.

They made another try at borrowing horses from Breen and Graves when the party stopped for an early midday rest and a scanty meal at the spot where Applegate's cutoff forked off to Oregon. Once more they received a violent refusal.

As if in retribution for deserting the helpless old man, the party struck a long stretch of deep, loose sand late in the afternoon. It took them twelve hours to struggle through it. It was four o'clock in the morning before the last wagons worked their way clear.

The party found the Donner families camped a little farther on, and learned that they had found the grave of the emigrant who had been slain by the Indians—the same one Reed had spoken of in his note. He was a man named Sallee, who had come by way of Fort Hall with Governor Boggs. (Boggs had taken Jim Clyman's warning so much to heart that he not only gave up the idea of taking the Hastings cutoff but also decided to go to Oregon instead of California. But he changed his mind again and arrived in California in October.) The Indians had dug up Sallee's grave and robbed the corpse of its clothes. Then the wolves had their turn and picked Sallee's bones bare. The Donners had hastily reburied them.

For the Reed family, there was encouraging news, however. James Reed was safe. For days the Donners had been scouting the trail for the ashes of his campfires. Whenever Reed had killed a wildfowl, he had left the feathers scattered conspicuously around the fireplace so that his family would know he had enough to eat.

Aside from the good news about Reed, the reunion was not a happy one. Arguments and quarrels about the deaths of Snyder and

Hardkoop broke out almost immediately. While the emigrants were wrangling, the Indians saw their chance and made off with all Graves's horses. Another wagon had to be abandoned. That night the party camped glumly by the river, which had been shrinking steadily as they traveled down it. The grass was scarce, and only scattered pools of stinking water remained in the riverbed. It was October 10, and they should have been in California by now.

In the night the Indians pounced again and ran off eighteen oxen and a cow. The cow, which belonged to Graves, was in no condition to give milk by now, but she could still have been used to pull a wagon in an emergency. However, it was Wolfinger and the Donners who suffered the greatest losses. The Donners, indeed, lost so many of their oxen that they had to yoke up some of their cows.

The beleaguered group struggled on, and that evening (October 11), they made camp at an equally unattractive spot. There was hardly any grass at all for the animals. The foul-smelling water lay in puddles surrounded by wide expanses of soft mud, in which the feet of people and animals alike sank when they crossed it to reach the water.

A fine mare belonging to Breen bogged down in a deep sinkhole filled with mud. He begged for help to get her out. Refused in turn by everyone he approached, he appealed to Eddy. Eddy coldly reminded Breen that he had refused to help Hardkoop, and the poor mare was left to smother in the mud.

During the night a party of Indians, aided by the darkness of the waning moon, crept up and shot some of the oxen full of arrows. It did not kill them—the Diggers' bows were weak, not being designed for game larger than a jackrabbit—but it made an amusing spectacle to see the beasts running about, lowing in pain and bristling with arrows like porcupines with quills erected.

The emigrants were now close to the Humboldt Sink, and they pushed ahead in a long drive. They reached the sink about midnight, although one of Eddy's oxen collapsed and had to be left beside the trail. They guarded the cattle carefully that night, but when the guards came in for breakfast no one went out to replace them. The ever-vigilant Diggers took the opportunity for some more target practice on the oxen and shot twenty-one of the meager herd. This time some of the oxen died; others were so badly injured that they could not keep up, even walking free behind the wagons. Their owners put them out of their misery, cut off the better portions of the meat, and bitterly left the rest behind for the Indians.

Eddy now had only one ox left, Wolfinger likewise, and one tired ox could not possibly pull a wagon through this terrain. The Donners generously offered to take care of the Reeds, although they had no room for even the few possessions that remained to the luckless family. So the Reeds stowed their modest bundles in one of Breen's wagons and walked on beside the Donners. The two littlest Reeds, five-year-old Jimmy and three-year-old Tommy, sat on their father's two remaining horses, which the Donners had taken charge of.

Billy, Virginia's cream-colored pony, had given out long ago, on the plains somewhere west of Fort Laramie, and was left behind, too exhausted to follow. Virginia had sat looking out of the back of the wagon, weeping as she saw her pet slowly dwindle to a little speck among the sagebrush, then disappear from view. Now she took her turn walking beside the horse that carried Tommy and holding the child on the saddle.

Eddy was in an even worse situation: He had no transportation at all. So he cached virtually everything he owned except the clothes he and his wife and children were wearing and three pounds of lump sugar. His gun he left behind—it was broken and would only be useless weight. But there was always the chance that he could borrow a gun from another member of the party, so he took his powderhorn and a supply of bullets.

Eddy, his wife, and the two small children then ate up the little food they had left and set off on foot, the parents carrying the children. Their shoes had long since worn out, and they wore homemade moccasins, not the most comfortable of footgear for trudging over jagged rocks and spiny prickly-pear cactuses.

Wealthy Wolfinger had no children to worry about, but he was understandably reluctant to jettison his possessions and enter California as a pauper, bringing only what he could carry on his back. His traveling companions, predictably, refused to carry anything for him in their wagons. They would not even wait while he made a cache. Finally his fellow-Germans Reinhardt and Spitzer offered to stay and help him, while Mrs. Wolfinger walked ahead with the other women.

The Humboldt Sink, which they were now leaving, was a most unpleasant spot at this time of year, a stinking marsh where dead cattails rustled above the mud in a harsh desert wind. The water was so vile that a member of Hastings's party later compared it to a strong solution of tepid water and Epsom salts, flavored with several rotten eggs. On either side were desolate wastes of sand with a little sagebrush. Farther off, the naked hillsides rose in giant steps, like bleachers. The emigrants were glad to leave this desolate spot, even though they faced another forty-mile stretch of desert.

It was a nightmare journey through the heat of the day. The sand was so fine that the animals kept sinking in to their knees. On the ridges there was no sand, but there were sharp rocks instead. To lighten the load of the faltering oxen, the emigrants carried as much as they could themselves. One of the Murphy boys wore a copper kettle on his head, like a bizarre helmet.

Eddy and his wife, burdened with their children, lagged far behind the wagons. Eddy looked up at the grandstandlike hills and saw them lined with Indians who were laughing at their calamity. He trudged on resolutely, following the wagon tracks. Night fell, and there was nothing to eat. The children sucked on lumps of sugar but became weak from dehydration. The waning moon came up and gave them a little light to travel by. At last, about four in the morning, the exhausted Eddy family caught up with the wagons, which had stopped at a group of hot springs.

To the fatigued and nerve-strained emigrants it must have seemed like a pocket of hell. One of the springs jetted boiling water in a column twenty feet tall—something to stay clear of if you didn't want

---

I asked him [Bryant's traveling companion, Hiram Miller] if he had found water. He answered that he had, but that his mule in attempting to drink out of a hole, had nearly scalded its tongue off. . . . I found myself in the midst of a hundred or more holes or small basins, varying from two to ten feet in diameter, of boiling water. [Edwin Bryant, *What I Saw in California*]

to be painfully scalded. The water of the other springs was also boiling hot; it had to be collected in buckets and cooled off before they could drink it. Even then, it was horribly bitter.

One of the Donner women gave Eddy a little coffee, which he brewed in the water of one of the boiling springs. Under happier circumstances this would have been a lark to laugh about for years afterward; now it was a bizarre necessity. Eddy took none of the bitter beverage for himself but gave it all to his wife and children. To his great relief, it revived them.

The party rested until about 9 a.m. and pushed on across the final stretch of desert, spurred by thoughts of the cool, fresh water and lush grass that waited for them along the banks of the Truckee River. The sun beat down cruelly. Neither Eddy nor his wife had a canteen, and the children suffered badly from thirst. After a while they became so weak from dehydration that Eddy feared they would die. He walked to Breen's wagon and asked for a drink for the children. And here in the Nevada desert Patrick Breen, family man, successful farmer, respected citizen, and presumably good Catholic, sank to the lowest point of his career. He refused the desperate father's request.

Breen mumbled that he had no water—Eddy knew this was a lie because he himself had helped Breen fill a ten-gallon cask that very morning. Faced with this, Breen admitted that he did have some water, but just enough for his own family, and he didn't know how far they still had to go before they reached the next source. In desperation, Eddy told Breen that he would have either the water or Breen's life. Breen sulked in silence, but did not resist as Eddy took the life-giving water for his children.

At sunset the party reached an exceedingly difficult ridge of deep sand about ten miles wide. Hastings's party, which had retained a modicum of discipline and cohesion, had double-teamed across this obstacle. But the Donner Party, at this point minus the Donners, had neither. So each family overstrained its own oxen in a surly and self-defeating show of independence. Once more they traveled all night, coaxing the half-dead oxen step by wearisome step. Six oxen dropped dead of exhaustion along the way. But at daybreak they finally came clear of the sand.

There, ahead of them, lay the tree-lined banks of the Truckee River. The tall cottonwoods cast a shade in which the emigrants would rest gratefully that day—the first real trees they had seen in a month of desert-crawling. For the famished animals there were grass and wild pea-vines. Best of all was the water—pure, clear water from the Sierras with no taint of mud or alkali. From now until they crossed the mountains, the guidebooks told them, they would never be far from it. It was now October 15, and the Donner Party took a day off for desperately needed rest.

Some, however, were in no position to enjoy the respite. Eddy and his wife had been without food for two days and nights of arduous travel, and their children had only the last of the sugar. No one offered to share with them; that was not the way of Westerners. In times of plenty, they were glad to share. When the going got tough, it was every man for himself. If you could not look out for yourself, well, it was just too bad.

Scorning to beg for charity for himself or his Eleanor, Eddy went to Betsy Graves and asked for a little piece of meat for his hungry children. She refused. So did hard-bitten Peggy Breen. Just then, Eddy heard wild geese honking from the river. He borrowed a gun from Keseberg and came back with nine fine, plump geese. He gave two each to Mrs. Graves and Mrs. Breen, despite their hard-hearted behavior. Keseberg received one goose as rent for the gun. Soon beef was added to the general supply of food when the Indians killed more oxen.

Despite the Indian raid, the emigrants' morale had gotten a boost. They had crossed the last desert; the oxen had had a day to feed and rest; and all the people had come through safely, except for Snyder, Hardkoop, and Wolfinger and his two German friends, who still had not appeared. Stanton and McCutchen had not returned either, and this was cause for worry, since they had expected to meet the two men much earlier.

On October 16 the bedraggled emigrants started up the Truckee, which would lead them into the high Sierras. The first couple of miles were easy going, but then the road led into a narrow, winding canyon between high mountains. The river bent and turned like a manic snake, and the trail crossed it more than once a mile. The oxen, many of them suffering from Indian arrow wounds, found it hard going.

That same day Reinhardt and Spitzer came into camp—without Wolfinger. They told a hair-raising tale. Indians had attacked them, they said, while they were caching Wolfinger's goods. Wolfinger had been killed, and the other two had fled. From a distance, they had watched the Indians loot and burn the wagons. No one quite knew whether to believe them, for Wolfinger was known as a wealthy man, and men did ugly things for money. In the end, the story was accepted at face value, and the Donners took in the newly widowed Mrs. Wolfinger.

On the fourth morning of working their way up the serpentine Truckee Canyon, the lead wagons had a welcome surprise. Down the canyon came chipper little Charley Stanton, with seven pack mules from Sutter's Fort, all loaded with flour and dried beef generously donated by Sutter. He had also sent two of his favorite Indian *vaqueros* to help Stanton with the mules.

CHAPTER 11

A Handicap Race Against Time

Without Stanton's aid the entire party would have been lost; not a single soul would have escaped. The provisions, though scant, were enough to entirely alter the situation of affairs.
— Charles F. McGlashan, journalist/historian, 1879

Many a man, placed in Stanton's position, would have disregarded his promise to his companions and stayed safe and comfortable at Sutter's Fort. Stanton stayed true to his word and returned over the dangerous mountain trails with his life-saving cargo of food. It is hard to say whether his erstwhile comrades were more glad to see him, or surprised that he had kept his promise.

The two Indian servants were another matter. After their recent experience with the Diggers, the members of the party were mistrustful of all Indians. But Stanton calmed their fears, assuring them that these young Indians, Salvador and Luis, were among Sutter's most trusted servants. He sent the two Indians down the trail with food for the stragglers in the rear while he told the eager gathering about his trip across the mountains and gave them news of the banished Reed.

Stanton and McCutchen had had an uneventful, if exhausting, trip to Sutter's. Along the way they had caught up with Hastings's wagon party. Here McCutchen found friends with whom he had traveled earlier. They tried to persuade him to turn back and bring his wife and baby to safety. McCutchen honorably put his promise to the Donner Party first and refused. But crossing the Sierras had taken more of a toll on the big, muscular McCutchen than on the small and wiry Stanton, for Mac had collapsed and was even now resting at Sutter's.

Stanton assured his listeners that Reed and Herron had gotten through safely, although by a narrow margin. Although the men had eaten sparingly, the rations donated by the Donners were used up in a few days. But Reed managed to keep them fed by shooting wild geese along the Humboldt and the Truckee. They had taken turns riding the mare, Glaucus, until she gave out. Then they led her along, for Reed could not bring himself to abandon his favorite horse.

Soon after the trail entered the mountains, the valley of the Truckee became impassable, and the trail had to make a wide swing away from the river. There were no more geese to hunt, and the men had nothing to eat. Reed could probably have killed some game in the pine forests of the Sierra, but he was afraid to take the time to hunt. If he did so, and found no game, he and Herron would just be that much closer to starvation.

For several days the two men pushed along with nothing to eat but two scanty meals of wild onions, growing weaker and weaker. At last the famished Herron demanded that they kill and eat the useless mare. Reed persuaded him against it, saying that they might find relief soon, and that he himself would kill poor Glaucus before they actually starved.

Herron soon became delirious, but they trudged on. Then Reed's keen eyes spied a bean on the road. A single bean, spilled from some jolting emigrant wagon. But to starving men it was cause for rejoicing. Reed gave the bean to Herron. For several miles they searched the road closely for more beans. They found four more and divided them equally.

The next morning they came upon some abandoned wagons. The men ransacked them desperately but found nothing to eat. The departing emigrants had taken all their food with them. On a whim, Reed unhooked the tar bucket that hung beneath one of the wagons. The tar bucket was a standard wagon fixture. It carried a mixture of tar and animal fat that was used for greasing the axles. This tar bucket was nearly empty, but Reed scraped away the last of the tar and found beneath it a streak of rancid tallow (beef fat) at the bottom.

Reed announced his find to Herron, who was sitting on a rock nearby. The young teamster raised as much of a cheer as he was capable of and came over to get his share. Reed scraped up a portion of fat about the size of a walnut and handed it to Herron on the tar paddle. Herron swallowed it greedily. Reed took a glob himself, but found it extremely repulsive. Herron wanted more, and Reed gave him a second helping. Herron was still hungry, but Reed refused to give him any more of the rancid tallow, warning him that it would kill him.

It nearly killed Reed himself. After he had walked on about fifty yards, he became deathly sick, vomiting uncontrollably and momentarily going blind. He rested against a rock and leaned his head against the muzzle of his gun, in a pose unintentionally suggesting suicide. Herron, seeing him, ran up in alarm, crying out: "My God, Mr. Reed, are you dying?" But in a few minutes Reed recovered. Herron, strangely enough, suffered no ill effects at all.

A little way beyond the abandoned wagons, the slope grew steeper and plunged down into Bear Valley, a favorite camping place for emigrants. At the end of the first steep pitch Reed looked down and saw some wagons far below.

"Herron," cried Reed, "there are wagons in the valley!" When Herron saw the wagons he shouted with joy, but he was so weak he could not be heard fifty yards away.

The two men stumbled down the slope, leading the tottering mare, who was so weak she could barely keep her feet. At the wagons they found hospitable people who gave them bread. Here, too, they found Stanton, on his way up from Sutter's Fort with his pack mules and Indians. At first Stanton could not recognize his old comrades, they were so thin and worn.

The men exchanged news, and the next morning Stanton headed

up toward the pass while Reed and Herron continued down toward Sutter's. It was four days ago that he had met them, said Stanton, and by now they should be safe at the fort. As for the crucial pass, he reported that there had been some snow on the ground when he and the Indians came through, but the pass was still open.

Stanton's arrival was doubly welcome to Margaret Reed and her children. In addition to bringing news that Reed was alive, Stanton was another friend they could count on in case of trouble with their traveling companions. Also, it meant an end of walking for a while, for Stanton let them ride on Sutter's mules. One mule carried what was left of their belongings; Mrs. Reed and little Tommy rode on another; Patty and Jimmy each perched behind one of the Indians; and Virginia rode behind Stanton.

With new energy now that they had food, the emigrants pressed on to Truckee Meadows, a pleasant, grass-covered flat near the foot of the Sierras. (The city of Reno stands there now.) They reached the meadows on October 20, only to find themselves in still another dilemma.

Prudence called for them to stop and rest the teams, now at the limit of their endurance. The ascent up the steep eastern face of the Sierras, as Stanton could tell them, was difficult. On the last stretch, above Truckee Lake, the slope was so steep that even with strong, well-rested oxen you had to double-team or even triple-team. Even then, the men had to help the oxen by heaving on the spokes of each wagon wheel. On some particularly steep stretches earlier parties rigged windlasses or ingenious devices with rollers, in which a chain attached to the wagon tongue was passed around the roller, and the oxen were hitched to the free end. Then the oxen, walking downhill, could pull the wagon uphill. Some emigrants, lacking the materials to build these mechanical aids, unloaded their wagons and carried their possessions up to the pass on their backs, so that the oxen had only the empty wagon to draw. Facing such obstacles, it was imperative that the animals of the Donner Party recover their strength.

On the other hand, each day they remained increased the peril of being caught in the snow, which had already begun to cover the high peaks above them. Hastings's *Emigrant's Guide* had warned that they must be over the pass by October, and it was now getting close to

November. Not that they had much faith any longer in anything Hastings had to say, but others had warned them, too. And there had been snow when Charley Stanton came riding back to their rescue.

Finally Stanton offered his opinion. It was true, he said, that there had been snow in the pass when he crossed. But at Sutter's Fort they had told him that at this time of the year the snow melted between storms. And Hastings's own party had made it through only two weeks earlier in the midst of a snowstorm. He would advise resting the oxen and taking their chances with the snow. Stanton was an educated man and had been over Truckee Pass twice, so with some misgivings they took his advice.

> In order to avoid the misfortunes which so frequently befall emigrants from the accidental discharge of firearms, guns should never be carried capped or primed. . . . More danger is to be apprehended, from your own guns, without . . . the above precautions, than from those of the enemy. [Lansford W. Hastings, *The Emigrant's Guide to Oregon and California,* pp. 149-150]

That night the big Murphy family, lately of Tennessee, suffered a tragedy. The two sons-in-law, William Foster and William Pike, were sitting by the campfire as Pike cleaned his pepperbox pistol. The pepperbox was an early type of revolver. Compact and easily concealed, it was a favorite weapon for self-defense, although it was not accurate beyond a few paces and had a distressing tendency to go off accidentally. Pike stood up to get more wood for the fire and handed or tossed the pistol to his brother-in-law. The gun went off; the unaimed shot from his own weapon struck Pike in the back, and he died within an hour. He left a young wife and two baby girls. And his death meant that the family now had only one grown man to defend it, for the next oldest male was fifteen-year-old Landrum Murphy.

They buried Pike as a snowfall briefly whitened the grass of Truckee Meadows. The oxen got a few more days of rest and grazing, but the party grew increasingly nervous about the snow. On the morning of October 25, Patrick Breen started up toward the pass. The Breens had lost fewer oxen to the Indians than anybody else, and they were the most anxious to move on. With the Breens went Patrick

Dolan, the Eddys, and Keseberg. Later in the day Stanton, the Reeds, the Graveses, and the Murphys left together. The Donner brothers brought up the rear.

The emigrant trail followed the Truckee for a day's journey beyond the meadows. As it entered the mountains the valley became deeper, steeper, and increasingly canyonlike, with nearly vertical slopes soaring above its narrow floor. An observant traveler would have noticed that the north-facing slopes, shaded and damp, were densely covered with tall conifers, while the sunny south-facing slopes were dry and grassy, with relatively few trees.

After the forty-ninth river crossing in eighty miles, wagons could go no farther up the river, and the trail turned off to the right, looping gradually upward over ridges and grassy valleys. Then it swung left, or south, along the main ridge of the Sierras, crossing several creeks. Finally it came to a cold, blue mountain lake that drained into the Truckee. Above the western end of the lake towered the forbiddingly steep summit ridge of the Sierras, notched by the pass that would at long last lead the Donner Party to California.

The eastern face of the mountain, up which the wagons had to be taken to the pass, was a formidable obstacle course, filled with high cliffs, great granite boulders wedged loose from the cliffs by frost, and sudden drop-offs. Scrub made the going more difficult and concealed many pitfalls. The wagon trail wound a tentative way among these dangers. Tall, grim crags loomed on either side of the pass, which was a narrow opening between some lower rocks. Even in summer there could be bone-chilling winds at the summit almost strong enough to knock a man down.

The distance from the meadows to the lake, then called Truckee Lake, was about fifty miles, and with good oxen the trip could be made in about three days. Breen and his companions in the faster section needed six days. The others took even longer.

Their troubles with the Indians were not quite over. When the first section camped for the night, an Indian crept up and shot arrows into the oxen. He was economical—one arrow apiece for nineteen animals. Eddy caught the Indian in the act, drew a bead, and shot him. With a horrible scream the Indian leaped into the air and fell down a bank into a willow thicket. The oxen were not killed, but they were too badly injured to work.

Snow kept falling as they crept along the trail, covering the grass and the wheel tracks. When the emigrants looked nervously up at the mountain peaks, they could see them mantled in white. The air was cold; storm clouds filled the cheerless sky. The smell of winter was in the air.

At dusk on October 31 the first section camped below Truckee Lake, about a mile from an abandoned cabin built two winters earlier by members of the Stevens-Murphy party. That party, which opened up the trail over Truckee Pass, had also reached the Sierras late—about November 15. They found the way blocked by snow. By herculean efforts five of the eleven wagons were manhandled up to the pass. These started down by a roundabout route and were stopped by the snow partway down the western slope. There the families—the big Irish-Canadian Murphy clan (not related to the Donner Party Murphys)—camped for the winter in their wagons.

The other six Stevens-Murphy wagons had to be left at the lake while their passengers went ahead on foot. Three young men volunteered to stay over and guard them until spring. They were Joseph Foster, Allen Montgomery, and Moses Schallenberger, an orphaned Ohio farm boy who had just turned eighteen. On a little flat about a quarter mile below the lake's outlet, they built a log cabin, a simple affair only twelve by fourteen feet, with a door but no windows. They roofed it over with brush. A primitive chimney of logs smeared with clay let the smoke out. Two worn-out cows had been left with them, and they used these to haul the logs to the cabin site.

Mose and his friends, not expecting the snow to get more than two or three feet deep, looked forward to a pleasant winter's adventure in the wilderness, tramping through the beautiful, snow-clad pine forests to stalk the wary game, and in general living the bold and hardy life of a frontiersman. They were soon disappointed. The snow began to fall in earnest about December 1, and in a short time nearly covered the cabin.

The men became worried and decided to leave. The snow was far too deep to walk in, so they made crude snowshoes out of the hickory bows that had held up the wagon tops. For strings they used the hides of the two cows, which they had killed when the snow got too deep for them to forage. Unfortunately, none of the three knew how to make or use snowshoes, never having seen one, although they had probably heard the Canadian-raised Murphys talk about them.

A snowshoe was supposed to be fastened to your foot at the toe only, so that you could drag it over the snow when you stepped forward. But these snowshoes were fastened at both toe and heel, and the men had to lift them clear up at every step. The snowshoes immediately picked up a load of snow on top, making the going even more difficult.

The three set off for California about December 15. Mose soon tired and could not keep up with the other two. After a couple of miles he turned back. He was so exhausted when he reached the cabin that he had to take his foot in his hand to lift it over the doorsill.

Young Mose lived on the beef from the slaughtered cows until it ran out. Then he set out steel traps that he found in one of the wagons. With these he caught coyotes and foxes. The first coyote he caught tasted so unpleasant that he just hung the others up outside the cabin for an emergency. But the foxes were delicious. Once Mose shot a crow, but he thought it tasted just as bad as the coyote.

Mose was in no danger of starvation, but the loneliness was a real hardship. There were books in one of the wagons (they belonged to Mose's uncle, Dr. John Townsend, with whom he had been traveling), and he read these to pass the time. Sometimes he read aloud to break the silence; sometimes he talked to himself.

He had been living alone in the cabin for about two and a half months when one day at sunset a man on snowshoes approached the cabin. It was Dennis Martin, of the Murphy clan. Mose's sister had persuaded him to come up and see how her little brother was getting on. Martin came from Canada and was familiar with snowshoes, and he soon made a new pair for Mose. In two days the men reached the rest of the party at their camp on the Yuba River.

This story, at least, had a happy ending, and Stanton had probably heard it at Sutter's Fort. But would it be of any help to the Donner Party?

While the faster section was already settling in, George Donner's family wagon, back on the trail, broke its front axle on a steep downgrade. The high-piled load tumbled helter-skelter, boxes and barrels and bundles, onto the little girls, Georgia and Eliza, who were sleeping inside. They pulled Georgia out through the back of the wagon cover; though shaken and frightened, she was all right. But Eliza was nowhere to be seen. After some frantic rummaging through the pile they found her, limp and unconscious. They feared for her life, but she recovered.

George and Jake Donner cut a tree to replace the broken axle. They had nearly finished trimming it to fit, and Jake was putting the finishing touches on one end while George held the big timber steady. Suddenly Jake's chisel slipped and cut a long gash in the back of George's hand. Blood spurted, but George did not want to worry his brother. He said the wound was nothing to worry about, wrapped a rag around it, and finished the job.

There was a covering of snow on the ground at Truckee Lake when the Breens, Eddys, Kesebergs, and Dolan arrived. It was too deep for the cattle to paw aside to reach the grass, and the men and boys had to cut boughs for them to munch on. It was not a food they ate naturally, and they showed little taste for it.

The next morning the first section started for the pass. The clouds that had obscured the mountains for the past few days blew aside now and then to reveal an unbroken cover of snow. The emigrants' hearts sank at the sight, but they pushed on along the shore of the lake, toward the slope that would confront them with their final test.

It was about six miles from the cabin to the pass, and the soft snow grew deeper as they neared the final ridge, which loomed a thousand feet above them. About halfway to the pass they ran into five feet of snow. The oxen could not get through this, and neither could the people, since the trail was obliterated. Discouraged, they turned back to the lake.

The Breens, probably first on the spot and in any case the most numerous family, laid claim to the cabin. That night, however, it rained hard, and the cabin roof was leaky. The Breens ended up in their wagon. The rain kept up all the next day—the emigrants took this as a good sign, thinking it would wash the snow away. At nightfall a drenched and depleted second section reached the cabin and camped nearby. The Donners were still far behind on the trail.

By morning the rain had stopped, and some of the party yoked up their teams to make a fresh start, with Stanton and the Indians leading the way. Others, thoroughly disheartened, could not muster the willpower to move from the spot. It made little difference in the end, for the rain, far from washing away the snow, had only added to it at the higher elevations. Even on the flats at the upper end of the lake, far below the pass, it now lay three feet deep. The oxen were too weak to make headway, and the men had to break a trail for them. It was soon obvious that they could not hope to get the wagons through.

It might still be possible to get through on foot, however, and the families decided to pack what they could on the backs of their oxen and try it that way. Unfortunately, this wasted an inordinate amount of time, because the family members could not agree on what things were the most worth saving. Should they take the box of tobacco or the bale of calico? Which would fetch the best price in California? By the time they made their minds up, it was rather late in the day. Then the oxen disliked having things tied onto their backs. Such a thing had never happened to them before, and it frightened them. They bucked and kicked, trying to get rid of the unfamiliar burdens. Some lay down in the snow and wallowed while their owners fretted.

At last the oxen gave up the struggle and accepted their fate as pack animals. Forward the party marched again, each adult carrying one of the smaller children. Keseberg had injured his foot on a sharp stub while hunting along the Truckee and could not walk; so he was hoisted onto a horse, and his foot was secured in a sling tied to the saddle.

The waist-deep snow made the trail impossible to find as well as hindering motion. Stanton and the Indians groped their way forward as best they could; the others floundered behind them. They noticed that one of Sutter's mules was a particularly good trail-breaker, and they put it at the head of the column. One of the Indians rode the mule, with Patty Reed clinging on behind. The mule plunged into the drifts and worked its way laboriously up the slope. The rest of the party, driving their unwilling oxen, followed in the track it broke.

After two or three miles of this exhausting travel everyone stopped while Stanton and the Indian who rode the mule went ahead to scout out a way.

Somehow they located the trail beneath the snow and reached the summit. As almost everyone who has written about the Donner Party likes to point out, Stanton could have abandoned his companions and crossed the pass to safety. It is almost certain that any one of them would have done so in his place, even if they had regrets. But Stanton, faithful to his trust, pushed his way through the snow three miles back to the waiting emigrants. The Indian must have wondered what the white man was doing, but he followed along dutifully.

The sun had set by the time Stanton got back to the halting place, and the weary, bone-chilled emigrants had set fire to a dead, standing pine tree. They all gathered around the burning trunk in the deepening twilight, grateful for the warmth. The oxen, unguarded, were trying to rub their packs off against other trees. Some of the emigrants had begun to make camp.

In the brief winter twilight, Stanton told his listeners that he thought they could get through if it didn't snow. Keseberg and others urged a final push. But the majority, men, women, and children, insisted that they could not go a step farther. They were played out, and they must have a rest. They would go onward in the morning. The majority carried the day.

The families made little campfires and fixed something to eat. Parents spread buffalo robes and blankets on the snow for their children to lie snug in. The snow began to fall as they slept or huddled in their blankets near the fires.

As Keseberg remembered it some thirty years later, ". . . it would have taken a determined man to induce the party to leave the fire. Had I been well, and able to push ahead over the ridge, some, if not all, would have followed. As it was, all lay down upon the snow, and from exhaustion were soon asleep. In the night, I felt something impeding my breath. A heavy weight seemed to be resting upon me. Springing up to a sitting posture, I found myself covered with freshly-fallen snow. The camp, the cattle, my companions, had all disappeared. All I could see was snow everywhere. I shouted at the top of my voice. Suddenly, here and there, all about me, heads popped up through the snow. The scene was not unlike what one might imagine at the resurrection, when people rise up out of the earth. The terror amounted to a panic."

The snow was a good foot deeper on the ground than when they had lain down to sleep, and in places it had drifted ten feet deep. They were trapped. It was November 4.

CHAPTER 12

Snowbound

With heavy hearts we turned back to a cabin that had been built by the Murphy-Schallenberger party two years before. We built more cabins and prepared as best we could for the winter.
— Virginia Reed Murphy, "Across the Plains in the Donner Party (1846)," *The Century Magazine,* July 1891

With numb despair the emigrants struggled through the snow back down to the lake. They did not reach the cabin until four o'clock; darkness was not far off. The Breens promptly reoccupied the leaky-roofed, windowless cabin; the other families had to wait until the next day, when they had enough daylight to work by, to construct their own shelters.

Keseberg, handicapped by his infected foot, built a lean-to for himself and his family along one side of the Breens' cabin. The arrogant German evidently concluded that proximity meant safety even if you were barely on speaking terms with the neighbors.

The ground at the outlet of Truckee Lake, where the cabins were built, was generally pretty level, but peppered with large boulders left by an ancient glacier. About a hundred and fifty yards upstream from the Breen-Keseberg complex, Eddy found a giant rock with a vertical face ten or twelve feet high and twenty feet wide; he built his cabin against this, using the cliff as one wall. Since Eddy and his wife and children shared this cabin with the large Murphy clan, he probably had help from Foster and such Murphy boys as were old enough to be useful.

Had it not been for their desperate situation, the site would have been delightful. The cabin stood close to the creek—only about forty-five steps away—and the big pines that covered the area promised an ample supply of firewood as well as timber for building. Many of the trees were lodgepole pines, whose long, straight trunks made excellent logs for a cabin. Others were Jeffrey pines, with bark that smelled like vanilla. Along the creek grew willows and alders, good for firewood.

Evidently craving to get away from the other families, the Graveses built a double cabin about half a mile down the creek from the Breens. They shared this structure with the Reed contingent—a bizarre and surely uncomfortable combination considering that Mrs. Reed's husband had killed the Graveses' prospective son-in-law. Still, they managed to keep peace. The Graves clan lived in one end of the cabin; Mrs. Reed, the children, and the hired hands, plus Stanton and the two Indians he had brought from Sutter's Fort, lived in the other. A log wall across the middle of the cabin separated the two groups and helped reduce the tension.

Hastily built, the cabins had flat roofs of green (unseasoned) pine saplings trimmed into poles. Over these were spread tents, canvas wagontops, hides from slaughtered oxen, and anything else that might serve to keep out the rain and snow. The cabins were fearfully crowded: Sixty people lived in this little, temporary, antagonistic community by the lake. Almost half of them were children.

The two Donner families had never made it up to the lake, much less the pass. They had stopped, probably late in the day on November 3, about five miles back on the trail near a little stream called Alder Creek. There, on a wide flat through which a tiny brooklet trickles today, the men decided to make camp. They began to cut logs for the cabins, but had to stop when the daylight failed.

The next day, with snow on the ground up to mid thigh, they abandoned their plans for the time-consuming construction of a cabin and quickly put up makeshift shelters. Under a huge pine tree the George Donner family cleared away the snow and put up their tent. Next to the tent they built a semicircular lean-to of pine branches around the tree, whose massive trunk served as the north wall. They covered the lean-to with rubber raincoats, buffalo robes, and old quilts. Inside tent and lean-to the resourceful Donners (no doubt inspired by Tamsen) built bedsteads by driving stakes into the ground and lashing poles across their tops. The beds were crude, but at least everyone could sleep off the ground.

Uncle Jake and his family put up a similar shelter nearby, and across the little stream the four young teamsters erected a bachelor lodge that looked something like an Indian tepee. Once everyone had settled in, they soon began visiting back and forth between the camp at Alder Creek and the bigger camp up by the lake.

Shelter was now secured, but food was the critical item. The emigrants had by now eaten up all their supplies, even the extra rations that Stanton and his little pack train had brought up from Sutter's. They could not hunt, for the game had all gone down to the valleys for the winter, and they dared not return to Truckee Meadows for fear of the Indians. (Though adequately armed, the men of fighting age were few. Most of the party consisted of vulnerable women and children, and they dared not take the risk.) Fishing parties prowled the banks of the lake, which was still unfrozen. In the clear water they could see huge trout, but the fish were logy with the cold and would not bite. It never occurred to anyone to make nets to catch the plentiful fish.

Eddy borrowed a gun and went out to try his luck at hunting, but his only bag was a coyote. His whole cabin—fifteen people in all—shared its flesh for supper. Another day that he spent in the woods yielded only an owl, again shared with all his cabin mates. It could not have gone very far among fifteen people, even if some of them were only small children.

It became clear to the snowbound emigrants that they would have to fall back on their own animals, and in fact some of them had already begun to slaughter their worn-out oxen. The carcasses, cut into quarters, were stacked outside the cabins, where the freezing cold preserved them.

Not all the cattle had been killed yet—some of the emigrants still had a faint hope that the snow would melt away or that the banished Reed would send a rescue party over the mountains. But the animals were getting weaker by the day, and leaner too, since the snow was too deep for them to paw through to reach the winter-killed grass that lay beneath.

The Eddy and Reed families were in a precarious situation. Eddy had only one ox on which to feed his family for God knew how many months. Margaret Reed had no cattle at all, and probably her two horses had given out before she reached the lake. The Reeds' five dogs were still with them, but no one would have thought of eating them until they were much, much more desperate.

The Breens, however, were relatively well fixed. Not only did they still have a fair number of oxen, but also their friend Patrick Dolan had several. In addition, Uncle Billy Graves had a few yoke remaining.

So the foodless were compelled to do business with those who owned the food supply, and the cattle barons drove some incredibly harsh bargains with those who had to buy from them or starve. Greed alone could not account for this mean-spirited behavior. For example, about November 9 one of Graves's oxen died of starvation. He did not consider the skeletal carcass worth salvaging for his own family, but he refused to give the worthless remains to Eddy, who had two small children. Instead, the grim old backwoodsman demanded twenty-five dollars for the dead ox! (Back in Independence, Missouri, you could get two oxen, alive, stout and meaty, and ready for hard work, for less than that.)

Margaret Reed managed to buy two oxen from Breen and two from Graves. They charged her two oxen for one, payable when they reached California.

The snow fell steadily, with few interruptions, for more than a week. Then the clouds blew away, the sun shone, and the snow melted. The strongest of the emigrants prepared to cross the pass on foot. Their reasons were two: Once they got through, they could send a rescue party up from Sutter's Fort, and while they were gone, there would be that many fewer mouths to feed.

So on November 12 fifteen people said good-bye to their families and friends and headed for Sutter's. They were William Eddy,

Charles Stanton, the two Indians Luis and Salvador, the recently wed Jay and Sarah Fosdick, Uncle Billy Graves and his daughter Mary, William Foster, the German Spitzer, Milt Elliott and his fellow teamsters—James Smith, Dutch Charley Burger, and Jean-Baptiste Trudeau—and the Spanish-American herder Antoine. Their rations for the long and strenuous journey were one small piece of beef apiece. They would have to rely on hunting after that ran out.

As it turned out, they never got far enough to run out of food. About three miles below the pass they encountered soft snow about ten feet deep, a roadblock they could not possibly get through. Deeply disappointed, they turned around and reached their cabins at about midnight.

In times of frustration, action is more satisfying than inaction, and Eddy borrowed a gun from Foster—for the fee of half of what he killed—and went off hunting again. Very faint from lack of food, he tramped through the woods and came upon the tracks of an enormous grizzly bear.

A lone hunter who knew his business left grizzlies alone. The grizzly was dreaded for its size, strength, and ferocity, and it was also very hard to kill. Even when badly wounded, a grizzly had amazing tenacity of life. And a muzzle-loading rifle, such as Eddy had, took time to load. You had to stand the weapon on the ground, take your powder horn and pour a measured charge of powder down the bore, and then reach into your bullet pouch, take out a bullet, wrap it in a patch of greased cloth, and push it down the bore with your ramrod. (Military guns had ready-made cartridges, but hunters did not use them.) Finally you pulled the hammer back to half cock, placed a percussion cap (it looked like a little copper hat) on the nipple that led to the chamber, pulled back the hammer to full cock, aimed, and fired. All this took time, and while you were busy with these unavoidable steps of reloading, your target, the grizzly bear, might be tearing you to pieces. Even if you inflicted a mortal wound with your first shot, the grizzly tended to take its time about dying.

Under normal circumstances Eddy would much rather have seen the bear's tracks and let the animal go, but his children needed food; so he followed the tracks. He soon caught sight of the monstrous animal as it dug up roots in a thicket about ninety yards from him.

The bear had its head to the ground as it munched the roots and did not notice him. Eddy sneaked closer and hid behind a big tree. He took his one spare bullet—all he had—and put it in his mouth to save precious seconds in reloading.

Eddy came out from behind the tree, took aim, and fired. The bear stood up and charged him, its mouth wide open and its fearsome teeth showing. He finished reloading just as the bear reached his tree. The wounded animal chased him around and around the trunk, growling hideously. Fear lent the exhausted Eddy speed, and he managed to run faster than the infuriated grizzly. Eventually he came up behind it and managed to disable it with a shot in the shoulder. Now out of ammunition, Eddy managed to kill the bear by knocking it on the head with a club. When he had caught his breath, Eddy examined the carcass and found that his first shot had pierced the bear's heart!

The successful hunter returned to the camp by the lake, which they now called the Mountain Camp, to get help in bringing home his quarry. Only Uncle Billy Graves offered to go with him—the other men could not be bothered. As they walked toward the kill site, leading one of Graves's remaining oxen to haul the bear, Uncle Billy fell into a gloomy mood. He feared that God would let him perish on the mountain, he confessed to Eddy, for refusing to help Hardkoop in the desert and for his part in driving Reed out of the camp. But the sight of the bear was enough to still the old backwoodsman's forebodings for a time. It was huge—they judged its weight at 800 pounds. There would be meat on the table for a while!

Eddy gave half the bear, as promised, to Foster for the use of his gun. He also gave shares to Mrs. Reed and to Graves, in return for his help.

The bear meat dwindled, and Eddy went out on the hunt again, but this time he returned with only a duck and a gray squirrel. Morale at the Mountain Camp sank again as the emigrants worried about starvation. Visits between the Mountain Camp and the Donner camp down by Alder Creek had ceased—five miles was too far to walk through deep snow when one was starving.

Patrick Breen began keeping a diary, perhaps in the hope that, even if the entire party perished, someone—be it trapper, emigrant, or would-be rescuer—would find it in the spring and tell the world of how they met their deaths.

"Friday Nov. 20, 1846," began the first entry. "Came to this place on the 31st of last month that it snowed we went on to the pass the snow so deep we were unable to find the road. when within 3 miles of the summit then turned back to this shanty on the lake. Stanton came one day after we arrived here. we again took our teams & waggons & made another unsuccessful attempt to cross in company with Stanton . . . We now have killed most part of our cattle having to stay here until next spring & live on poor beef without bread or salt . . . "

The pent-up emigrants at the Mountain Camp, feeling like captives, waited impatiently for a chance to escape from their prison of snow. Their first opportunity came on November 21, a fine morning with a northwest wind. Sixteen men and women set out for the pass that towered over the far end of the lake. Stanton and the Indians took Sutter's seven mules. This time they were luckier—the snow on the upper slopes was crusted over, hard and strong enough to bear a man's weight. Eddy, curious, broke a hole in the crust at the pass and measured the depth of the snow beneath. It was twenty-five feet!

Secure on the firm crust, the little party crossed over the pass and camped in a little valley on the west side of the mighty ridge. They passed an uncomfortable night there, so weak that they could barely gather firewood and start a fire. Then they had a great deal of trouble keeping the fire going in six-foot-deep snow. Adding to the unhappiness, Stanton announced that he and his Indians would go no farther. The mules, whose weight had caused them to break through the crust repeatedly, were exhausted by their climb, and the Indians were sure they could not make it down the western slope of the Sierras, where the going was even tougher.

Stanton felt honorbound to return the mules to Sutter, and he would listen to no argument. The Indians, on their part, were afraid that Sutter would hang them if they returned without the mules. The autocrat of New Helvetia frequently issued such threats to keep his Indian workers under control, although in fact he was too softhearted to carry them out. The Indians took them in deadly earnest, however.

Eddy used every argument he could think of to change Stanton's mind. He pointed out the danger that the whole group down below would starve if they went back. He pleaded with Stanton that Sutter would surely rather lose the mules than know that fellow human beings had perished in a foolish attempt to save them. He even offered to pay for the seven mules himself. But Stanton, grown stubborn from frustration and apprehension of the dangers that lay both ahead on the trail and behind at the lake, was adamant. Sutter had entrusted these valuable animals to him, and he was not going to come back without them. Period. And without Stanton to guide them the others dared not go ahead.

Eddy tried another gambit: He suggested that he and the others in the party compel Stanton to continue down the mountain. Surely this would clear him and the Indians of all blame. But Stanton, in a fit of righteousness, would not be budged. The fearful Indians backed him up. Eddy lost his temper, but this did not change Stanton's mind either. At last everyone went to sleep as best they could in the bitter cold of the mountain night.

The next morning they trudged back across the pass and returned to the cabins. The fair weather, with the sun shining brightly on the snow, could not disguise their fiasco. Eddy suggested that they kill Sutter's mules to eke out the food supply, but Graves and some other adults vetoed the suggestion. If they killed the mules, they would have to pay for them, and this thought galled their frugal souls.

A few days dragged by. . . . November 25 dawned as a gray, overcast day after an intensely cold night. It looked like snow, but the emigrants voted to make another try at crossing the pass on the next day, which happened to be Thanksgiving. That afternoon the snow began to fall again, in great flakes that made it impossible to see more than a few feet. The snowstorm continued for eight days, with a few brief respites, while even the most venturesome remained cabin-bound. During the storm Breen made a profitable deal, selling two oxen to Foster and taking his gold watch and some other valuables as security.

When the snow finally stopped falling, it lay over six feet deep. The few surviving cattle, the horses, and Sutter's precious mules were all gone without trace, buried somewhere under the vast, white blanket of snow. There was no hope of finding them until a thaw melted the snow away. This meant that a great part of their food reserve was lost. To make matters worse, the deep snow prevented anyone from going out and cutting firewood. The housebound emigrants, in desperation, began chipping away at the logs of their cabins to keep the fires going.

At last the sun came out, and the emigrants' spirits rose again, so much so that on December 3 Uncle Billy Graves and Charley Stanton began to make snowshoes for everyone. Graves, who had grown up in the Green Mountains of Vermont, had probably used snowshoes for half his life. Stanton, from the snow belt of upstate New York, was certainly familiar with them too. None of the other men had ever seen a snowshoe. There was no need for them in Illinois and Missouri, where the snow was seldom deep and usually melted within a few days. Everyone now agreed that they had made a mistake in not slaughtering Sutter's mules. But talking and self-reproach did not uncover the poor animals' carcasses.

The effects of hunger began to manifest themselves alarmingly. On December 8, a fine, clear day, Spitzer was too weak to get up without help. Breen took the starving man into his cabin; in his diary he incongruously noted, "all in good health."

With the meat supply nearing its end, those who still had a little were not willing to share with those who had none. Stanton went from family to family pleading for something to eat for his Indians and himself. "Not likely to get much," Breen noted. This was the gratitude the snow-trapped emigrants showed to the man who had twice risked his own life to save theirs. But then they probably blamed him for persuading them to rest for five days at Truckee Meadows and for insisting on turning back beyond the pass to save Sutter's mules.

The day after Spitzer collapsed, it began to snow again. When the storm ended five days later, the snow was eight feet deep. The emigrants began to be obsessed with the thought of starving to death on the mountain, for they realized all too well how slim their chances of survival were. Even before the snow stopped falling, Eddy, with Graves, Stanton, and others, was planning another escape.

CHAPTER 13

The Forlorn Hope

Dec. 6, The morning fine and clear—Stanton and Graves manufacturing snowshoes for another mountain scrabble. . . . Dec. 16, Fair and pleasant, froze hard last night—the company started on snowshoes to cross the mountains, wind S.E.

—Diary of Patrick Breen, printed anonymously in
The California Star, May 22, 1847

The escape party—they dubbed themselves "the Forlorn Hope"—strapped on their snowshoes and left the morning of December 16. Their determination was increased by the death of Baylis Williams, the Reeds' handyman, the day before. There were seventeen in the party, twelve men and five women, mostly young adults. Eddy and Stanton were the leaders; with them were Sutter's two Indian trail guides, Luis and Salvador. Uncle Billy Graves, still vigorous at fifty-seven, led a detachment from his family: Sarah and Jay Fosdick and the beautiful Mary. From the Murphy clan there were William and Sarah Foster, twelve-year-old Lemuel and eleven-year-old Billy, and the recently widowed Harriet Pike. Amanda McCutchen joined them; she was anxious to join her husband down in the settlements. She left her year-old baby behind, probably in the care of Aunt Betsy

Graves. She was not the only young mother to leave a child behind at the Mountain Camp. Sarah Foster left one and Harriet Pike left two. It was a heartrending choice to make. But it was impossible to carry small children over the difficult terrain, deep in snow, and at the cabins the little ones would at least be warm and sheltered.

The remainder of the party were Dutch Charley Burger, Antoine the herder, and Patrick Dolan. Lewis Keseberg could not go because his foot had not yet healed, and Patrick Breen, another still-vigorous man, was ailing with "the gravel," an old term for kidney and bladder stones.

Historians have done a great deal of moralizing about the decision of the men and women of the Forlorn Hope. Were they selfishly taking a gamble on saving their own lives while leaving their families behind? Or were they being noble in risking their lives to bring help for the others? Probably both selfish and altruistic motives were at work here—but in fact the real choice was between dying of exhaustion on the trail or dying of starvation at the cabins.

The Forlorn Hope took little enough in the way of provisions. In their packs, each member had a small ration of tough, dried beef—enough to give them a two-finger-wide strip three times a day for five or six days. This amounted to about one ounce per meal. They also had a little coffee and sugar, but no salt—that essential had run out by the time they reached the lake. The men had a little tobacco, considered a manly necessity. Each person had a single blanket or quilt to keep warm with, but no extra clothing. The tents were now serving as cabin roofs and could not be spared—the snowshoers would have to sleep out in the open after a day's exhausting slogging through the snow.

They took with them a single hatchet to chop firewood, a few pistols for defense, a little powder and shot, and Foster's hunting rifle in case they should sight any game. The rifle was a heavy burden for the half-starved men and women, but they could manage by taking turns carrying it. That was all—not an ounce of unnecessary weight.

It was a poignant moment when the Forlorn Hope said farewell to their families, knowing they might never see them again. They had reason to worry, for those they left behind were already painfully thin. Patrick Dolan, who had no family to provide for, generously requested that Mrs. Reed and her children should have a share of the beef he owned. Eddy felt like crying at the sight of his wife's hollow cheeks, sunken eyes, and wasted figure. But stress numbed him, and the tears did not come.

The morning of the departure offered favorable travel conditions. The snow was dry and feathery, which meant it would not cling to the snowshoes, and the weather was fair and cold, so that the snow would not thaw into a wet, clinging mass. The party planned to follow the established emigrant trail, if only they could find it beneath the snow. The route ran along the ridgelines of the mountains as much as possible, since the going for the wagons was easiest there. But there were many steep descents and climbs between one ridge and the next.

After crossing the pass, the trail led through a pleasant mountain meadow called Summit Valley, about two miles long. following the headwaters of the south fork of the Yuba River, which rises near the pass. Then the river (at this point a shallow stream only a few yards wide) dropped into a canyonlike valley, while the trail held to the valley rim for several miles before slanting steeply down to the valley floor and rejoining the Yuba. Then there were a few miles of level going along the Yuba Bottoms, until the trail climbed over a divide to the watershed of the American River. The trail then dipped down into a small hollow called Dry Valley and went through a notch in the mountains that formed the valley's north side, called Emigrant Gap. On the far side of Emigrant Gap the slope was so steep that wagons had to be let down by ropes that were snubbed around trees to provide friction. At the bottom of this hazardous slope, about twelve miles from the Yuba Bottoms, lay the lovely, parklike Bear Valley, where the precipitous canyon of the Bear River widened out.

Bear Valley was far from the end of the trail, however. At the foot of the valley the road entered another canyon carved by the Bear River, but soon climbed up to a dividing ridge. Bear Canyon lay on the right; another canyon, called Steep Hollow, lay on the left. The road followed the ridge top because the slopes on either side were too steep for a wagon to remain upright, and in places the ridge top itself was so narrow that the wagon tracks straddled it.

About ten miles beyond Bear Valley was a spot called Mule Springs, a favored campground of the emigrants and their tired teams. About another ten miles farther on, the ridge ended precipitously where Steep Hollow ran into Bear Canyon. This was another spot where wagons had to be lowered with ropes, while oxen and horses slipped and stumbled down the slopes as best they could. But this cliff marked the end of the high mountains and canyons. The road now led down over foothills that grew gentler and gentler, until it entered the plains of the great central valley that Hastings had described in such alluring terms. From there it was about thirty-seven miles to the first settlement, Johnson's Ranch. Sutter's Fort lay another forty miles beyond Johnson's Ranch.

The distance from the lake to Bear Valley was about thirty miles, and Stanton had ridden it in a day that fall. The whole distance from the lake to the end of the foothills was about fifty miles. Hastings's wagons had made it in seven days. However, they had done it on mostly snow-free ground and with people in good condition—a far cry from a malnourished and poorly clad band of desperate souls struggling through deep snow.

The snowshoe party calculated that they had enough food to see them to Bear Valley, about halfway across the mountains. There, with luck, they might find deer to shoot or even locate a cache of food left by a family trying to lighten its wagonload.

The Forlorn Hope started off in single file, the leaders breaking a trail for the others. Even with their snowshoes they sank halfway to their knees in the soft, powdery snow at each step. There were not enough snowshoes to go around, so Burger and the two Murphy boys brought up the rear, stepping carefully in the snowshoe tracks. However, the snow was not packed hard enough to bear their weight, and they kept breaking through and floundering.

Billy Murphy gave out and had to turn back; he got back to the cabins that evening. Burger also dropped out, but no one noticed his absence for some time. Then they simply assumed that he had turned back to the cabins and did not bother to search for him. (He did get back safely, but long after Billy Murphy.) Lemuel Murphy struggled on gamely in the grown-ups' snowshoe tracks until the party reached some packsaddles from Sutter's mules that had been jettisoned by the trail. Graves and Stanton ripped these apart and fashioned a pair of snowshoes for Lem out of their components.

That first day the Forlorn Hope made only four miles, camping a little way above the head of the lake. From their campsite they could see the smoke of the cabins, a discouraging reminder of how little progress they had made. The next day, however, they crossed the pass. As they climbed, Mary Graves, at the rear of the column, looked up at her heavily muffled companions and thought that they looked like a picture of Norwegian trappers among the icebergs that she had seen in a book long ago.

The party paused at the top of the pass for a last look at their loved ones. Although by now they loathed the snow and the mountains, they could not help admiring the magnificent view. Someone said jokingly that they must be about as close to heaven as they could get.

They made camp that afternoon a short distance west of the pass, being too tired to go farther. They judged they had traveled about six miles that day. The snow at the campsite was twelve feet deep, but the Forlorn Hope had learned one thing since their first fiasco: how to keep a fire going in deep snow.

The trick was to cut two green saplings and lay them parallel on top of the snow, a few feet apart. Over these one laid crosspieces of green wood to make a platform. The fire was built on top of this. As long as someone kept the fire going all night, the travelers would stay warm even without tents and with only one blanket apiece.

The following day, December 18, they had a downhill slope to help them. This was well, for they were beginning to weaken after two days' arduous climbing with only a few tiny strips of lean, saltless beef to sustain them. It was an excellent reducing regimen, but losing flesh was the last thing the Forlorn Hope needed. Another trouble now struck them: The glare of the sun on the snow of Summit Valley caused Stanton to go snowblind. He had to stop, but was able to continue when the sun got low, and caught up with his comrades about an hour after they had made camp. That day they made about five miles.

For the next few days the Forlorn Hope kept on along the highlands, making a few miles each day. They were favored with clear, pleasant weather most of the time, and they used the sun as a guide. Stanton, however, kept going snowblind, dropping behind, and coming in each evening after sunset. Since he was the only one who really knew the trail, his misfortune affected the whole group.

By now the hard-pressed little band of refugees were not only horribly emaciated, but in bad mental shape as well. They began to hallucinate as they dragged themselves through the snow. Fine, big farmhouses, fields full of crops, and lovely gardens appeared before their eyes. When they camped at night they heard familiar farm sounds where there was nothing to make them: dogs barking, roosters crowing, cowbells tinkling, and the voices of men talking. When they slept, they dreamed of food—huge banquets of their favorite dishes prepared just the way they liked best. Yet, as their vitality drained away, they gradually lost their sense of hunger and wanted above all to sleep.

One morning—it was December 21—Eddy searched through his little pack to see if there was anything he could discard to lighten his load. At the bottom he found a half pound of bear meat with a note from his wife attached. The note told him to save the meat for the last extremity, as it might save his life. It was signed "Your own dear Eleanor." The loyal Eleanor had hoarded the meat from her own share of the grizzly bear for just such an emergency. Eddy made this self-sacrificing gift from his wife last a long time.

That morning, Stanton did not start out with his comrades but stayed by the campfire, calmly smoking his pipe. Don't worry, he told the others; he would catch up with them later. The Forlorn Hope started off, guided rather uncertainly by the Indians, who had been over the trail only once, and then when the ground was free of snow. Moreover, the Indians had been going in the other direction. So it was not surprising that the party gradually veered in the wrong direction, away from Bear Valley. (This would cost them many painful days and miles, but they didn't discover how badly lost they were for more than a week.) That night they used up the last of the beef they had brought with them from the Mountain Camp and waited for Stanton to come in to the warmth and light of the campfire. He did not come.

The next day they had traveled only about a mile when the snow began to fall. They halted and made camp, and waited again for

Stanton. It was a foodless day for all—Eddy would surely not have dared nibble on his secret hoard of bear meat in front of his starving companions. They waited and waited, but Stanton still did not come staggering through the snow. At nightfall they gave him up for dead. A gentleman to the last, little Charley Stanton had sacrificed his own life rather than endanger his companions by holding them back.

The following day, December 23, they climbed the barren, rocky dome of Cisco Butte, the highest peak in the vicinity, and tried to take their bearings. Now that Stanton was no longer there to guide them, they had to plot their own route. The easiest way appeared to be toward the south, where the mountains looked less menacing than those to the north and west. Unfortunately, this led them away from Bear Valley—but they had no way of knowing this.

A foot of snow fell that night, but the painful journey continued the next morning, December 24, the day before Christmas. The party limped two or three miles before the wind shifted to the southwest, and a heavy snow began to fall. By now the members of the Forlorn Hope had become experts at forecasting snow. A wind from the south or southwest brought snow (on moisture-laden winds from the ocean), while an east or northeast wind (from the dry interior) meant clear weather.

The fourteen remaining members of the Forlorn Hope sat down among the falling flakes and took counsel. All the men except Eddy wanted to give up and return to the Mountain Camp, reasoning they had not tasted food for two days and had been on starvation rations for a week before that. It was a suicidally foolish idea, since, in their weakened condition, they could not possibly have made it back. Eddy and the women stood firm, however. They vowed they would go through with their mission or perish. Strangely, the women bore the physical and mental stress far better than the men, a phenomenon that would happen again and again before their trials were over.

Finally Patrick Dolan, the once-carefree bachelor, voiced the thought that must have crossed everyone's mind: One must die to save the rest. Dolan proposed that they draw lots to determine who should be killed so that the rest might eat. (At this point the starving emigrants back at the Mountain Camp and Alder Creek had not yet begun to eat their dead.) Eddy seconded the motion, but Foster did not want to take the risk of being the one who made the sacrifice, and he opposed it.

Eddy then proposed that two men each take a revolver and shoot it out until one or both were killed. This sporting proposition was also turned down. Finally Eddy, by now the de facto leader, suggested that they simply travel on until someone died, letting nature solve the problem. After some querulous argument the others finally agreed, and they staggered on through the storm for another two or three miles.

Disasters now fell on them almost as thickly as the snowflakes. The snow and wind made it almost impossible to get a fire started. But at last the flame caught, and the bone-chilled emigrants piled on fuel to make a big, cheering bonfire. If they had nothing to eat, they could at least be warm. But one of them did not enjoy it for long. Antoine, the Mexican cattle herder, lay in an exhausted slumber by the blaze. The others could hear that he breathed with difficulty, for his breath rattled gruesomely in his throat. In his sleep, he flung out an arm, and his hand landed in the fire. Eddy saw it happen, but was too exhausted to help the sleeping young man. Unable to rouse himself, he thought that the pain would surely wake Antoine soon enough, and he would pull his hand out of the fire by himself. Antoine slumbered on, breathing heavily and unnaturally. His hand doubled up and began to roast in the fire. This was more than Eddy could bear, and he pulled the unconscious herder's hand and arm away from danger. Antoine soon flung out his arm again, and Eddy realized that it was no use to help him. Antoine died without showing a sign of pain as his hand burned to a crisp.

Shortly after this, a terrible storm of wind, snow, and hail swept down upon them. At the same time, the fire began to eat its way down into the snow from its own intense heat. The dismayed emigrants watched helplessly as it sank slowly down, blazing logs, platform, and all. Then the supply of firewood ran out. One of the men took the party's lone hatchet and went to cut more. As he chopped away, the head flew off the hatchet and was lost in the depths of the snow, impossible to find in the dark and the howling storm even if they had had the strength to dig for it.

Still the fire kept burning, shielded from the storm by its

self-made well in the snow. By midnight it had sunk to ground level, eight feet below the surface of the snow, and the emigrants crouched miserably around it with their feet in the ice-cold meltwater.

It was obvious even to the starvation-dulled minds of the emigrants that the fire would soon sputter out in the melted snow if something were not done. A few who were a little more alive than the rest stood the half-burned foundation logs on end and built the fire up again on top. At this point one of the Indians stood up to get closer to the warmth. Clumsy with cold and weariness, he lurched against the fire platform. Down went the rickety structure, and the flames hissed out in the icy pool of water in which the men and women stood. It looked as if everyone was doomed to perish from the cold. Despair set in, and everyone began to pray to God for a merciful death—everyone but Eddy and one or two of the women.

The resourceful Eddy finally persuaded his companions to try a trick he had heard about from someone on the trail, before the Donner Party made its fatal turn onto the Hastings cutoff. It was a mountain man's way of surviving a blizzard. One way or another, he prodded them out of the pit and made them spread blankets on the surface of the snow. The people sat on the blankets in a tight circle with their feet in the center, while Eddy dragged himself around the circle and spread other blankets over them. Last of all, he slipped into the circle himself. The blankets, with the snow that fell on top of them, formed a snug, insulated tent that held in their body heat and kept them warm.

It was a simple enough procedure, but some of the emigrants were so apathetic that they didn't want to move. It took an hour or more before Eddy had coaxed and bullied everyone into position beneath the blankets. Uncle Billy Graves had been weakening visibly since early in the evening. Now Eddy told him he was dying. Uncle Billy replied feebly that he didn't care; he soon sank into death. But before he died, he urged his daughters to eat his body so that they might live.

Christmas morning brought no holiday cheer to the wretched snowshoe party. The storm still raged outside their tent of blankets. Then Patrick Dolan became delirious and began to babble senselessly, in vague and disjointed phrases. He cried out to Eddy that he,

Dolan, was the only one in the group who could be counted on. The deranged man then pulled off his boots and most of his clothes and shouted to Eddy to follow him down to the settlements. They would get there in just a few hours, cried Dolan.

With a great deal of difficulty the others managed to overpower him and bring him back under the blankets. He thrashed about for a while, but they held him down. After a while, his energy exhausted, Dolan became quiet and submissive, like an obedient child, as one of the survivors later commented. As he drifted into death, his companions thought he looked as if he were enjoying a calm and pleasant sleep. Thus died jolly Patrick Dolan, the children's favorite.

In the evening, with the storm still raging, Lemuel Murphy became delirious and started talking uncontrollably about food. In fact, none of the party had eaten for four days, for so far neither men nor women had been able to eat the flesh of any of the three corpses they had on hand.

The next morning—December 26—Eddy tried to start a fire beneath the blanket tent with the aid of gunpowder. His cold, weak hands were clumsy; there was a flareback; and the powderhorn exploded, burning Eddy's face and hands severely. Amanda McCutchen and Sarah Foster, who were sitting nearby, were also burned, though not seriously.

That afternoon the storm finally blew over. Eddy, despite his injuries, immediately climbed out from under the blankets and found a huge, dead pine tree standing nearby. He commandeered some shreds from the cotton lining of Harriet Pike's cloak and dried them in the sun. Using these as tinder, he lit them with sparks from flint and steel and coaxed them into a precarious flame. He fed the tiny flame with bits of dead twigs until it grew; before long he managed to set fire to the dead pine's dry, resin-laden trunk.

The emigrants lay down around the burning tree to enjoy the warmth. The flames roared up the massive trunk in a most gratifying fashion, but then big, burning limbs began to fall in their midst. The people of the Forlorn Hope were now so weak and uncaring that they didn't even try to dodge the flaming menaces. But fortunately none of the falling limbs struck anyone.

It is hard to tell just what happened during the next few days, for the survivors' memories were understandably confused, and the early historians of the Donner Party, unable to straighten out the sequence of events, were equally confused. But at some point the remaining emigrants realized that they had to eat something or die. Up to then, their horror of cannibalism had held them back from eating the flesh of their dead comrades. And they had lost their appetites, a characteristic of the later stages of starvation. But still they wanted to live.

Someone again brought up the dreaded subject of eating human flesh, and this time they did not reject it. They cut strips of flesh from Patrick Dolan's arms and legs, which was fitting, because he had been the first to propose cannibalism and moreover was not related to any of the survivors.

They roasted the lean, stringy meat over the campfire and ate it, turning their faces away from each other. Overcome by guilt and grief, Eddy and the two Indians did not share in the loathsome meal.

This rare map of 1826 shows the West as mainly Indian territory.
Conditions had not changed greatly by 1846, when the Donner Party
started on their fateful journey. (The Beinecke Rare Book and Manuscript
Library, Yale University)

James Frazier Reed, de facto leader of the Donner Party, and his wife, Margaret. The photograph was taken years after their harrowing experience crossing the plains and mountains. (Illinois State Historical Library)

Colonel William Henry "Owl" Russell, original leader of the wagon company with which the Donners and Reeds traveled west from Kansas to the Little Sandy Creek. (United States History, Local History & Genealogy Division, The New York Public Library, Astor, Lenox, and Tilden Foundations.)

Patty Reed, seven years old at the time of her family's misfortunes, grew into this somber but rather pretty young woman. (State of California Department of Parks and Recreation)

Emigrants expected something like this romanticized view of a wagon train.
(Baldwin H. Ward/Corbis-Bettmann)

The reality was more often like this, with toiling oxen and worried men.
(Corbis)

Above, members of the Russell-Boggs company, with which the Donners and Reeds traveled, carved the name of this picturesque spring in northern Kansas in the soft limestone rock. (United States History, Local History & Genealogy Division, The New York Public Library, Astor, Lenox, and Tilden Foundations.)

James Frazier Reed left his initials and the date for posterity at the same spot. (United States History, Local History & Genealogy Division, The New York Public Library, Astor, Lenox, and Tilden Foundations.)

If the river were shallow and the bottom firm and level, the crossing was easy. (Utah State Historical Society)

The Platte River, with its swift currents, potholes, and quicksands, was always a problem to cross. (Corbis-Bettmann)

Wagons line up for an orderly river crossing in this nineteenth century print. Strangely unconcerned Indians camp in left foreground as dramatic clouds tower in the sky. (Utah State Historical Society)

The famed trading post of Fort Laramie was still in business in 1849, the date of this engraving, catering to Indians, emigrants, and traders. Heavy palisades and near-windowless walls guarded against attacks by Indian clients. (Corbis-Bettmann)

Neat in his formal clothing, William Eddy looks the very model of a prosperous citizen. The Illinois coachmaker and his family were among those who joined the Donner and Reed families on the untried Hastings Cutoff. (State of California Department of Parks and Recreation)

(Left, top) The title of this classic print, "A Desperate Situation," all too accurately describes the case of emigrants whose oxen gave out. (Corbis-Bettmann)

Eleanor Eddy's stern face belies the generous nature that led her to hide a life-saving gift of bear meat in her husband's pack. (State of California Department of Parks and Recreation)

Harriet Murphy Pike
and her younger brother
William Murphy,
apparently photographed
in California in later,
more prosperous times.
Harriet's face may still
show grief at the loss
of her husband, mother,
and several siblings.
(State of California
Department of Parks
and Recreation)

Patrick Breen, from Ireland via Iowa, prospered as a farmer in California. (State of California Department of Parks and Recreation)

A grim-looking Margaret Breen, Patrick's wife, looks at the portrait photographer's camera. Her strict and frugal management may have saved her family's lives. (State of California Department of Parks and Recreation)

Ramshackle Fort Bridger was the last stop for travelers on Hastings' new route. Supplies and repairs, and water and grass for the oxen, could all be obtained here. (Corbis-Bettmann)

Lansford W. Hastings, author of the famous guidebook, here depicted in middle life. (State of California Department of Parks and Recreation)

Cresting a pass through the rugged peaks of the Wasatch range, these post-1846 emigrants catch their first sight of the Salt Lake Valley. They may be using the road that the Donner party cleared. (Corbis-Bettmann)

Rusted wheel hubs from abandoned wagons bear mute testimony to the passage of the Donner Party through the Salt Lake Desert. The photo was taken in the late 1920s. (Utah State Historical Society)

This bountiful spring at the entrance to Skull Valley gave the Donner party their last drinking water before the dreadful 80-mile dry drive. (United States History, Local History & Genealogy Division, The New York Public Library, Astor, Lenox, and Tilden Foundations.)

Pilot Peak rises above the far edge of the desolate salt flats. A spring at its foot saved the lives of the Donner Party and their remaining livestock. Rain had apparently flooded the salt flats when this photo was taken. (United States History, Local History & Genealogy Division, The New York Public Library, Astor, Lenox, and Tilden Foundations.)

"Captain" John Augustus Sutter, proprietor of Sutter's Fort, was something of a patron saint to hard-pressed emigrants on the last stage of their journey west. (State of California Department of Parks and Recreation)

SUTTER'S FORT IN 1849

Sutter's Fort did a lively business with emigrants, for whom it was a goal. Since this engraving was made in 1849, the American flag flies over the fort. (State of California Department of Parks and Recreation)

On difficult pitches in the Sierras, emigrants often had to help their oxen by heaving on wheel spokes and pushing the wagon from behind. In foreground, a dog investigates the bones of an ox that didn't make it. (Corbis-Bettmann)

Travelers who made it to the summit of the Sierras were confronted by a tumbled sea of jagged peaks. The western slope of the Sierras was the toughest portion of the trail. (Corbis-Bettmann)

An artist's concept of the Donner Party building their winter quarters at the lake. The two Donner families themselves never got that far, camping five miles downslope. (Corbis)

Artist's concept of the arrival of the Second Relief at the lakeside camp in March 1847. Note how the cabin chimneys barely protrude above the snow. (Corbis)

(Left, top) Those who crossed the Sierras in timely fashion were rewarded by vistas of the great central valley, here seen from the west end of Madelin Pass. (The Beinecke Rare Book and Manuscript Library, Yale University)

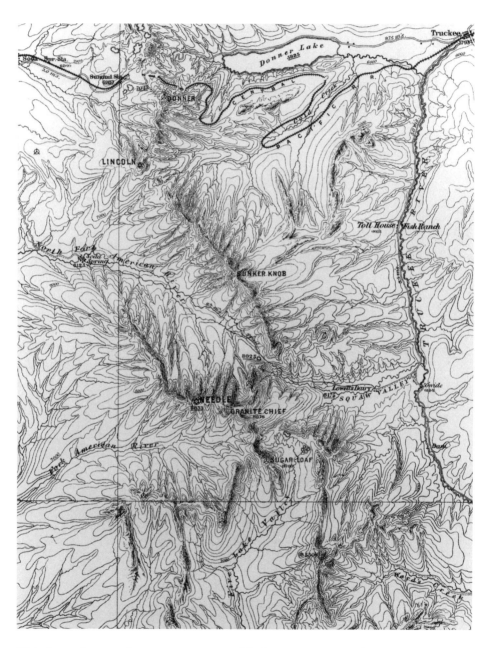

This late nineteenth century topographical map suggests the precipitous terrain at Donner Pass. (The Beinecke Rare Book and Manuscript Library, Yale University)

Heavy snow like this was a nearly insuperable obstacle to the Forlorn Hope. The scene is near Donner Lake. (State of California Department of Parks and Recreation)

Rugged topography of the Sierras near Donner Lake was a sore trial to emigrants even in summer, when the ground was clear of snow. (State of California Department of Parks and Recreation)

Snow-clad Donner Peak rears a mighty barricade for westbound travelers. (The Society of California Pioneers)

Donner Lake, seen from the slope leading up to the pass. The modern railroad line can be seen at center right. Trains and highway traffic are still occasionally blocked by snow. (State of California Department of Parks and Recreation)

A rowdy crowd of American interlopers hails Frémont as he raises the banner of the Bear Flag Rebellion in California on July 7, 1846. At this point, the Donners and Reeds had not yet reached the Continental Divide. (Corbis-Bettmann)

Ever eager for martial glory, a middle-aged Frémont poses for famed Civil War photographer Matthew Brady in his Union general's uniform. (Corbis)

Towering tree stumps in Summit Valley, just across the pass, show the depth of the snow where the Forlorn Hope cut their tops for firewood. (The Society of California Pioneers)

The emigrant trail crossed the rocky bed of the upper Yuba River near here; it was buried under ten to twelve feet of snow when the Forlorn Hope crossed it. (The Society of California Pioneers)

Britton Greenwood, son of a famed mountain man and a member of the Second Relief, in a photograph of unknown date. (State of California Department of Parks and Recreation)

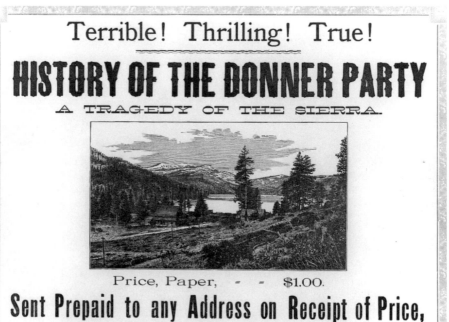

Terrible! Thrilling! True!

HISTORY OF THE DONNER PARTY

A TRAGEDY OF THE SIERRA.

Price, Paper, - - $1.00.

Sent Prepaid to any Address on Receipt of Price,

By the Author, C. F. McGLASHAN, Truckee, Cal.

H. S. Crocker & Co., Printers, Sacramento, Cal.

This early book on the Donner Party, based on extensive interviews and correspondence with survivors, appeared in 1880. (The Beinecke Rare Book and Manuscript Library, Yale University)

A frail, timorous Patty Reed Lewis (left) poses at the dedication of the Pioneer Monument on June 6, 1918. With her are Eliza Donner Houghton (center) and Frances Donner Wilder (right). The men are the Governor of California and the president of the University of California. (State of California Department of Parks and Recreation)

Eliza (right, with tall hat) and Frances (left) stand with two unidentified women and an unidentified man in front of a reconstruction of a cabin at Donner State Memorial Park. (State of California Department of Parks and Recreation)

Leanna Donner App, half-sister of Frances, Georgia, and Eliza, outlived her younger half-siblings, dying in 1930 at the age of ninety-six. (United States History, Local History & Genealogy Division, The New York Public Library, Astor, Lenox, and Tilden Foundations.)

The Pioneer Monument stands proudly at Donner Memorial State Park, by Donner Lake, a reminder of the tragedies that occurred there and on the trail. (Lenscapes)

CHAPTER 14
Suffering and Safety

I could state several most horrid circumstances connected with this affair: such as one of the women being obliged to eat part of the body of her father and her brother, another saw her husband's heart cooked &c; which would be more suitable for a hangmans [sic] journal than the columns of a family newspaper.

—From an anonymous letter printed in
The California Star, February 13, 1847

Sarah Murphy Foster and Harriet Murphy Pike tried to feed a little of Dolan's flesh to their young brother, Lemuel Murphy, but he was beyond help. The boy grew steadily weaker and died in the early morning hours, with his head in his oldest sister's lap. The living members of the Forlorn Hope were not so far from death themselves. As Thornton described them, they were mere walking skeletons. The skin on their faces was drawn tight over the bones, like a mummy's, and from their ghastly countenances their eyes glared out fierce and wild.

By this time most of them had resigned themselves to dying. When Eddy, hiding his own fears, tried to cheer them up, they responded with sighs, tears, and moans. But the meal of human flesh, repellent as it was, had given them new strength. The women regained a bit of spirit, although the men remained sunk in despondency.

The depleted band of survivors stayed on at the scene of their tragedies four days after Christmas, resting and drying the meager flesh of their dead relatives and friends for rations on the trail. Although the first taboo—against eating human flesh—had been broken, no one touched the flesh of his or her own kin. But Sarah Murphy Foster was almost prostrated when she saw one of her companions roasting the heart of her younger brother over a campfire.

On December 30 the Forlorn Hope left the Camp of Death, as they had christened the dreadful spot. It was a wonder that they were able to travel at all, for their feet had swollen so badly that the skin burst. They wrapped their injured feet in rags and pieces of blanket (for the dead no longer needed their blankets to keep them warm) to cushion them, but the pain was still so excruciating that they made little progress.

The Indian Luis, who spoke a little broken English, now confessed to Eddy that he and Salvador were lost. This was not their own country, and without familiar landmarks to guide them they were as helpless as the white strangers they were guiding. Still the expedition kept on going mechanically, bushwhacking their way westward. Their only alternative was to die where they were.

That night it was Eddy who gave out. He had long since used up the half pound of bear meat that his wife had so carefully hidden in his knapsack, and he was faint and weak from starvation. His companions looked at him and told him he was dying—he'd better have something to eat. At first he pooh-poohed the idea, but then he recognized that he had the same symptoms of lassitude and weakness that he'd seen in those who had died. To save his life, and bring help to his wife and children, he reluctantly took his first cannibal meal. The others willingly shared their rations of human flesh with him (he had evidently taken none himself) because they knew that without his leadership they would not make it.

As Eddy ate, the thought crossed his mind that he was committing a horrifying act. But he actually felt no loathing or disgust. As Thornton later wrote, "The hard hand of necessity was on him, and he was compelled to eat or die."

The night passed as quietly as could be expected for people who had just gone through such soul-wrenching experiences. Eddy, once more able to attempt to raise the group's morale, assured them that everyone would get through to safety. They did not believe him, but they recovered enough to curse Lansford W. Hastings bitterly, and to vow vengeance on him for having lured them onto his cutoff.

All the last day of 1846 they traveled along a high, sharp-crested ridge. Although they had no idea of where they were, they had actually blundered back on the trail, for this was the ridge that divided Steep Hollow from the canyon of the Bear River. It was the most terrifying journey they had yet made. They crossed ravines on frail bridges of snow; now and then they could look down through a hole in the snow and see the icy torrent far below. The men and women of the Forlorn Hope had their hearts in their throats as they inched apprehensively over the snow bridges, teetering on their clumsy snowshoes. But their luck held. No one lost his or her balance, and the snow held firm under their weight.

After an eternity of negotiating these terrors, they reached a high spot along the spine of the ridge and paused for a view. In the distance, off to the west, they could see a vast, green plain that seemed to spread out forever—the Sacramento Valley, their goal. But their joy was damped by the sight of the mountains and canyons that still lay across their path. As Mary Graves later remembered, each time they reached the summit of a mountain, another mountain, even higher, lay ahead.

Late that afternoon they reached the end of the ridge. Before them lay a slope that plunged precipitously to a canyon bottom two thousand feet or more below. (This was, in fact, one of the spots where the wagons had to be gingerly let down with ropes.) The exhausted men and women could see that the canyon on the left (Steep Hollow) made a bend below them and joined the canyon (Bear River) on their right. Unable to go farther, they made camp.

New Year's Day 1847 brought the Forlorn Hope no more cheer than Christmas had. The only difference was that there were no storms, and no one had died. The entire day was spent negotiating the formidable canyon. Going down was not too difficult—on the gentler slopes the people squatted down on their snowshoes and slid to the bottom, where they usually fetched up in a snowdrift. Then, hampered by their packs and snowshoes, they laboriously worked themselves free and went on. It would have been comical if the situation had not been so grave.

The fierce cold of the mountains had done them one favor: It had frozen the headwaters of the Bear River so that the stream was low. They were able to cross it without any difficulty severe enough to be remembered. But the climb up the far slope more than made up for this lucky break. For the first fifty feet, the slope was so steep that the hunger-weakened men and women had to cling to bushes and cracks in the rock to avoid sliding back to the bottom. Then the slope became a little less vertical, enough so that snow could cling and trees grow. They dug their snowshoes into the snow and stairstepped up. They moved very slowly, for each step was an effort, and blood from their damaged feet marked the trail. It was evening before they reached the top, and Fosdick barely made it. That night they ate the last of the human flesh they had brought with them.

They were now on a broad plateau with fairly level ground. Although they were foodless, they had a compensation. The snow was so firm that they could walk on it without their snowshoes, a great relief. But their feet could not heal while walking through the snow, and this day they were worse than ever. Fosdick's weakness held the whole group back, and one of the Indians was in even worse condition: His frostbitten toes began to drop off at the first joint.

But on January 3 there were encouraging signs. The snow remained firm, and it looked as if they were at last coming down from the mountain heights, for there were oaks among the conifers. When they camped that night the snow was only three feet deep, an occasion for rejoicing. Figuring that they no longer needed their snowshoes, whose rawhide strings had begun to rot, they toasted the strings over the campfire and dined on them. Eddy also toasted and ate a worn-out pair of moccasins. At least their stomachs had something to work on, even if the leather held no nourishment.

The next day, again, they had nothing to eat, and Fosdick was so weak that they made only two miles. But that night they camped for the first time on bare ground, in a grove of oak trees!

Foster now proposed that the whites kill and eat the Indians. To most white Westerners, an Indian was not quite human, and an enemy at that, so no one was shocked by the suggestion. Except for Eddy. To him, these two dark-skinned youths were fellow human beings and moreover faithful companions. To kill them would be a shabby reward for their having brought food over the Sierras to the whole Donner Party, perhaps saving their lives.

One can imagine the responses he got when he reproached his companions: The Indians were just savages! The Indians had gotten them lost! It was those Indians' fault that they had turned back beyond the pass on their first attempt, just because of Sutter's mules! And so on.

Unable to change his fellow travelers' minds, Eddy secretly warned Luis. Luis looked stunned for a moment, then concealed his emotions as a respectable man of his tribe was brought up to do. He whispered briefly to Salvador, and the two Indian *vaqueros* silently disappeared.

The Forlorn Hope still had its lone rifle and meager supply of munitions, faithfully dragged through snow and mountains and canyons. Eddy decided to take the gun and go hunting. It was a no-lose gamble. If he had luck, he would save the lives of his seven remaining companions. If he failed, they would be no worse off. But when he dropped a hint of his plan to the women, they wept and carried on and begged him to remain, pleading that their lives depended on his staying with them.

But Eddy's mind was made up. The next morning he took the gun, only to be assailed by a reproachful, weeping chorus of women. Harriet Pike threw her arms around his neck and implored him not to go, and the others joined in, fearing he might never come back. But Mary Graves decided to go with Eddy. She was the only one still strong enough to keep up with him.

Eddy was not acting on a deranged whim. An experienced hunter, he thought that the fact that they were now on snow-free ground meant there might be animals around. After he and Mary had trudged about two miles, his keen eyes caught sight of a place where a deer had lain down for the night. Eddy burst into tears of happiness—his first since he had left the Mountain Camp. He turned around and saw Mary also weeping like a child. Although neither was in the least bit religious, both of them fell on their knees and prayed in gratitude. (Some recent commentators believe that Thornton made up this whole passage because he thought that this was how Eddy and Mary Graves *ought* to have behaved. I cannot say.)

Now emotionally relieved, they went on and soon saw a large buck about eighty-five yards away. Eddy raised his gun, but found to his dismay that he was too weak to aim it. Try as he might to hold it still, the gun wavered uncontrollably. He changed his grip and tried again. Again he failed. He heard Mary sobbing behind him. Alarmed and afraid that she would frighten the deer off, Eddy whispered to her to be quiet. "Oh, I am afraid you will not kill it!" she exclaimed, and then fell silent.

For the third time Eddy lifted his rifle to his shoulder. He raised the muzzle above the deer and lowered it slowly. As soon as the deer was in the sights, he pulled the trigger. The rifle cracked; the deer leaped three feet into the air and then stood still. Mary lost her self-control and wept, "O merciful God, you have missed it!"

Eddy told her that he knew his aim was on the deer at the instant he fired. Also, he explained, the deer had dropped its tail between its legs, a sign that it was wounded. At this, the deer recovered its wits and ran off. Eddy and Mary limped after it as fast as they could, sliding down a thirty-foot drop-off cushioned by a snowbank at the bottom. The deer ran about two hundred yards and fell. It was still alive when Eddy reached it, seized it by the antlers, and cut its throat with his penknife. Before he had finished, Mary was at his side, and the two famished humans drank the deer's blood as it gushed out.

They rested a bit and then found the strength to roll the deer's carcass to a spot where they could make a fire. Their faces were covered with blood, but they didn't care. They were going to eat.

They ate part of the deer's liver and some other internal organs for supper, then enjoyed a good night's sleep without dreams of food. During the night Eddy fired his gun several times to alert his comrades. Up on the plateau, Fosdick had heard the first crack of all, and knew what it meant. To his wife he exclaimed feebly, "There! Eddy has killed a deer! Now, if only I can get to him, I shall live!"

Fosdick's hopes were vain. During the night he died. He and Sarah Graves had been married less than a year. Sarah, heartbroken, wrapped his body in their one remaining blanket and lay down on the bare ground to die herself. Somehow she survived the subfreezing cold of the night and revived with morning. To her horror she saw two of her traveling companions (the early chroniclers discreetly suppressed their names, but they were probably William and Sarah Foster) approaching her campsite. They were sure that both she and her husband had died during the cold night, and were coming up to help themselves to their flesh as well as their jewelry, watches, and money. Embarrassed at finding Sarah Fosdick still alive, they turned back to their own campsite and there met Eddy, who had come up from the valley with roasted venison for all hands.

As Eddy dried the remaining deer meat by the fire, Mrs. Fosdick and the two Fosters returned to Jay Fosdick's body. Sarah Fosdick gave her dead husband a last kiss. Then, in spite of her entreaties, the Fosters cut out her newly dead husband's heart and liver before her eyes and also took his arms and legs, the meatiest parts of the body.

The poor young widow, only twenty-two, made a little bundle of her valuables and went back to the campsites with the two people who had just callously butchered her husband. Uncaring, they impaled Fosdick's heart on a stick and began to roast it as she looked on. Sarah Fosdick could bear no more, and retreated to Eddy's campsite, which was a little way off.

During the next couple of days the handful that remained of the Forlorn Hope struck the north branch of the American River and crossed it. They had to climb another steep canyon wall by clinging to the bushes and small trees that grew in crevices. Their bleeding feet soaked their wretched wrappings of blanket scraps. But the weather, at least, was good, and everyone sat down peacefully to eat the last of the venison. Eddy made a little speech, mourning their lost companions. He tactfully avoided mentioning that they had been eaten by the survivors.

After supper, Foster took Eddy aside. Ever since the Forlorn Hope had left the Mountain Camp, Foster had been strangely apathetic and unhelpful, incapable of making a decision on his own and totally dependent on Eddy. Suddenly taking the initiative, he wanted Eddy to help him kill Amanda McCutchen, on the excuse that she was a nuisance and could not keep up.

Eddy, shocked and revolted, told Foster that she had a husband and children. Besides, she was one of their comrades, she was helpless, and she depended on them for protection. Foster kept whimpering objections, until Eddy finally told him sternly that Mrs. McCutchen was not going to die for his sake.

Foster's hunger-crazed mind turned to the sisters Sarah Fosdick and Mary Graves. Neither of them had a child, he slyly pointed out, and Sarah Fosdick no longer had a husband. After hearing this heartless proposal, Eddy warned the two women in the presence of the whole company.

Foster became angry and boasted that he didn't care what Eddy said; he could handle Eddy. Eddy, losing patience, challenged Foster to settle their differences on the spot. He grabbed a large stick, whacked it on a log to test its soundness, and threw it to Foster, telling him to defend himself. He seized a knife that had belonged to the late Jay Fosdick and went for Foster as fast as his weakness would permit. Eddy was almost within striking distance when the women, three of whom Foster had just proposed to kill and eat, seized him, dragged him to the ground, and took the knife away. Luckily, Foster stood dazed, missing this opportunity to kill Eddy.

Eddy, recovering, warned Foster once more that he would kill him if he ever again showed the slightest inclination to take the life of any member of the party. If anyone were to die, he said, it would be either Foster or himself. And they would settle the question of who was to die by fighting, since Foster had never been willing to take his chances by drawing lots, the only fair way, said Eddy, of selecting a victim.

On January 8 they left the Camp of Strife, as they named the place, and after about two miles found the bloody tracks of Sutter's Indians. Foster, sunk into a deranged bestiality, vowed that he would track down the Indians and kill them. Another couple of miles farther on, they found the two Indian *vaqueros,* collapsed on the ground and dying. It was no wonder, for they had been without food for a week and without fire for four days.

Eddy wanted to let the poor Indians die in peace—surely they could not last for more than a few hours—but Foster would not wait. Eddy felt there was no point in trying to stop him, since the Indians would soon be dead anyway, but he walked away so as not to witness the evil deed.

Foster, savoring his triumph, hobbled over to Luis, callously told him what he was about to do, and shot him through the head. He killed Salvador a moment later. Then, perhaps helped by the women, he cut the Indians' flesh from their bones and dried it.

That night Eddy ate only dried grass, refusing the flesh of the slain Indian youths. And from that night on only Foster's wife and his sister-in-law, Harriet Pike, camped with the slayer. The others slept a safe distance away, and one of them always stayed awake to keep an eye on their former friend, no longer trustworthy.

By now they saw numerous deer, but Eddy was so weak that he could no longer aim the gun. When he walked, he staggered like a drunk, and when he came to a fallen log only a foot high, he lacked the strength to step over it. Instead, he had to stoop down, put both hands on the log, and roll himself over it. All the survivors were now so enfeebled that they had to sit down and rest every quarter mile. The slightest obstacle caused them to stumble and fall. When the women fell, they wept like babies, got up, and tottered on again. There is no record of how the men behaved.

They had to cross rough terrain. Eddy still lived on grass, refusing to touch the flesh of his slain Indian companions. A cold rain began to fall on the wretched wanderers and did not stop. At last, on January 12, they reached an Indian village in the foothills. Dreadful experiences with the Spaniards had taught these Indians to fear and mistrust the white man. Yet when they saw these miserable wraiths, skeleton-thin and wrapped in rags, they burst into tears of pity.

After their first outburst of emotion, the Indians hurried to bring the survivors their own staple food of acorn bread. The starving whites did not get much nourishment from this unaccustomed food, and Eddy got sick and had to go back to eating grass.

The next day the chief of the village sent runners ahead to the next village, telling them to take care of the emigrants and have food ready for them. An escort from the village accompanied them, with an Indian on either side of each emigrant to support them and help them along. In this way they were passed along from village to village toward the white settlements.

On January 17 they reached a village where the chief had

managed to collect a large handful of pine nuts. He gave them to Eddy, who ate them and felt miraculously restored. With new energy he led his comrades on. But the others gave out after a mile and collapsed on the ground, ready to die. The Indians, greatly distressed, were unable to help them.

Eddy thought again of his wife and children starving up in the snows of the Sierras and resolved to get through or die in the attempt. The elderly chief detailed one of his men to guide Eddy to the nearest white settlement, but after about five miles Eddy's new strength began to run out. Luckily, another Indian happened by, and Eddy prevailed on him to join them in return for some tobacco. After another five miles Eddy's strength failed completely, but the Indians half-carried him along, his bleeding feet dragging on the ground.

About half an hour before sunset they arrived at the home of a settler named M. D. Ritchie, who had arrived late in the fall of 1846 and built a shack on Johnson's ranch to spend the winter in. Come spring, he would go out and claim his own spread. Several other emigrants lived in winter quarters nearby.

Ritchie's young daughter, Harriet, heard a noise outside the shack and went to the door. There she saw the two Indians supporting a hideous bundle between them. The bundle spoke in English and asked for bread. Harriet burst into tears and led Eddy into the house. They instantly put him to bed, fed him, and heard his story. For four days he remained in bed, too exhausted even to turn over. He had traveled eighteen miles on foot that day, and he had been thirty-one days on the trail from the cabins by the lake.

Harriet Ritchie ran immediately to the neighbors with the news of the starving refugees who had escaped from the snow. The housewives collected all the bread they could spare. To this they added sugar, tea, and coffee—what was left of the limited supplies that they had brought over the mountains last fall. Beef from California's huge herds of half-wild cattle went into the food packets as well. Husbands and bachelors, not to miss out on the excitement, leaped on their horses and dashed importantly back and forth between the cabins bearing messages and collecting food.

Four men took backpacks loaded with as much food as they could carry and set off on foot, guided by the Indians (they did not want to risk their horses by riding at night). They reached the remaining members of the Forlorn Hope about midnight. One man stayed up all night cooking for them. Eddy had warned the rescue party not to give the survivors too much to eat, but they wept and begged for food so pathetically that the men gave them all they asked for, until all the food was gone. The result of this gorging on starved stomachs was that they all got sick.

In the morning came more men carrying food, this time on horseback. They had no trouble following the trail—for the past six miles it was marked by the blood from Eddy's feet. The rescuers could hardly believe that a starving man could cover such a distance. Indeed, they would not have believed it at all if they had not just traveled the same route and seen his tracks themselves.

That night the five women and Foster were brought to the settlement. The Forlorn Hope had reached a haven in California at last. But only seven had lived to reach it out of fifteen who began the deadly journey from the far side of the mountains.

CHAPTER 15

Slow Starvation in the Snow

Poor little children were crying with hunger, and mothers were crying because they had so little to give their children.
—Virginia Reed Murphy, "Across the Plains in the Donner Party (1846)," *The Century Magazine*, July 1891

While the Forlorn Hope had been undergoing their incredible sufferings, life proceeded quietly at the Mountain Camp and Alder Creek. The days came and went in a monotonous procession; storms came and dumped new layers of snow; the stranded emigrants watched the weather and tried to calculate how much longer their scanty stock of food would last. Patrick Breen's diary recorded mostly the weather.

But on Monday, December 21, the same day that the Forlorn Hope ran out of food, Breen had something different to say:

"Milt got back last night from Donos camp sad news. Jake Donno, Sam Shoemaker Rinehart & Smith are dead the rest of them in a low condition." (Breen persistently tried to turn the name Donner into something resembling Donough. Perhaps it gave him comfort to imagine the Donners as fellow Irishmen.)

It was at about this time that Breen turned to religion and began to mention God in his daily entries. He also began to read the Bible and the Thirty Days' Prayer.

Uncle Jake's health had failed again; he lost his will to live, and slipped away. The same thing may have happened to the two teamsters Sam Shoemaker and James Smith, and the German Reinhardt. It was later said that before Reinhardt died he whispered a confession to Uncle George, telling him how he and Spitzer had slain and robbed Wolfinger in the desert. But George Donner kept Reinhardt's secret. Wolfinger's widow was living in his shelter, and he may have wished to spare her feelings.

The four dead men at the Donner camp were buried in the snow, and life went on. Despite the family tragedy, things were still better in some ways down at Alder Creek than up at the lake. For one thing, there was love and cooperation among the families at the Donner camp. For another, Tamsen Donner was an excellent organizer. However, they were short of food. The first big snowstorm had taken the Donners by surprise before they had slaughtered their oxen. The animals had wandered during the storm, and their carcasses could not be found. The men and older boys went out and prodded the snow with long poles to locate the dead oxen, but without success.

The days dragged on in the cabins, now buried so deeply beneath the snow that the inhabitants had to dig tunnels to reach the surface. Down below, the cabins were dark, damp, and filthy as well as unbearably crowded. Neither people, clothing, nor bedding had been washed in months, and lice plagued them. All the dogs but two had been eaten. The last of the tasteless beef from the starved oxen was running out, and most families were reduced to eating ox hides.

These were prepared by a simple process. First they were cut into pieces and held over the fire to singe off the hair. Then they were scraped as clean as possible and boiled in a kettle for hours until they turned to a gluelike paste (in fact, hide makes a very strong glue that is still used by fine furniture craftsmen). The thick glue soup was removed from the fire and allowed to cool to a jelly. There was no more salt to season the gluey mess, but some families used pepper. Either straight or seasoned, the dish was disgusting, and some of the trapped emigrants, starving as they were, barely managed to choke down a few mouthfuls.

There was not much nutrition in the hides, and the lack of salt may also have contributed to the general poor health of the stranded Donner Party. In fact, it was malnutrition rather than outright starvation that first caused people to sicken and die.

The distasteful diet was sometimes varied by boiling bones to make a watery soup. Then someone discovered that if bones were boiled long enough, they became soft and crumbly enough to be eaten. Alternatively, they could be toasted over the fire until they were charred and brittle. Down at Alder Creek the Donners were trapping and eating the mice that came into their dwellings for the warmth. The despised Digger Indians ate such fare—but it was fresh meat even if the quantity was sadly insufficient.

The stench in the cabins must have been almost unbearable: unwashed people and clothing, boiling hides, excrement, and no ventilation. Yet the people who lived in these noisome warrens became so apathetic that they spent much of their time in bed and seldom went out except to get firewood. In the midst of unspoiled forest and mountain scenery they were living in a tiny, crowded slum. They were, in effect, prisoners in a death camp, but their jailer was no human. It was the weather itself.

Christmas brought but little cheer to most of the Donner Party. Patrick Breen was still ailing with "the gravel," and his sons had to go out into the severe snowstorm to get wood. His comment for that day was: "the prospect is appalling but hope in God."

But in the Reed family quarters there was a real celebration. During the preceding weeks Margaret Reed had somehow squirreled away a few dried apples, some beans, a piece of tripe, a two-inch square of bacon, and half a cup of rice. The children were beside themselves with delight as their mother brought these treasures out from their hiding places, and they stood around the fire and watched them cook. They danced and shouted with glee each time the boiling water carried a bean, a tiny cube of bacon, or some other delicacy to the top of the kettle. When dinner was finally ready, Mrs. Reed told them, "Children, eat slowly. There is plenty for all." The proprieties must be observed, even in adversity.

On December 29, Breen noted that Keseberg's teamster, Burger, was sick. That night he died. On his corpse were found $1.50 in cash, a gold pin, and two handsome silver watches. His other valuables consisted of a razor and three boxes of percussion caps for guns. Spitzer took the dead man's coat and raincoat, and Keseberg appropriated the rest.

Before the New Year the Reeds were out of food again. They killed and ate their little dog Cash, the children's pet. They lived on him for a week—his meat, entrails, feet, tail, "and everything about him." When that was gone they made soup of the bones.

Then the last of the dog soup was eaten, and they had to live on hides. Very well in itself, but the only hides they had were those that formed the roof of their cabin. If they ate those hides, they would destroy their own shelter and die of exposure instead of starvation. So Margaret Reed organized her own escape party: herself, Milt Elliott, Eliza the hired girl, and Virginia.

Milt was still relatively vigorous and utterly loyal, so much a part of the family that he called Mrs. Reed "Ma." They could depend on him for anything that required strength. Eliza had become more childish than ever and was useless—but she could not fend for herself if she were left behind, and she would be eating food of which Patty, Jimmy, and Tommy might otherwise get a share. Virginia, now thirteen, was plucky and big enough to keep up with the adults. As for Margaret Reed herself, she was a semi-invalid to begin with, and weeks of malnutrition and close confinement had surely not improved her health. But she had a strength of character that rose above these difficulties.

The three small children, Patty, Jimmy, and Tommy, were parceled out among the neighbors, who for once were helpful. Patty went to the Kesebergs, Jimmy to the Graveses, and little Tommy to the Breens. Mrs. Reed had a hard time getting away, for the children wept with despair and begged to be taken along. She was able to calm them only by telling them that she was going off to get bread for them.

It was a mad idea, this expedition, and bound to fail. But Mrs. Reed was desperate and no longer thinking rationally. For food they had only a tiny portion of dried meat apiece, much less than the Forlorn Hope had taken.

The four left the cabins about eleven-thirty in the morning of

January 4. It was a beautiful, sunny day—Patrick Breen thought it looked like spring—and the snow began to melt away. Milt led the party, breaking a trail with his snowshoes, and the others stepped in his tracks. It was tiring work. Eliza soon became discouraged and was sent back the next morning.

Now came the test of scaling the slope to the pass. Virginia was so weak that she often had to crawl instead of walking, but bravely kept on. Once beyond the pass, the three had to halt while Milt fashioned snowshoes for the women. For two more days they dragged themselves on, getting thoroughly lost. Milt had a compass, but it was not working properly, and they wandered into the rugged country north of the pass, a wilderness of peaks, boulders, and small, frozen lakes.

On the third night, Virginia's feet became frostbitten, and they had to turn back. Fortunately, there were no storms, so they were able to follow their own tracks back to the relative safety of the cabins. They got back on January 8, one day before the onset of a severe storm that would surely have killed them had they been in the open. Virginia wrote later: "I could go on very well while I thought we were getting along, but as soon as we had to turn back I could hardly get along." (During this same period, the members of the Forlorn Hope were working their way down the western slope of the Sierras, Foster had proposed killing the two Indians, and Eddy shot the deer.)

There was no jubilation to greet the returning Reeds—three more mouths to feed—but the Breens made room for Virginia in their cabin. Milt and Eliza went down to the Donners, and Mrs. Reed moved in with Keseberg, where three-year-old Tommy was already lodging. This solved the problem of shelter, and Mrs. Reed could now use her own oxhide roof for food.

The snow continued to accumulate. On January 13 Breen judged it at thirteen feet deep. "Don't know how to get wood this morning," he confided to his diary, "it is dredful to look at."

Margaret Breen ran a frugal household, and her family had begun to eat hides before the other emigrants, so they still had a little meat left. Mrs. Breen took a fancy to Virginia and now and then secretly gave her a bit of the hoarded supply. There were now fifteen people in the Breen cabin, for all the Reeds had moved in. They shared a floor space of twelve by fourteen feet. A simple calculation shows that each person had a space of a little more than five feet long and two feet wide. Of course, this does not allow for the space that the hearth and various utensils took up. The occupants could hardly move without stepping on someone; many found it simpler not to get out of bed.

Patrick Breen led family prayers morning and evening and read often from his big Bible. Virginia took turns with the others holding resinous splints of pine to provide reading light. So impressed was she by the magical mystery of these torchlit ceremonies that she made a vow to become a Catholic if God spared her life and got her safely to California.

There were other books, too, and Virginia read them over and over. In later life she remembered particularly a biography of Daniel Boone, whose adventures in the wilderness fascinated her.

Things were worse in the other cabins. One day Billy Murphy came to take the hides off Keseberg's lean-to (the Keseberg family had now moved in with the Murphys) and told Breen that his brother Landrum, the oldest son in the Murphy family, had gone crazy. Two days later (January 19), Breen wrote in his diary, "Lanthrom very low in danger if relief don't soon come." The Breen family had its own mishap when Mrs. Breen and young Edward Breen ate some meat on which Patrick Dolan had spat his chaw of tobacco weeks ago, and got violently sick.

Jean-Baptiste and Denton came up one day from the Donner camp at Alder Creek. They had the hired girl Eliza with them. She refused to eat hides, and in her childish mind was convinced that there was meat at the Mountain Camp. Of course, there was none, and Mrs. Reed sent her back "to live or die on hides," as Breen noted. That same day, Milt Elliott's toes were frozen.

Now and then Breen wrote in his diary of his hope that a rescue party from Sutter's would arrive, for he clung to the belief that either Reed or the Forlorn Hope had gotten through to summon help. But the days came and went, and no rescuers appeared. On January 6 he wrote: "those that went to Suitors not yet returned. provisions getting very scant. people getting very weak living on short allowance of hides."

The next day brought even more depressing news. Mrs. Keseberg came for a visit and told them that her little son had died. Landrum Murphy was now in bed, too weak to get up. Billy and Simon Murphy were sick, too. Keseberg himself was still incapacitated with his badly infected foot. With no one able to cut firewood, they did not have enough fuel to cook hides.

January 30, a Saturday, was a fine, pleasant morning, and the snow thawed where the sun struck it. On this cheery day, Mrs. Graves seized the Reed family's goods as security for what she said the Reeds owed her. She even took all but two of the hides on which Mrs. Reed was depending to feed her family. Even if Betsy Graves still blamed Margaret Reed for the death of John Snyder an eternity ago, it is hard to account for such inhuman behavior. But, as Thornton wrote, "Untold sufferings had broken their spirits and prostrated anything like an honorable and commendable pride. Misfortune had dried up the fountains of the heart."

By now, most of the suffering prisoners of the snow had lost all self-respect and were living an animal existence, concerned only with their own precarious survival and that of their children. All of them realized that they would die soon if help did not get through. Some began to prepare for death by praying industriously. Others frantically "cursed God, cursed the snow, cursed the mountain, and in the wildest frenzy deplored their hard and miserable fate." Almost everyone cursed Hastings bitterly for having lied to them about his so-called cutoff.

The next few days brought a terrible death toll. Landrum Murphy died the night of January 30. Baby Harriet McCutchen, entrusted to the dubious care of Mrs. Graves, died February 2. Eddy's little girl died February 4; the mother lingered a few days more. That left only one in the Eddy family, three-year-old James. He was living with the elderly Mrs. Murphy, now childish and half-blind from malnutrition.

Spitzer died in the dark hours of the morning of February 8. Patty Reed recalled that he begged Mrs. Breen for a little bit of meat to put in his mouth so that he could die content. She did not give him one.

On February 9 the faithful recorder of disaster, Patrick Breen, reported that the Pike baby was all but dead. Milt Elliott had collapsed at the Murphy cabin and was too weak to get up. He died that night. Mrs. Reed and Virginia dragged the body up the snow tunnel from the cabin and buried their last friend in a shallow grave of snow. They now had no protector among the hostile people at the lake.

A few days later, on February 15, Mrs. Reed again pleaded with Betsy Graves for a hide to feed her children. Once more she was coldly refused. Breen noted the following day, "we all feel very weakly today."

But at sundown on February 19 seven men on snowshoes, carrying bulging packs on their backs, appeared at the Mountain Camp. The long-awaited rescue expedition had arrived!

CHAPTER 16
Delays and Disappointments

Here we found that it was utterly impossible to proceed further with the horses. Leaving them, we proceeded further on foot. . . . found that impossible, the snow being soft and deep. I may here state that neither of us knew anything about snow shoes, having always lived in a country where they were never used.
—James Frazier Reed, "The Snow-Bound, Starved Emigrants of 1846," *Pacific Rural Press*, Mar. 25, 1871

At this point the story of the Donner Party becomes extremely complex, with many new characters and a number of different episodes unfolding simultaneously.

We will now flash back to James Frazier Reed, of whom we have not heard since his near-fatal journey across the mountains. Reed had not been idle since he came down half-starved from the Sierras. Reaching Sutter's Fort on October 28, he went instantly to Sutter himself to plead for help. It was late in the season, he knew, but there was still a chance that he might get back to his family and fellow travelers with supplies. With his customary generosity, Sutter donated ample supplies of jerked meat and flour, and provided horses and pack mules with Indian *vaqueros* to lead them. Reed was ready to start back across the mountains the next morning—but that night a courier from Colonel Frémont's headquarters in Monterey arrived at the fort. The courier bore letters from Frémont that told of turmoil and war in the United States' new possession of California.

The United States and Mexico had been formally at war since May 13, 1846, although the Donner Party and the rest of the Russell-Boggs wagon company did not learn of it until they reached California. An expansionist-minded Congress had maneuvered Mexico into warlike action, first by annexing the sovereign Republic of Texas and then by sending troops to the Texas-Mexico border zone. Acquiring California, of course, was always in the expansionists' plans.

In June Frémont had come riding down from Oregon at the head of a motley force of mountain men and adventurers to seize California from Mexico. Without authorization from his superiors, he had instigated a revolt among the American settlers. Success crowned his maneuverings, and the short-lived Bear Flag Republic was born, soon to be annexed by the mother country. Giddy with triumph, Frémont forcibly commandeered Sutter's Fort for his temporary headquarters. U.S. Navy ships sailed into Californian ports to complete the conquest.

But the native Californios (the people of Spanish California) soon came to resent this forcible occupation, and they had risen in arms to drive out the hated gringos. They were succeeding so well that Frémont now found it necessary to raise an army of American volunteers. This meant every available able-bodied man, including Reed.

Reed was in a dreadful position. He ached to get back to his family. But he dared not risk incurring Frémont's displeasure. If he declined to enlist in Frémont's makeshift army, he risked being arrested and thrown into prison. (The imperious Pathfinder had already thus disciplined several American settlers who had objected to his high-handed methods.) So Reed enlisted, along with his friend and former traveling companion Edwin Bryant, who was also at Sutter's Fort.

Luckily, Reed was a skillful negotiator, and he was able to strike a fairly good bargain with Frémont. Pointing out that his first duty was to the endangered emigrant group in the mountains, he was able to decline the command of a volunteer company. Instead, he was permitted to head back to the mountains on condition that he recruit volunteers along the route between Sutter's Fort and Bear Valley, in the foothills of the Sierras. To give him the necessary official status, Reed was given the title of lieutenant. (He was actually able to sign up twelve or thirteen men.)

All this military business delayed Reed's departure by a couple of days. It rained in the great central valley the night of October 29, and the next morning snow was visible on the distant mountains. Ominously, Sutter told Reed that the snow lay lower than normal, and that it looked unusually heavy for the first snowfall of the season (just how heavy, the luckless group at Truckee Lake were finding out at firsthhand). The sight of the snow, and Sutter's comments, did nothing to ease Reed's fears for his family.

Not until the morning of October 31 was Reed finally able to get away. With him he took William McCutchen, now recovered from his physical breakdown. The big Missourian's legs hung ludicrously down below his horse's belly, but he was not concerned with making a smart impression. He was happy to be going back at last to his Amanda and the baby, and to fulfill the pledge he had made to the members of the Donner Party back in the Nevada desert. With them the two fathers had twenty-six packhorses loaded with food, and two Indian helpers.

They proceeded up the muddy road, stopping at Johnson's Ranch to pick up four more horses and a mule, plus extra supplies of beans and dried beef. The pack train proceeded without hindrance as far as Bear Valley, where they found snow almost knee-deep on the ground but no trace of the Donner Party, which the men had expected to be camping there with their wagons and belongings.

A heavy storm of rain and sleet swept down, but Reed and McCutchen pushed on until late at night. Getting the flour and the horses under cover as best they could, they spent a miserably sleepless night, as they could not get a fire started in the downpour. The next morning they continued up Bear Valley toward the mountains and, to their astonishment, saw smoke drifting from a tent.

It was the camp of a Mr. and Mrs. Jotham Curtis. Curtis had quarreled with his wagon company and decided to spend the winter in the pleasant meadows of Bear Valley, having no idea that it snowed there. Now he and his wife were marooned. With their food supply exhausted, they had decided to sacrifice their dog—he was old, and not good for much any more—and at that moment were cooking the last of his remains in a Dutch oven.

The stranded couple hailed Reed and McCutchen as angels sent for their deliverance. The two men generously offered them flour and beef from their ample supplies. Mrs. Curtis, not to be outdone, invited them to stay for supper and share the baked dog. After some initial reluctance Reed and McCutchen, who had not eaten since the morning of the day before, accepted the offer.

Reed warily lifted the heavy lid of the Dutch oven. The dog appeared to be well baked, and it had a savory smell. He cut off a rib, smelled it, and took a taste. He found it quite palatable. He passed the rib on to McCutchen, who sniffed at it suspiciously for a while, then ate it and pronounced it "very good dog." With this encouragement, Mrs. Curtis immediately began baking bread, and in a short time there was supper for all.

In the morning Reed and McCutchen set off promptly, following a trail that Curtis's oxen had beaten in the two-foot-deep snow as they drifted back up the mountain before the force of the storm. Before the two men left, they promised to take the stranded Curtises down to the settlements on their return journey. They also left them a few days' supply of beef and flour, and left behind nine packhorses, guarded by one of the Indians.

As they had hoped, the ox trail led them up into the mountains, but once on the first ridge they ran into dry, loose snow three feet deep—too much for the horses. The floundering animals made no more than three miles before the rescuers had to make camp. During the night they awoke to the sound of horses moving down the trail. Leaping to their feet, they hurried to the spot where the Indian helper had been sleeping. He was gone, and three of the horses were missing with him.

McCutchen immediately saddled his horse and rode back down the night-shrouded trail to Curtis's camp. Curtis whined that both Indians had been there, warmed themselves by the fire, and gone back down the valley. He had not tried to stop them, he said, because it would have been useless. McCutchen suspected, however, that Curtis had actually encouraged the Indians to desert, thinking it would force the anxious fathers to abandon their mission and rescue him on the way back.

It was midnight before McCutchen rejoined Reed at their camp in the snow, but in the morning he was eager to go again. It was their sixth day out from Sutter's, and each day of delay increased the peril to their families. Both of them knew what even one additional day without food could do.

The helpful trail left by Curtis's oxen soon veered off to the left, and they had to leave it. The snow now deepened rapidly, and the horses could barely force their way through it. At each step, they had to rear up on their hind legs to get their forequarters above the snow, then plunge forward and down. At the end of each plunge they sank so deep that the men could see nothing of them but their noses and a bit of their heads. The exhausted packhorses soon gave out, but the men managed to push forward another mile on their saddle horses. Then these, too, gave out, and the men struggled ahead on foot in snow up to their armpits. Snowshoes would have been a great help, but neither man knew how to make or use them.

Reed and McCutchen got as far as the ridge above Yuba Bottoms and halted there, exhausted. They saw no sign of an emigrant party, heard no sound but the whistling of the wind through the pine trees. They looked at the empty, snow-covered landscape and back at each other, and gave up any hope of getting through. Even if they had been able to cross the mountains on foot, the risky exploit would be useless without food for the starving people of the Donner Party, and the packhorses obviously could not make it. They floundered back to the horses, dug them out of the snow, and returned to Curtis's camp, deeply dejected.

Curtis, far from being glad to see his rescuers, turned surly and began to abuse McCutchen as the big Missourian cooked supper. McCutchen replied with a volley of thundering Shakespearean imprecations, but Curtis continued to vomit out his venom. At last McCutchen, exasperated, threatened to thrash Curtis if he didn't hold his tongue. This worked, for cowardice was one of Curtis's more amiable qualities.

McCutchen offered to share supper with their unpleasant hosts.

Mrs. Curtis accepted, but her husband sulked and refused until McCutchen picked him up and told him he would shake him out of his trousers if he didn't eat.

The following day Reed and McCutchen cached their supplies for the next attempt. The flour went into Curtis's wagon; the meat they stored high up in trees, where they hoped it would be safe from marauding carnivores. Then they drove the unladen packhorses back down the valley until they reached a place where the snow was light enough for the poor animals to browse on the underbrush—they had not had anything to eat for several days.

The next morning, the two men packed Curtis's belongings on a horse for him. Curtis, now in splendid form, repaid the favor with a fresh stream of complaints and abuse. Then he left the horse for his benefactors to lead, although they had their hands full managing their own animals.

Next, Curtis's pack ropes came loose, and the pack flopped down beneath his horse's belly. Reed and McCutchen asked him to give them a hand in fixing it. He ignored them and sauntered on ahead. This was too much for McCutchen, who caught up with Curtis and gave him a few wallops with a rope. At this, Curtis's arrogance collapsed, and he whimpered that he would come back and take care of his own packhorse if only McCutchen would not kill him. In this disharmonious fashion they proceeded back to the settlements.

Once back at the fort, Reed unburdened his fears to Sutter. The Swiss land baron did his best to console the distraught father, saying that it didn't surprise him at all that the two men had failed to get through the snow. How many oxen did the Donner Party have with them? asked Sutter. Reed reckoned up how many there had been when he was banished from the wagon train. (He could not know, of course, how many the Indians had killed or run off, or how many had dropped dead of exhaustion.) Sutter made some rapid mental calculations and assured Reed that the party would have enough to last them to the beginning of spring if they slaughtered the animals now. The cold, as they knew, would preserve the meat.

That was some comfort. But a moment later Sutter added that no relief expedition could possibly get through until February, when the winter storms were normally over and the snow had a crust firm enough for men to walk on without falling through. In the meantime, he suggested, Reed should travel down to Yerba Buena (now a part of San Francisco) and seek help from the U.S. naval commander there.

Once more, events kept Reed from his goal. The Mexican forces had retaken the San Francisco side of the San Francisco Bay from the gringos, and Reed had to cool his heels in San Jose. His time there was not entirely wasted, however, for he filed a number of applications for land grants and planted grapevines and fruit trees on one of his claims. We should note that Reed had not come over the Sierras as a pauper, for he carried $10,000 in a secret money belt. With the business formalities completed, Reed joined a volunteer company of mounted riflemen, rode about a bit, and finally on January 2 saw action in a cavalry skirmish at Santa Clara.

After this engagement the Mexican Californians decided that the time was ripe to make peace, but the negotiations took much time, and it was February 1 before Reed was free to depart for Yerba Buena and plead the case of the snowbound emigrants to Commander Hull of the U.S. Navy.

The navy could do nothing to help a private citizen, but Hull and other officers called a mass meeting of the resident Americans for February 3 and invited Reed to speak. Almost every man in the area attended. Many had known Reed from the Russell-Boggs wagon company; others he had met while playing soldier in Frémont's military drama. Reed stood up to make his appeal, faced the crowd, and burst into tears. He had to sit down, his speech unfinished. A Reverend Dunleavy, who had come across the plains that same summer with a different party, carried on for him. At this point neither Reed nor anyone else knew anything about the Forlorn Hope or the fate of the others stranded somewhere in the Sierras. However, Dunleavy guessed accurately that they must be at Truckee Lake, and in desperate straits.

Hardly had the Reverend finished than men rushed up to the chairman's table to offer money. The embarrassed chairman had to ask them to wait until he could appoint a committee to receive the funds. This was speedily done, and more than $700 was collected to recruit and outfit a relief party.

A renowned old mountain man was living in Redwood, forty miles away, and a courier dashed off at once to hire him as a guide. Back came the message that the old man already had an engagement. (The truth was almost surely that he didn't want to risk his life in one of the worst Sierra winters in memory for a bunch of strangers.)

Preparations went on undeterred. February 4 was a busy day of raising more money and purchasing supplies. The expedition was to start up the Sacramento River by boat the next day with the evening tide. All was ready for departure when Sutter's launch came sailing down from upcountry. On board was a courier bearing news of the Forlorn Hope and its horrifying story.

We segue now to William Eddy. When Eddy finally woke up at Ritchie's house (he had slept thirty-six hours straight after his frightful journey), he dictated a letter to John Sinclair, the local *alcalde,* who lived nearby. (An *alcalde* was a Spanish official, a combination of mayor and judge.) An Indian runner carried the letter, for the California rains had made the unpaved roads so soft and muddy that a horse would have bogged down. Sinclair, in turn, sent an urgent message by courier and Sutter's launch to Yerba Buena, where it caused consternation. The committee decided that the desperate condition of the Donner Party's survivors called for better organization and more food. Once more the rescue was held up while men scoured the area for extra supplies.

It was clear, too, that the rescue party would have to establish a halfway camp in the foothills, where both victims and rescuers could rest and regain their strength. A certain Passed Midshipman Selim E. Woodworth, U.S. Navy—presently on leave—volunteered to take charge of this halfway station. Woodworth, thirty-one, was the son of the man who had written "The Old Oaken Bucket," a favorite sentimental song of generations of Americans. Personable and persuasive, Woodworth made a fine impression on people.

The delay of the expedition was not all bad, for later that same evening the legendary mountain man Caleb Greenwood arrived from Sonoma, north of San Francisco Bay, where McCutchen had hurried off to raise volunteers. Old Greenwood was eighty-three years old, he boasted, and he knew the Sierras like his own backyard. He had come west to Oregon with John Jacob Astor's fur traders in 1810, and he claimed to have made the overland journey as long ago as 1826. For the past couple of years he had been guiding "emigrators" to the Golden West.

Greenwood had lived for years with the Crow tribe, and he brought with him several of his sons by his Indian wife. Dressed in an ancient and filthy suit of buckskin, Greenwood was still fit and energetic despite his age. Six feet tall, rawboned and wiry, he still stood erect and moved with the ease of a young man. His only weakness was badly inflamed eyes.

Up in Sonoma, the wealthier citizens had offered Greenwood $500 on condition that he actually get together a relief party and set out. Even some of the Mexican elite, overcome with pity for the suffering gringos, had chipped in. Now Greenwood had come to the San Francisco area to raise volunteers and ready cash. The old mountain man said that he needed only ten or twelve men he could depend on in the snow, but he must have money to hire them.

The pickings were slim, however. Most of the men in California (excluding Mexicans and Indians) were sailors of a dozen nationalities who had deserted their ships, and the rest were mainly American farmers who had come overland. Hardy and brave they might be, but they simply could not cope with the Sierras in winter, even if any had cared to try. So Greenwood planned to make a swing around Laguna Lake and Mount St. Helena to pick up a few hunters and trappers who were spending the slack season there.

This threatened further delay, but after much haggling and last-minute changes of plan by the harassed relief committee, Reed was finally able to leave Yerba Buena on February 7. In the meantime, a different and entirely separate relief expedition had already left from Johnson's Ranch.

CHAPTER 17
The Rescuers Come Through

I will again give you a list of their names, as I think they ought to be recorded in letters of gold.
— Sheriff George McKinstry, *The California Star,* Mar. 13, 1847

The second expedition had been organized by the dauntless William Eddy, who, isolated in the back country, was not aware of Reed's frantic efforts. It came to be known as the First Relief, because it was the first to leave and the first to arrive at the scene.

Still barely back on his feet after his brush with death, Eddy was desperate to bring help to his wife and children—and whoever else was still alive. (He could not know, of course, that his wife and daughter had already succumbed to cold and hunger.)

The first result of Eddy's letter to Alcalde Sinclair was a bit of an anticlimax. When the panting, mud-covered Indian runner reached Sinclair's house, the *alcalde* was away, and his wife read the message. She responded instinctively by sending a load of underclothes over to the five women survivors of the Forlorn Hope, who had arrived in a state of almost total nudity.

With modesty's requirements appeased, she took the message to the commander of the American troops at Sutter's Fort, a Captain Kern. Kern called a meeting of the few men left in the area—most of them were still off trying to fight the Californios— and offered three dollars a day to anyone who would volunteer to rescue the families trapped in the snow. Three dollars a day was excellent pay, but Kern had few takers. Even these greenhorns knew enough about the Sierra winters to stay far, far away.

Three men did come forward. Two of them had crossed the plains and mountains with Owl Russell's party the previous summer, and felt some kinship with the Donner Party. They were Aquila Glover, a well-to-do gentleman, and Riley Septimus Mootrey, the young man who had married the beautiful Miss Lard in her father's tent that soft summer night on the prairie. The third was Joseph Sels, who also went by the name of Joe Foster. People suspected he was a runaway sailor, but in California it was not wise to ask too much about a stranger.

These three volunteers offered to go without pay. It was a noble offer, but three men were not enough for a relief expedition, and things stood still until Sinclair returned. Sinclair and Sutter perceived that the U.S. government's credit rating was not high on the California frontier. They offered to pay the volunteers personally if the government failed to honor Kern's promise. This was a more attractive offer, and more names were added to the list of volunteers, until on January 31 seven men rode north from Sutter's Fort with a string of packhorses.

Rain, with the consequent muddy roads and swollen streams, so delayed the little cavalcade that it took them two days to cover the forty miles to Johnson's Ranch. Arriving in the morning, the men immediately set to work preparing supplies, no easy task since they had to start from scratch by slaughtering cattle. Then the meat had to be cut into strips and dried over fires, both to preserve it and to reduce its weight. Another urgent task was to grind flour. Johnson had no mill at his ranch; so the volunteers pounded grain to a powder in Indian mortars of stone and ground some in hand-cranked coffee grinders. The men took only a few hours out for meals and sleep; yet it took them two days and nights of frantic labor to get the food ready.

By the morning of February 4, a Thursday, the relief party was ready to set off, strengthened by more volunteers they had picked up at Johnson's. One was M. D. Ritchie, at whose house Eddy was recuperating. Then there were two young Mormon emigrants, the brothers John and Daniel Rhoads. There were Reasin P. Tucker and his sixteen-year-old son John. (Reasin Tucker was generally called Dan, a nickname taken from the popular comic song "Old Dan Tucker." Chroniclers of the Donner Party often refer to him thus, for the sake of informality.) Jotham Curtis, whom Reed and McCutchen had rescued earlier, actually offered his services and did go, an odd twist for that surly misanthrope. Five more rounded out the party: a runaway sailor named Ned Coffeemeyer; a German known as "Greasy Jim" (real name, Adolph Brueheim); a Joseph Verrot or Varro, who had come to California with Frémont in 1844; and a mentally retarded youth named Billy Coon. Finally, there was stouthearted William Eddy himself, still too weak to mount his horse without help but insisting on going.

The skies were leaden when the relief party left Johnson's Ranch that morning. The road was a quagmire, and the horses kept bogging down. One horse bucked his pack off and ran back toward Johnson's. Eddy and the teenaged John Tucker were sent back to catch the runaway, while the other men slogged miserably ahead.

The next day—Friday—the relief party was stopped by a deluge of chilly rain that made the road impassable. They found a little flat to halt at and managed to get a fire going in the shelter of two fallen pines. But the ground was flooded two or three inches deep, and they had to build a platform of pine bark and branches to keep the food packs above the water. They put the pack saddles over the valuable goods in an attempt to keep the rain off.

That evening Eddy came in alone to the drenched campsite with the runaway horse. Young Tucker's horse had given out, he told them, and he had had to leave the youth behind. The men spent a cheerless night standing around the fire in the pouring rain—there was no dry spot where they could lie down to snatch some badly needed sleep.

Young Tucker dragged himself in by the sullen gray light of daybreak. He had gotten lost in the dark and spent the night sitting under a pine tree. As he warmed himself by the campfire, his arms and legs swelled so badly that he could not move. This proved no delay to the rescuers, however, for the rain held them up all day. (Up in the mountains it was snowing, the fourth great storm of the season. Breen noted in his diary that the storm dropped another four feet of snow on the cabins by Truckee Lake.)

On Sunday morning the sun finally came out, but by now the rain had thoroughly soaked the food supplies. The men had to unpack everything and use up the day drying it out in the sun to keep it from spoiling.

With the rain ended, the party got a good sleep that night, their first in forty-eight hours. They set off on Monday, February 8, cheered by the fact that the ground had dried out somewhat. They made good progress until they reached the minor canyon called Steep Hollow, where nature's forces again compelled them to halt.

In summer and fall, an insignificant creek that didn't even have a name trickled down the canyon floor. But the torrential rains had flooded the canyon, and a raging river twenty feet deep, a hundred feet wide, and too cold to swim blocked their way.

Racing against time, the men could not afford to wait for the stream to go down. They felled a giant pine to bridge the roiling flood. It spanned the torrent, all right, but its sheer weight made the trunk sag until its middle was a foot under swift-flowing, icy water.

Someone managed to inch his way across and rig up guide ropes. With this aid, the men were able to carry the packs of meat and flour across to the far side.

The packhorses were a different matter. They were terrified of the shaky, water-covered pine-tree bridge and refused to go near it. Finally the men managed to get two horses into the water above the bridge. One managed to swim to the other bank. The other was sucked under by the turbulent current and carried a hundred yards downstream before he was flung ashore, half drowned. All else failing, the men had to drag each remaining horse across the river at the end of a long rope, one at a time. This used up the remainder of that day, and each day was precious.

On Tuesday, February 9, the relief party ran into snow after four miles, on the same ridge between Steep Hollow and Bear River Canyon where the Forlorn Hope had wandered blindly and without food. The snow was soon three or four feet deep, and the horses were unable to get through, so it was decided to leave them. Even if they could have coped with the snow, it covered any vegetation they could have eaten, and weakness would have stopped them long before they reached the pass.

Fuming at the delay, the men built a halfway camp at Mule Springs, a lean-to of brush and boughs in which they stored most of the provisions. Young John Tucker and the half-witted Billy Coon were detailed to guard the supplies from animals. Eddy and Verrot were assigned to take the now useless horses back to Johnson's to keep them from starving in the mountains. Eddy, desperate to reach his family, protested, but his companions overruled him because he was too weak to travel on foot.

On Wednesday morning the remaining men shouldered their packs and started off on foot. Each man carried a load of fifty to seventy-five pounds, except the complaining Curtis, who carried only half a load. The men walked single file, each stepping in the footprints of the man ahead. Every few minutes the leader, exhausted, had to drop back to the rear of the file while the next man took his turn breaking trail. They headed down into Bear River Canyon but found they couldn't get through, so they had to turn around and retrace their steps in frustration.

At one point the men stopped to make snowshoes, but the sun made the snow soft and mushy, and it clung to the snowshoes in great, heavy masses. They abandoned the snowshoes and went on, sinking knee-deep at each step. It was Friday before they reached Bear Valley.

There the snow was ten feet deep, but to their relief they could walk on the crust without sinking in. At the upper end of the valley they dug down through the snow for the cache of food that Reed and McCutchen had left in November, but when they reached bottom they found that Curtis's wagon had been ripped to pieces by grizzly bears, and the food was gone. That night it rained and snowed again, and the men spent the miserable hours on a platform of logs atop the snow. The next day was consumed in once more drying out the soaked provisions. Some they cached to lighten their load and to provide sustenance for the arduous trip back down the mountains.

To foil marauding animals they hung the food bundles from tree limbs on ropes.

Sunday morning, February 14, dawned beautiful and clear, but it almost brought failure. Three of the men—Ritchie, Brueheim, and the abominable Curtis—had had enough and insisted on turning back. Their defection discouraged the others, and for a moment it looked as if the expedition would be aborted after so much effort.

But Reasin Tucker saved the day by offering five dollars a day from his own pocket to everyone who stuck it out to the end, making it retroactive to the day they entered the snow. Six remained with him: Glover, Mootrey, Sels, the Rhoads brothers, and Coffeemeyer. Not one of the seven had ever roughed it in the mountains in the winter, and it was surely not the money alone that drew them back to their mission.

Hard as the going had been, the worst still lay ahead: the country of the high peaks. The men looked up at the snow-covered precipice of Emigrant Gap and decided to take an alternate route that one emigrant party had discovered. Instead of clambering over Emigrant Gap they would follow the Bear River and cross an easy divide over to the Yuba. Then they could follow the Yuba until it led them back to the emigrant road. It was a longer route, but not nearly so dangerous or exhausting. As they traveled, they set fire to dead pines along the way so that the blackened stumps would serve as trail markers for the return journey.

They made a good day's march that took them twelve miles closer to their goal and spent the night above Yuba Bottoms. But the next day it snowed again; once more the men had to stop and fashion snowshoes, and that day they made only eight miles.

Five more hard-slogging miles on Tuesday and eight on Wednesday brought them across the windswept Summit Valley, and they camped at the head of the Yuba, only five miles from Truckee Pass. From their campsite they could see the jagged peaks that flanked the pass on either side. Here they cached still more food for the return trip.

On Thursday, February 18, the men began the five-hundred-foot climb to the pass itself. Even with the lightened packs it was tough going, and the exertion in the thin air began to affect them. John and Daniel Rhoads became so ill that the others had to carry their packs for them. But the determined men pushed on and over the pass. Nothing was going to stop them now.

At the far side they stopped to scan the lakeshore below for signs of life. They saw none. But, having come this far, they reasoned that they must see their mission through to the finish.

A little after noon they began the descent to the frozen, snow-buried lake, easier than the climb up but more perilous, since a single slip could mean broken bones—and no doctor or shelter at hand. The sun had sunk behind the towering mountain wall as the men came down the lake, and it was almost dark when they reached the spot where Eddy had told them the cabins stood. No cabins could they find, not even a wisp of smoke—just the flat, white expanse of featureless snow. The place was quiet as a grave. The rescuers were seized by a horrible feeling that they had arrived too late.

Still, they raised a shout to see if anyone really were left alive. To their surprise and shock, the figure of a woman emerged from a hole in the snow. The scarecrow being tottered toward them as they approached, floundering in the snow. It spoke in a strange, hollow, nervous voice. "Are you men from California," it said, "or do you come from heaven?"

The First Relief had arrived.

Other figures now emerged from the snow, women, children, and men, like sick animals crawling out of a den. They greeted the rescuers in thin, feeble, mewing voices, weeping and laughing hysterically as they cried, "Relief, thank God! Relief!" and, perhaps closer to the heart, "Have you brought anything for me?"

The survivors looked like living corpses—barely living. As Thornton later wrote, they were emaciated and ghastly pale, and their skin seemed to have dried tight on their bones. To the appalled rescuers it seemed as if their shout had awakened the dead from their tombs in the snow. All of the survivors had, in fact, expected to die.

The rescue party handed out as much food as they thought safe and sent Tucker down into the Graves cabin to look after the people there. Then, exhausted, they turned in for the night. But first they prudently placed a guard over the little store of provisions that they had lugged so far.

In the morning Mootrey, Tucker, and John Rhoads, the three strongest of the relief party, went down the mountain to the Donner camp with a little beef. There they found the Donners in desperate straits, with only one ox hide left to live on. Jake, never robust, had died and lay buried in the snow. George, whose infection had spread from his hand to his arm, was helpless in bed and looked as if he did not have long to live. Tamsen, weak but otherwise healthy, could have walked back to Sutter's with the rescuers but refused to leave her dying husband and her small children. Betsy Donner chose unselfishly to stay on and help her sister-in-law. Jean-Baptiste, the young teamster, wanted very badly to leave, but the rescuers told him he had to stay and look after the women and children. He accepted this decision with very ill grace and sulked frightfully.

The three rescuers chopped a tree into firewood and left the tiny supply of beef they had brought. Then they departed with the six people who were strong enough to make the trek. These were the young teamster Noah James; the widowed Mrs. Wolfinger; and four of the older children: George Donner's daughters Elitha and Leanna, plus Billy Hook, and George Donner II from Jake's family. Before they left, Tamsen confided to Tucker that when the beef and their lone remaining hide were gone they would have to begin eating the dead.

In the meantime, the four rescuers who had stayed at the Mountain Camp received shock after shock. They may have expected to find the survivors ennobled by suffering and doing their enfeebled best to comfort and help one another, as prescribed by the moral fiction of the time. What they actually witnessed was appalling.

The indescribable filth of the camp was bad enough, but worse yet was the way the survivors behaved. To quote from Thornton again, they seemed to have lost all sense of decency and respect. They showed not the slightest sympathy for each other's sufferings, and they seemed unable to distinguish between right and wrong. Many behaved as if they were deranged, and they almost certainly were.

As for the dead, the enfeebled survivors had simply dragged them up from the deeply buried cabins and laid them to rest in the snow. (They could not possibly have done otherwise, but Thornton was recording the feelings of the rescue party.) Some of the bodies were not even buried, but lay on top of the snow wrapped in their tattered, filthy quilts.

It took three days for the men of the First Relief to give the survivors what care they could and to organize a group of the fittest for the return journey. When they left on Monday, February 22, the Reeds and their hired girl Eliza Williams, no longer fat, went with them. The Reeds had run out of provisions a week ago and had been trying to live on discarded bones from which Mrs. Breen had carefully scraped every shred of meat. Two of the older Breen boys, Eddie and Simon, went, too. Two of the Graves girls were picked to go; then eighteen-year-old Billy Graves begged for a chance. His mother let him go on condition that he chop enough wood to last her and the remaining children for a while. Somehow he found the energy to cut and stack two cords over the weekend. (A standard cord of wood measures 8 feet long by 4 feet wide by 4 feet high, a substantial amount.)

Others went, too. John Denton, the English gunsmith, had been in poor shape for weeks but still seemed strong enough to travel. Keseberg was still incapacitated by his injured foot, but Mrs. Keseberg went, taking little Ada, while Keseberg moved into the Murphy cabin. There was room for him there, since Mary and Billy Murphy were leaving with the rescue party. Baby Catherine Pike had died two days ago, but her three-year-old sister Naomi was still alive, and John Rhoads offered to carry her, slung on his back in a blanket. The little group from the Donner camp rounded off the hopeful caravan.

The rescuers had carefully kept the news about the fate of the Forlorn Hope from the survivors, partly to spare their feelings, but also because they feared the truth would so demoralize their charges that they would refuse to risk the journey. So everyone was in reasonably good spirits as they set off. They even had something to nibble on as they traveled, for the rescuers had prudently set aside enough food to give everyone an ounce of beef and a spoonful of flour twice a day until they reached the cache just over the pass.

All the children but Naomi Pike and Ada Keseberg had to walk; after two miles Patty and Tommy Reed gave out. Glover and Tucker told their mother that they must go back to the cabins. Otherwise, he said, they would endanger the lives of all the others by delaying them.

Margaret Reed was faced with the terrible choice between rejoining her husband and staying with the little ones to care for them.

Glover urged her to go on with Virginia and Jimmy, promising to return for Patty and Tommy as soon as he had led the others to safety. Mrs. Reed was dubious about the promise of a stranger—she had suffered enough betrayals from her traveling companions. Suddenly it struck her that this man might be a Mason, like her husband. Masons kept their promises to each other. It was one of the attractions of the Masonic Order. She asked him anxiously. Glover was indeed a Mason, and he swore on a Mason's word that he would turn around at Bear Valley and come back for the little ones unless he met Reed himself coming up. This satisfied her, and she said good-bye to her youngest children.

Patty took the decision with fatalistic calm, saying only, "Well, Ma, if you never see me again, do the best you can."

At this stoical farewell, the rough-hewn rescuers burst into tears, but there was no help for it. The little ones obviously could not keep up. And, equally obviously, the least delay might be fatal.

Glover and Mootrey took the two children back to the Breen cabin. As they walked, Patty told them that she didn't mind going back to take care of her little brother, but she never expected to see her mother again. She was sure she would die, and the reception she and her brother were given by the Breens might have been scripted to bear out her worst fears. Patrick and Peggy Breen were indignant at the intrusion and refused even to let the cold, tired children inside. Two more mouths to feed? Impossible!

Glover had to work on the Breens for some time, promising that another relief expedition was on the way and bribing them with some of the skimpy food supply that he and Mootrey still had with them. Even then the Breens accepted the children reluctantly and with hostility. Glover and Mootrey left them with some forebodings, but concealed the unpleasant facts from their mother and the other rescuees.

The party camped at the usual spot at the head of the lake. During the night some hunger-crazed person ate the rawhide strings from Ned Coffeemeyer's snowshoes, to his great annoyance. The next morning they began the climb to the pass.

Mrs. Keseberg soon tired and put Ada down to walk. The child gave out, in turn, and Mrs. Keseberg became hysterical at the thought of abandoning her. She offered twenty-five dollars and a gold watch to anyone who would carry her baby; she found a taker. John Denton, too, weakened rapidly and collapsed in the snow after crossing the pass. Someone noticed he was missing, and two of the rescuers hurried back to fetch him. They found him unconscious; it took an hour before they could rouse him and, with great difficulty, get him to the campsite. There they discovered a calamity almost as bad as those that had struck the Forlorn Hope.

Some animal—a pine marten or a wolverine, they suspected—had climbed the tree and gnawed through the rope that held the pack of food. Then it had scurried down and ransacked the contents. It was four days' travel to the next food cache, and most members of the party were already weak from starvation. Four men hurried forward the next morning to the cache at Bear Valley to bring back as much food as they could—provided that cache had not been destroyed too. Sels, John Rhoads, and Tucker were left to shepherd the emigrants along with as little delay as possible. However, Denton gave out again after only a mile, and they stopped.

The Englishman told his companions that he could go no farther. They could do nothing to help him by staying with him, he said, and he urged them to go on and save their own lives. All that he asked was that they should, if possible, send a rescue party after him when they reached safety.

The three rescuers were moved by Denton's unselfish sacrifice, and before they left him they chopped a good supply of wood and started a fire. They gave him a little food—all they could spare—and left him propped up against a tree by the fire, snugly wrapped in Tucker's own quilt. The exhausted man looked so comfortable that little Jimmy Reed wanted to stay with him.

The party made eight miles after leaving Denton, but all of them, the rescuers now included, were growing weaker on their starvation rations. That night little Ada Keseberg died and was buried in the snow by the trailside. Her mother was inconsolable, but the party could not tarry because of her grief. They pushed on for two more days, guided by the charred pine stumps the rescue party had left on the way up.

Each morning they had good going on the hard-frozen snow crust, but when the sun softened the crust they broke through and floundered. Jimmy Reed gave up and had to be cajoled along. His mother and sister told him that every step brought him nearer to his father, and the men promised that when they got to California he would have a horse of his own and never have to walk again.

On Friday, February 26, they halted at noon, ate some roasted snowshoe strings, and continued on. After about half a mile they met Mootrey and Coffeemeyer toiling uphill with a load of dried beef from the cache. Overjoyed, they instantly made a fire and feasted on the beef. They traveled another mile and then made camp, as the snow was too soft to travel any farther.

Despite the hearty meal, the children were so weak the next day that they had to be carried. As the procession wound its way down the mountain with its living burdens, they caught sight of another group coming up in single file among the trees. It was Reed's expedition!

CHAPTER 18

The Second Relief Arrives

Here I met Mrs. Reed and the children. . . . I cannot describe the death like look they all had Bread Bread Bread Bread was the beging of every child and grown person except my wife.
——Diary of James F. Reed, Feb. 27, 1847

Mrs. Murphy said here yesterday that [she] thought she would commence on Milt. & eat him. I dout that she has done so yet it is distressing.
——Diary of Patrick Breen, Feb. 26, 1847

It was an emotional encounter. As the two columns approached each other, someone called out, "Is Mrs. Reed with you? Tell her Mr. Reed is here."

Mrs. Reed and Virginia both heard the shout. Mrs. Reed, overcome, collapsed in the snow. Virginia tried to run to her father, but she was so weak that she tripped and fell. She struggled up again, and her father caught her in his arms.

"Your mother, my child, your mother!" cried Reed. "Where is she?" Virginia, weeping with relief, could only point to her mother's crumpled form on the snow. But Mrs. Reed soon came around, and the long-parted husband and wife were reunited. Did they fall into each other's arms in a long, tearful embrace, relieved and grateful to find each other alive? Reed's journal is primly silent. There were certain private things that one did not commit to paper.

The meeting was no surprise to Reed, since he had met Glover and Daniel Rhoads on the trail and they had given him the news that the First Relief was on its way down. In anticipation, Reed had spent most of the night baking bread and sweet cakes for the children. These he distributed in prudently small amounts to the survivors. The children pleaded uncontrollably for more bread, and the adults joined in—except for Margaret Reed, for ladies do not beg.

The joyous reunion was brief, for Reed was consumed by the need to rescue his two children who were still on the far side of the mountain, and the men of the First Relief were equally anxious to get their charges down to the valley.

Tucker got the First Relief safely to Bear Valley and its plentiful food supply, but here the bad luck that had dogged the Donner Party ever since they left Fort Bridger struck again. Eleven-year-old Billy Hook could not restrain himself and overate grossly. He became deathly ill. But someone made him swallow tobacco juice; the crude frontiersman's emetic worked, and he recovered by morning. Unfortunately, he either sneaked out at night and gorged himself again or else overate at breakfast (the sources disagree). This time the tobacco juice did not work, and Billy Hook died in midmorning. Two other survivors also overate, but they recovered.

Two days later the First Relief reached the halfway station at Mule Springs, where Passed Midshipman Woodworth of the U.S. Navy had set up his base camp. Rescuers and refugees alike could hardly believe their eyes when they saw Woodworth lolling on a warm blanket, with two men rubbing his feet to prevent frostbite. But the sight of bare ground and patches of green grass, after four months in the snow, more than made up for their disappointment in Woodworth.

The next day the refugees were bundled onto horses—what luxury!—and led down the trail to Johnson's Ranch—a peculiar-looking cavalcade, since there were not enough saddles and bridles to go around, and most of the people had only one or the other of these necessary items. The people with bridles were better off than those with saddles only, because they could at least steer their mounts. The rest had to trust that their horses would follow the leader, which they did with varying degrees of cooperation. In this peculiar fashion the first contingent of survivors reached California at last.

One of the rescuers asked Virginia to marry him. (He was undoubtedly serious. Women were in great demand in California.) The emaciated thirteen-year-old girl giggled and declined the invitation.

Reed, for his part, pressed on with his relief party of ten men, fearful that another storm would come and imperil his expedition, as the Forlorn Hope had been imperiled. And he had suffered enough delay already.

After the frantic preparations in Yerba Buena, Reed had taken the boat to Sonoma and made a swing around the northern side of San Francisco Bay with old Greenwood, picking up his friend McCutchen and a number of recruits. Ten days later he and Greenwood brought the party to the place where the Feather River joins the Sacramento, north of Sutter's Fort. There they were to meet Woodworth and the schooner full of supplies.

Woodworth, who in some ways was distressingly like Lansford W. Hastings, was not at the rendezvous. Reed and McCutchen resolved to go ahead without him. They still had the flooded Sacramento River to cross, and no Woodworth to carry them over. Undaunted, the party cut timbers for boat frames, intending to cover them with skins from an immense herd of elks in the vicinity. Just as they were starting to put the elkskins on one of the boats, a little schooner sailed up the river to them. At the helm was an Irish sailor, Perry McCoon, who had jumped ship a year earlier and settled at Sutter's Fort. He knew of the Donner Party's plight, and he sympathized.

McCoon ferried Reed and McCutchen across with their horses, and they galloped off to Johnson's Ranch. The others were to follow as soon as their jerry-built emergency craft were ready, but high winds suddenly whipped up dangerous waves on the river and prevented them from crossing for three days.

Round-the-clock work by Reed and McCutchen, aided by Johnson's Indian servants, had supplies of dried beef and flour ready by the time old Caleb Greenwood arrived with the rest of the expedition.

In contrast to the First Relief's valiant but inexperienced mixture of farmers, sailors, and townsmen, Greenwood's crew was composed mainly of veteran outdoorsmen. One was his half-Indian son Britton Greenwood, who had spent almost his entire life in the wilderness. There was a veteran mountain man, John Turner, as big and powerful as McCutchen, and two seasoned French-Canadian trappers named Joseph Gendreau and Matthew Dofar. Hiram Miller, the blacksmith from Springfield, was there, too. Three young Americans—Charles Stone, Nicholas Clark, and Charles Cady—rounded off the group.

The Second Relief, as the newspapers soon dubbed it, got under way from Johnson's on February 22. Old Greenwood had planned to take the packhorses all the way across Truckee Pass to the lake and kill them there for food, if necessary. But the horses got only a few hundred yards beyond Mule Springs before the snow became too much for them, and they had to be sent back. Old Greenwood, whose eyes were troubling him, stayed with the horses and a couple of helpers at Mule Springs, where there was plentiful grazing. Woodworth was expected to join them there soon and set up a disciplined base camp.

Reed and his men now became the pack animals, and they moved ahead with desperate energy. They had no difficulty in finding the trail. They simply followed the path that the men of the First Relief had tramped out. It was firm, and no new snow had fallen to make walking difficult and hide the trail. They made good time, covering the twenty-one miles to the upper end of Bear Valley in two days. Along the way they met Glover and Daniel Rhoads, and from them learned of the First Relief and the survivors who were still up on the far side of the mountains. Here, too, the Second Relief lightened their packs by making a cache in the top of a small pine tree. As the man who took up the pack of food climbed down, he cut off the branches behind him to prevent animals from scaling the tree and getting at the food.

The sun was now strong enough to make the snow mushy and impassable by midafternoon, so the men altered their schedule to compensate. They camped early and got in their sleep. At midnight they began the next day's journey on the hard-frozen crust and kept going until the snow became soft again.

It was on the third morning out from Mule Springs that Reed's party met the First Relief coming down. The sight of the survivors in their wretched, near-dead condition made Reed even more anxious to reach the cabins before it was too late.

That night they camped at Yuba Bottoms, on snow that Reed judged to be fifteen feet deep. The next night they camped on top of thirty feet of snow. Cady, Clark, and Stone went ahead as the snow hardened.

The three young men almost lost the trail in the dark and were about to turn back when they saw a pathetic trail marker. It was the body of poor John Denton, sitting under his tree just as the First Relief had left him. Now the three knew they were on the right trail, and they went on over the pass and down the lake, stopping two miles short of the cabins. They had to do without fire, for they spotted a group of ten Indians, and they themselves were not armed.

The "boys" were afraid that the Indians had raided the camp and killed everyone, and they started on with a feeling of dread. To their relief, they found the inhabitants still alive. They distributed food to everyone, cabin by cabin, and then pushed on to the Donner Camp down on Alder Creek. Two pushed on, that is, for Stone stayed behind to make a start at cleaning things up.

Reed and the rest of the men arrived at the Mountain Camp about noon. The sun had melted away so much snow that the top of the Breen cabin was bare. There, sitting on the cabin roof with her feet in the snow, was Patty Reed. She jumped up and tried to run to her father, but fell down in her weakness. Reed rushed to his daughter and picked her up, hugging and kissing her.

As the sobbing child clung to him, Reed asked her where her brother was. She told him that Tommy was sleeping down below. Reed made his way down the snowhole and found Tommy. The child was skeletally thin, but that, for Reed, was not the worst. When he woke Tommy up, the little boy did not recognize him and kept asking Patty if "that man" was really his father. It was a while before he finally believed her.

Reed gave a little bread to each of his children and hurried over to the Murphy cabin, accompanied by McCutchen. The two men found young Stone busy washing some of the children's filth-soaked clothes. Down below in the cabin, conditions were almost unbelievably squalid. Keseberg lay by the fire, almost helpless. On another bed was old Mrs. Murphy, unable to get up without help, half blind, and childish. As she tried to talk to her rescuers she laughed and wept for no reason they could discern. It was hard to make sense of what she said. But the elderly woman was not in much worse mental shape than most of the other survivors.

On a bed were little Georgie Foster and Jimmy Eddy, lying in their own excrement. Mrs. Murphy told Reed they had been in that bed for two weeks. She had kept them fed but had been too weak to do more for them. The little boys held out their arms and begged pathetically for food. Although Stone had already given them as much as he thought was safe, Reed could not resist the children's pleas and gave them more. This was risky, but fortunately no harm came of it this time.

The next step was to do something about the nauseating filth. Reed and McCutchen built a fire and heated a big kettle of water. They took their clothes off and left them on the snow outside to keep them from being infested by the lice that swarmed inside the cabin. Then they took the two little boys and washed them thoroughly in soapsuds, oiled their raw and irritated skin, and wrapped them in warm flannel before returning them to the filthy bed. At least they would be more comfortable for a while.

Keseberg lay nearby on his wretched pile of blankets. This was the man who had wanted to hang Reed from his wagon tongue last October. Now Reed began to undress Keseberg to give him a bath. This return of good for evil was too much for even the self-centered Keseberg, and he begged Reed not to do this to him. Let someone else bathe him, he pleaded. Reed replied that this was something he had to do out of decency, and he was willing to let bygones be bygones.

Finally the two rescuers had time to look around the cabin. By now their eyes were accustomed to the dark, and they could see all too clearly. By the door lay the body of faithful Milt Elliott, who had stood by the Reed family through every danger. His face had not been touched, but the rest of his body had been pretty thoroughly utilized by the starving inmates of the cabin. Half-consumed limbs lay partly hidden in trunks, and human hair of different colors was strewn in tufts around the fireplace. The sight was too much to bear.

Reed and McCutchen cried out in grief and horror and burst into tears.

Things had rapidly gone from bad to worse in the Murphy cabin during the few days since the First Relief had left. Wolves had been prowling around the cabin at night, sniffing and scratching in the snow after the dead bodies. For the famished survivors, a wolf itself would have been a feast, but no one dared to risk sitting outside on a subfreezing night on the chance of getting in a shot.

On February 25, a fine, sunny day, Mrs. Murphy had tottered over to the Breen cabin for the infrequent treat of a visit. She had informed Patrick Breen that she was about to start eating Milt's body, as if to get his approval. The remains now lay on her cabin floor, under the grief-stricken eyes of Reed and McCutchen.

There is no record of what the men of the Second Relief found in the Graves cabin, but that night they slept outdoors in the clean air, away from the filth, the stench, and the bloodsucking vermin of the cabins.

That night also Patrick Breen made his last entry in his diary. "Mond. Mar. 1st. Fine & pleasant froze hard here last night there has 10 men arrived from Bear Valley with provisions we are to start in two three days & Cash [cache] our goods here. There is among them some old [mountain men]. they say the snow may be here untill June," he noted in his neat, well-formed handwriting.

The following morning Reed took Hiram Miller and Gendreau down to the Donner camp, leaving the other four men at the lake to tend the survivors, make sure they didn't eat too much, and get them ready for the journey down. An important part of the preparations was caching the valuables to hide them from wandering Indians. Starved and half-crazed as the adults were, they were not about to risk their property. They had suffered enough to get it this far. Mrs. Graves amazed the men when she had them pry up an ordinary-looking cleat in the bed of her wagon and turn it over. There was her money, about $800 in gold and silver coins, stuffed in the holes her husband had bored.

The Indians were already beginning to come up from their valley homes to investigate the white men's camp. Just two days before Reed's expedition arrived, Patrick Breen had spied a lone Indian coming down from the lake. From a heavy pack on his back the Indian produced five or six onion-shaped roots, which he laid on the snow for Breen to take—he commented that they tasted somewhat like sweet potatoes but were full of tough little fibers. And Cady, Stone, and Clark had spied ten Indians by the lake only two nights ago.

Up until recently, conditions at the George Donner Camp had not been nearly as bad as they were at the lake. Jean-Baptiste had gotten over his monumental sulk, and every day he took Frances, Georgia, and Eliza out on the snow to play and get some exercise. When he cut wood for the fire, he would bring out his long Navajo blanket from New Mexico, put one of the little girls at each end, and roll them up until they met in the middle. Then he would set them on a stump to watch him work and keep him company.

When Tamsen had done what she could to make her dying husband comfortable, she, too, would come out and sit with her little girls on a log. Never idle, she would write in her diary or draw pictures for the children—sketches of the mountains all covered with snow and the tops of pine trees sticking out of it. But the girls liked it best when she told them stories from the Bible, especially those with children in them.

Tamsen had another project as well. She prepared the children for being on their own in case she could not go with them when the rescuers came. She taught them how to behave with strangers and how to make friends. "Friends do not come easily to a crybaby child," said self-reliant Tamsen. She also taught them what to answer when people asked them whose children they were: "We are the children of Mr. and Mrs. George Donner."

The George and Jacob Donner shelters lay at most a hundred yards apart, and Tamsen and Betsy Donner visited back and forth often. The children, for some reason, did not. Eliza remembered one day when her mother dressed her up warmly and took her to a hole in the snow where she saw smoke coming up. There were steps in the hole, and her mother told her that they led down to Uncle Jacob's tent. They were going down to see Aunt Betsy and the little cousins. The children of the two families had not seen each other since the day they had camped at Alder Creek.

Eliza bent down and peered into the dark depths. She called to her cousins to come up, because she was afraid to go down inside. When they came up, she could barely recognize them. The children she remembered as plump and cheerful and lively were now scrawny, listless, and pallid-white. She was glad when her mother came up and took her back to her own tent, where everything was familiar and she knew the faces around her.

But the food situation now was desperate. Here, too, the gap between the relief expeditions had pushed them to the edge of survival. Lately they had been living on a thin slab of tallow that Tamsen had cooked out of the dried beef that the First Relief had left them. She cut this into tiny squares, and everyone got three squares a day. The children would nibble off the four corners very slowly and then work their way around and around the edges until the pieces were too small to hold in their fingers.

Only a short distance away, at Jake Donner's tent, the situation was horribly different. As Reed and his two companions approached the campsite, they were intercepted by Cady and Stone, and the two young men had a hair-raising tale to tell. They had arrived to find Jean-Baptiste leaving the tent of Jacob Donner carrying one of Jake's legs. He told them that George Donner had sent him for the flesh and that Aunt Betsy had said that she could spare no more after this, for Uncle Jake's body was all they had left.

Inside the shelter, Jake's children were sitting on a log, their faces messy with blood, eating the half-roasted heart and liver of their father. Conscious only of their own hunger, they paid no attention to the rescuers as they consumed their grisly meal.

Aunt Betsy was lying down to save her last strength. Her family had already eaten four of the dead, she said, and her husband's body was the last they had. But she would rather die herself than eat that. Around the fire, as at the Murphys' cabin, lay hair, bones, skulls, and fragments of partly eaten limbs.

Reed and the others immediately moved the tent to a new spot, made Betsy as comfortable as they could, and walked off to recover from the horrors they had just witnessed. Their walk brought them to a fresh horror not far away: the open snow-grave of Uncle Jake. His head had been cut off and was lying face up; the cold had preserved his features unaltered. But his arms and legs had been cut off and his body cut open to remove the nutritious heart and liver. On top of the mutilated corpse lay a leg—Jean-Baptiste had tossed it back when he saw the rescuers coming with more acceptable food. There were other open graves, too, but there was nothing left in them but a few fragments.

They went over to the tent of George Donner, not knowing what to expect. The old patriarch was in very bad shape. The infection had spread from his hand all the way up his arm, almost to the shoulder. It was obvious that he had not long to live. Tamsen, however, appeared strong and healthy, and Reed thought the three little girls looked stout and hearty. (They could have looked so only in comparison to the other starved children Reed had seen most recently.)

Reed announced that Woodworth was expected to arrive with a supply train within a few days. The news cheered Tamsen, who would not leave her dying husband. She also felt it best to keep the children with her until Woodworth came, for they were small. (Perhaps, too, George would be dead by then, and she would have no need to remain.) Meanwhile, young Cady and Clark would stay on to look after the two Donner families.

Reed dispatched Cady back to the lake to fetch seven days' worth of provisions for the Donners—enough to tide them over until Woodworth arrived, according to plan—and started back himself with all the Donner children who were big enough to walk by themselves. They included Mary and Isaac Donner and Solomon Hook, all of the Jacob Donner family. Teen-aged Sol Hook had had a bad time after the First Relief left. His mind had snapped and he had started off for Sutter's by himself. He wandered in the woods for forty-eight hours, going snow-blind, but luckily went in a great circle that brought him back to his family. Recovered, he was now ready for another try at escaping from the snow.

CHAPTER 19

The Rescuers Trapped

It has snowed already 12 inches, still the storm continues the light of Heaven, is as it ware shut in from us the snow blows so thick that we cannot see 20 feet. . . . I dread the coming night. . . .
—Diary of James Frazier Reed

The departure of the Second Relief was set for Wednesday, March 3. The Breens, the Graves family, the three older children of Jacob and Elizabeth Donner, and Reed's two remaining children—in short, almost everyone who could walk or had someone to carry them—was going. This left at the lake the crippled Keseberg, the enfeebled Mrs. Murphy, her ten-year-old son Simon, and the two little sons of Eddy and Foster. Stone was detailed to stay on and care for these helpless individuals until Woodworth's expedition arrived.

Down at Alder Creek there still remained Tamsen Donner with the dying husband she would not leave, their three little girls, and Jean-Baptiste; the recently widowed Betsy Donner with her two smallest children, Sammie and Lewis, all three very weak; and the rescue-party members Cady and Clark.

Reed had counted on an early start, but these emigrants would not be hurried. In part, they were too weak to make haste; in part, they may have been asserting their independence after months of enforced helplessness. At any rate, they did not get under way until midday. Once moving, they walked with agonizing slowness, and by evening had covered only two miles. They camped at a bare spot on the lakeshore—oh, what relief not to have snow! Mrs. Graves had brought along her son-in-law Jay Fosdick's violin—she had not been told he was dead—and Breen played happily on it for two hours. Everyone was in good spirits, joking and smiling and begging Uncle Patrick for another tune—except for Reed, who was deeply worried about another snowstorm.

Reed had another grave worry: Passed Midshipman Woodworth, who according to plan should by now have crossed the pass and been well on his way down to the lake. What was keeping the man? Had he no idea of how close to death the remaining survivors were?

Reed kept his misgivings to himself, and the next morning the men of the rescue party were in high good humor. They began cracking cruel frontier jokes. One, who was carrying Mrs. Graves's small fortune in coins, bawled to his friends that they ought to play euchre (a card game) to see who got the money. Mrs. Graves took their coarse horseplay seriously, demanded her money back, and stayed at the campsite to hide it after everyone else had left.

This day, too, the survivors took their time, as if they were on a pleasure outing. Now that they were released from their prison in the snow, they seemed unable to grasp the idea that they were not yet out of danger. It was all Reed could do to get them past the end of the lake, urge as he might. He forced himself to conceal his annoyance and foreboding.

They camped at the foot of the mountain. While Patrick Breen treated the company to another musical evening, Reed looked up at the pass, where threatening-looking clouds were forming. His apprehension deepened. A storm coming now would gravely endanger the party, for they had only a little food with them. The rest had been cached away at carefully planned locations—and he had counted on getting to the first cache at least a day earlier.

On Friday morning after breakfast only two scanty meals apiece remained for the Second Relief and their rescuees. Fearing that some accident had delayed Woodworth, Reed sent Gendreau, Dofar, and Turner ahead to the cache, telling them to send one man back with food. If animals had destroyed the cache, he said, they were to go on to the next cache, fifteen miles farther down the mountains. It was at least a full day's trip down there, and God alone knew how much longer it would take them to get back.

After much haranguing by Reed, who pointed out the threat of the storm clouds, the survivors pulled themselves together long enough to scale the pass by noon, helped by the four remaining rescuers. By three o'clock they had reached the First Relief's old campsite on the western slope of the mountain, near the head of the Yuba. It was a bad place for a campsite, open and exposed to the wind, but the survivors were exhausted and could go no farther. The rescuers themselves were weak, after four days on the minuscule ration of a pint and a half of gruel per day. On the credit side of the balance, the First Relief had left piles of firewood and the remains of log fire-platforms. Good—that meant the tired rescuers could save their strength!

Soon there was a cheerily crackling campfire, and the survivors lay at their ease around it on beds of fragrant pine boughs. But Reed was plagued by a premonition of disaster. There was no sign of the three men he had sent ahead for food, and the clouds were thickening fast as night came on.

The weather turned bitterly cold, and the rescuees began to complain. The cold they could fight by piling more wood on the fire, but if provisions did not arrive in a day or two it meant the end for all of them. Reed hastily scribbled his fears in his diary, but dared not confide them to anyone else.

"The sky look like snow," he scrawled with cold-numbed fingers, "and everything indicates a storm god forbid wood being got for the night & Bows [boughs] for the beds of all, and night closing fast, the clouds still thicking . . . terror . . . dare not communicate my mind to any, death to all if our provisions do not come, in a day or two if a storm should fall on us, very cold, a great lamentation about the cold."

During the night the storm Reed had dreaded hit them, with blindingly heavy snow and howling winds that sucked the warmth right out of the body. At times the snow was so thick that Reed could not see the fire only a few feet away from him.

The rescuers hastily built a windbreak of pine boughs packed with snow, and this deflected the worst of the wind. But the cold was still severe—enough to freeze everyone to death within a few hours if the fire should go out.

All night the debilitated survivors wept and prayed and lamented their fate, while the four rescuers toiled like madmen to keep the fire supplied with wood. Reed, exhausted, lost his vision for several hours. Morning brought no relief. The wind and snow were worse than ever, and only the faintest glimmer of daylight penetrated the turbulent, black storm clouds.

In the gloom, Reed issued the last of the food: one spoonful of flour per person. The children wailed their hunger, but there was nothing more to give them. The parents moaned about the cold but didn't lift a finger to help get firewood. Why should they? The rescuers were getting paid to do it, weren't they? Chances were, that smart-alecky rich man Jim Reed, with his superior ways, was getting more money than all the rest of them!

The rescuers were having a hard time, though. The snow was so thick they could not see more than a few paces, and the cold was so intense that no one could chop firewood for more than ten minutes before he had to come back and warm himself by the fire.

"It has already snowed 12 inches," Reed managed to scribble in a spare moment, "still the light of Heaven, is as it ware shut in from us the snow blows so thick that we cannot see 20 feet looking against the wind I dread the coming night . . . night closing fast and with it the Hurricane increases."

Night came on again as the storm increased in fury. Reed, for the sake of morale, took the first watch while the other rescuers slept. But he was so exhausted that he went blind again and then lost consciousness. The fire, with no one to feed it, burned low. What happened next almost proved fatal to the entire party.

The snow beneath the foundation logs had melted unevenly, and the log platform slowly tilted . . . more . . . and more . . . until suddenly most of the fire slid off it into the pool of melted snow beneath the platform. The cold woke some of the sleeping people, and the campsite was soon a scene of panic as the children cried and the women prayed hysterically. Reed lay unconscious and near death.

Patrick Breen did not attempt to help, but he discovered again that he was a religious man and dropped to his knees, praying frenziedly. The rescuer Britton Greenwood, intrepid son of the wilderness, succumbed to fear and joined Breen at his prayers while McCutchen and Miller tried frantically to revive the nearly dead fire. Miller's hands were so badly frozen that the skin split open when he grasped his ax to split kindling, but he ignored the pain as best he could and worked on.

McCutchen cursed Breen and Greenwood and shouted to them to leave off praying and help him get firewood. The two newly pious men paid him no attention.

Then Mrs. Breen burst into a vicious tirade. She shrieked at the unconscious Reed that the men were being paid three dollars a day to get them out of the snow, "and here they are a-lettin' us all fraze!" In her half-demented state she accused Reed of luring her family away from their comfortable cabin to murder them and let them freeze to death in the wilderness. She screamed that three of her children were dead and one had his legs burned off to the knees. None of this was true, although one of the Breen boys had fallen into the pit, which the fire had now melted about fifteen feet deep. The snow at the bottom cushioned his fall, however, and he was unharmed.

Mrs. Breen's fury, like a forest fire, seemed to feed on itself, until finally the exasperated McCutchen had to threaten her to make her hold her tongue.

Between them, McCutchen and Miller managed to get the fire going again. McCutchen did most of the work, for the pain of Miller's injured hands crippled him. This done, the two men dragged Reed, still unconscious, to the fire, warmed him, and revived him by rubbing his hands and feet. As the cheering blaze rose through the dry pine logs, the children exulted, "I'm glad, I'm glad we have got some fire! Oh, how good it feels! It is good our fire didn't go out!" Everyone's hopes revived along with the fire.

McCutchen finally had a chance to sit down and warm himself.

He was so chilled that he did not notice the fire burning the backs out of the four shirts he wore, one on top of the other, until he felt the flames on his bare skin.

The storm raged on all day Sunday; the party had been without food for two days. During the night little Isaac Donner, aged five, died, lying between his sister Mary and Patty Reed. He died so quietly that neither of the girls noticed it until morning.

Mary herself suffered a bad injury. Her feet were numb with cold, and in her sleep one foot slipped into the fire. The poor girl felt nothing, but woke up with her foot severely burned. (Later she lost four toes.)

But the storm was finally blowing itself out. There were blessed lulls in the wind, and around noon the snow stopped falling. Reed tried to get his group moving again, but the Graveses were too weakened to walk far, and the Breens refused to go. Reed argued with the Breens, but to no avail. Patrick declared that, if he had to die, he would rather die comfortably in camp than along the way. At last Reed called his men together as witnesses and declared that if any of the Breen family died, their blood would be upon Breen's head, not his.

Before leaving, the rescuers cut enough firewood to last several days. They had no food to leave, other than little Isaac Donner's body. However, Mrs. Breen was not worried. She had a secret hoard of seeds that she had collected, a little tea, and a pound of sugar.

It was a small party that set off for Mule Springs. Sol Hook was just able to walk. Mary Donner, despite the pain of her burned foot, hobbled along the best she could. To stay in the snow pit with the Graveses and Breens could well mean death, she knew, for who knew when Woodworth would arrive with food, if ever? But Mary, despite her courage, could not keep up long, and she had to be taken back to the pit in the snow where her brother had just died.

That left Reed, Miller, McCutchen, Brit Greenwood, Patty and Tommy Reed, and Sol Hook. Miller carried little Tommy Reed, but Patty steadfastly insisted on walking by herself. They had the usual trouble with the deep, soft, newly fallen snow, and a bitterly cold air mass had followed the storm, so that everyone soon suffered from frostbite. Starvation and cold weakened Patty as she trudged bravely along in her father's footprints. Suddenly she called out to her father that she could see stars and a crowd of angels, such a beautiful sight!

Reed realized that this hallucination meant his daughter was freezing to death. He quickly scooped her up and wrapped her in a blanket while the other men rubbed her hands and feet. Reed dug into the thumb of one of his mittens for his reserve food supply, a tiny portion of crumbs he had scraped from the seams of the empty food bags. He moistened the crumbs in his mouth and fed them to Patty bit by bit. Slowly the dying girl revived, and the miserable parade continued.

Patty rode in a blanket slung on her father's back, where his body heat could warm her. Some of the men began to voice their fears that this time they were all going to die.

"No! No!" cried Patty from her perch on her father's back. "God has not brought us so far to let us perish now!" Tears came to the eyes of McCutchen, who had only a few days ago learned of the death of his own child, and he exclaimed with an oath, "Boys, if there is an angel on earth, Patty is that angel!"

CHAPTER 20

A Trust Betrayed, and a Happy Ending—For Some

We heard no word of greeting and met no sign of welcome, but were given a dreary resting place near the foot of the steps, just inside the open doorway, with a bed of branches to lie upon and a blanket to cover us.
—Eliza Donner

As the men tried to treat their frostbitten toes that night by rubbing them with snow, they were surprised to see Cady and Stone come up to join them by their foodless campfire. The two young men had deserted their posts at the lakeside cabins and fled. They had with them small packs that looked heavy, but they did not say what was in them. Reed and his three companions must have felt outraged, but did nothing and probably said nothing. They were exhausted and unarmed; the two young men were relatively unwearied and strong. California was full of lawless characters, and the law did not reach into the mountains; indeed, it barely functioned in the settlements. Later on they learned the story of Cady and Stone's desertion, and what the mysterious packs contained.

After the Second Relief had traveled a safe distance away from the Mountain Camp, Cady and Stone left their posts and went down to the Donner camp on Alder Creek. Their friend Clark was out, hunting a bear whose tracks he had seen in the snow. The two young men talked with Tamsen. She, too, had looked at the sky over the mountain ridge and worried about a storm.

If a storm did come, then Woodworth could not get through, and the children would starve. She offered Cady and Stone $500 if they would take her little girls safely to Sutter's and deliver them to their half sisters, Elitha and Leanna. The men accepted, and Tamsen carefully counted out the coins. She also made up a couple of small bundles: keepsakes, silver spoons, and a fine silk dress for each girl.

Tamsen carefully combed her daughters' hair and took them to George's bedside to say good-bye to their father. Then she took them up on the snow to say good-bye herself. She put on their cloaks and hoods—garnet-red cloaks and red knitted hoods for Eliza and Georgia and a blue shawl and hood for Frances, the eldest. She said in a strange voice, as if talking to herself, "I may never see you again, but God will take care of you."

And so the three little girls started up toward the lake with their big escorts, for all the world as if they were going off to school. Georgia and Eliza tired soon and had to be carried. After a little while the men put the girls down on a blanket in the snow and went off to talk privately. Young as they were, the shivering little girls realized that Cady and Stone meant no good by this private discussion, and they guessed that the two young men were going to leave them there to freeze.

Frances tried to reassure her younger sisters. "Don't feel afraid," she said. "If they go off and leave us, I can lead you back to Mother by our foot tracks in the snow."

The two young men finished their discussion, came back, and picked up the girls. They carried them as far as the Murphy cabin and left them there without so much as a parting word. At the cabin, the girls were received coldly. Someone, probably Keseberg, pointed to a pile of pine boughs by the door and told them to sleep there.

It was dark and cold and malodorous inside the cabin, and the little girls were afraid. Soon they heard a child begin to cry, "Give me some bread! Oh, give me some meat!" Another child took up the vain plea. Then a hoarse voice shouted, "Be quiet, you crying children, or I'll shoot you!"

It was Keseberg, but the Donner children no longer recognized him. They saw only an ugly, bearded man with bushy hair who lay next to the fire. The crying children—they were the Foster and Eddy boys—fell silent, but soon began again. Keseberg replied with the same threat. This scenario was repeated several times. The little girls got no food that night.

The storm came, and Eliza and her sisters, lying by the open doorway, were soon covered by blowing snow. They were not allowed near the fire, which Keseberg reserved for himself. The big German ruled the little cabin like a tyrant. He shouted and threatened and made the children stay in bed. If they got up, they would be in the way, he grumbled.

That night Keseberg limped past the Donner girls' sleeping place and muttered that he wanted to take Eliza with him. Frances and Georgia feared that he was going to kill her, and they guarded Eliza for the next few days, never letting her out of their sight.

They had good reason for their fear, for not long afterward Keseberg took little Georgie Foster to bed with him. Perhaps he used the pretext of keeping the child warm. In the morning, Georgie was dead. Mrs. Murphy took her grandson's body in her lap and screamed that Keseberg had murdered him.

Keseberg, now deeply sunk into bestiality, snatched the body from her and hung it on the cabin wall, in plain view. He did not leave it there for long. In fairness, however, it must be pointed out that he gave the other children a share of the dead boy's meager flesh. Mrs. Murphy may have gotten some, too, if she could have borne the thought of eating her own grandchild.

Meanwhile, Cady and Stone had probably taken shelter from the approaching storm inside the abandoned Breen cabin. As soon as the storm died out, they took their packs of valuables and made tracks for the settlements. Being young and strong, with no children to slow them down, they made it easily over the summit, passed by the snow pit where the Breens and Graveses were staying, and reached Reed's campsite before stopping for the night. But the terrible cold had told on them, too. Cady had frostbitten feet.

At the Donner camp, Clark returned empty-handed from his bear hunt. Exhausted, he tumbled into the Jacob Donner tent and went to sleep. When he awoke in the morning, the storm was raging, although not so fiercely as on the other side of the mountains. They were short of firewood, but Clark decided he would rather go cold than set foot outside the tent to chop wood. He didn't ask the others what they thought.

Before the storm was over, Aunt Betsy Donner and her three-year-old son Lewis were dead. Nearby, Tamsen, Jean-Baptiste, and the dying George Donner survived. Four-year-old Sammie Donner was alive, too, and Tamsen took her orphaned nephew in.

At the Murphy cabin the nightmare existence continued. But one day, about a week and a half after the Second Relief had left (it was probably March 13), Tamsen appeared at the cabin. She had come to see what had happened to her children.

Tamsen was overjoyed to see her little daughters alive. Although Cady and Stone had heartlessly betrayed their promise to her, and cheated her out of a large sum of money, she realized that the children might have died if the men had kept their word and they had been caught out on the trail in the storm. She stayed overnight with the girls and lingered on the next morning to exchange sympathies with the pathetic Mrs. Murphy.

Tamsen was still there when a new rescue party appeared: Eddy, Foster, and the tireless blacksmith from Springfield, Hiram Miller. Eddy and Foster, who only a few weeks ago had been ready to kill each other, had patched up their quarrel and joined forces to rescue their little sons. Once back in a normal environment, Foster had recovered his sanity and was able to act like a decent human being again.

In the meantime, Reed's party struggled painfully along the western slopes. The men's feet left tracks of blood, as had the Forlorn Hope's. But they were in luck. Dangling from a tree they found a little cache of food that Dofar had left for them.

The three mountain men whom Reed had sent ahead—Dofar,

Gendreau, and Turner—had also run into trouble. They had found the first cache rifled by animals. Before they reached the next cache, the storm caught them. They had no food, and probably had trouble getting a fire started.

All three of these experienced outdoorsmen suffered bad frost injuries. The huge, powerful Turner was so badly frostbitten that the other two had to help him along like a cripple.

When they reached the second cache, they found that animals had been at it, too. But luckily part of it remained. Dofar, who was in the best shape of the three, limped back a short way on his frostbitten feet and left some of it hanging from a tree for the other members of the Second Relief to find. Then he rejoined his comrades, and the three of them dragged themselves to Bear Valley, too badly crippled to help the others.

Revived by the food, Reed's party straggled down toward Bear Valley, some of them far ahead of the others. The leaders made camp along the Yuba and waited for the others to come in. Cady and Brit Greenwood lagged far behind. Both men were in considerable pain from their frozen feet, and they gave vent to their feelings in a loud and continuous stream of curses and moans. They were so loud, in fact, that their outcries reached the ears of Passed Midshipman Woodworth, who was encamped a mile or so farther down the valley. He dispatched an aide to invite the group to join him, but only Cady and Greenwood went. The others had already made themselves comfortable for the night.

A short tramp through the snow had apparently persuaded Woodworth to stay at his comfortable advance camp in Bear Valley, disregarding his orders to bring food to the starving people trapped in the snow across the mountains. That would have entailed risking his own life for a handful of strangers, who might well be dead in any case before he reached them. But Eddy and Foster and Miller, on their way up to the pass, had spent the night with Woodworth, and the next morning they shamed the reluctant midshipman into following them onward for a few miles, bolstered by five of his own men. On the trail they met the frost-crippled mountain men of the Second Relief, Dofar, Gendreau, and Turner, and heard their doleful news.

Things looked bad for the survivors, very bad. But Eddy and Foster learned that their sons were still alive when the Second Relief had left, and the two fathers burned with anxiety to reach them before it was too late. However, Woodworth insisted on making camp early, and they felt the wisest course was to stay with him. That night they heard the shouts of Cady and Greenwood on the trail above them.

The next morning, Reed and his men, carrying Patty and Tommy, made their painful way down to Bear Valley. There Patty Reed, her ordeal over at last, sat down on the ground and pulled a little packet out from the bosom of her dress. She had kept it hidden because she knew the men would make her throw away even that negligible bit of extra weight. It was a piece of cloth with blue flowers on it, and in it were her treasures. A lock of gray hair from Grandma Keyes's head— Patty had snipped it herself before they buried Grandma back on the Big Blue in Kansas. A miniature glass saltcellar. And a battered little wooden doll with black eyes and hair, like Patty herself.

Patty, who had had to be grown up for so long, could now relax and be a child again. She picked up the doll and began to tell it what had happened in the past few days. And in another few days the Reed family was joyfully reunited at the house of Alcalde Sinclair, near Sutter's Fort.

CHAPTER 21
A Tale of Courage and Cowardice

With this little party Stark remained and had he not done so probably not one of them would have got out of the snow . . . he said that he would take them all to Bear Valley if they would only live long enough.
                                             —Memoirs of John Breen

After they came down from the mountains with the Forlorn Hope, Eddy and Foster had stayed at Johnson's Ranch until they felt recovered from their near-fatal ordeal. (Eddy's courageous attempt to go up with the First Relief had done him no good.) They waited at Johnson's until the First Relief came back.

From the rescuers, Eddy learned that his wife and baby daughter had died, but that only made him more anxious to save his son. Foster, too, had a son up there, and the news of Mrs. Murphy's condition was alarming. (She was his mother-in-law, and he was fond of her.)

That was March 3. Two days later, from their safe refuge in the settlements, they could see the storm raging in the mountains. They needed no imagination to tell them what was happening up there beneath the veil of white. They had been through it themselves.

They waited a day for the storm to cease, then another day. On the third day (March 7) they could wait no longer. They took horses from Johnson's herd, purchased by the U.S. Navy for the relief effort, and set off while the storm still hurled snow and life-chilling winds at anyone luckless enough to be on the mountains. The two fathers pushed their horses hard and covered fifty miles in a single day. They camped at Mule Springs and caught up with Woodworth at Bear Valley.

Passed Midshipman Woodworth's orders from Commander Hull had been very clear. Woodworth was instructed to use every possible effort to rescue the stranded emigrants, and he was authorized to use navy funds to pay whatever expenses were needed to fulfill his mission. Part of that mission was to go over the pass with a large pack train of supplies and bring back all the emigrants. He had reached Mule Springs on March 2, and from there he could easily have crossed the pass in good weather. In fact, he sent a letter back to Sheriff McKinstry at Sutter's that he was about to start up with four men and three mules, with four hundred pounds of flour. He added that he would not return until all the emigrants were in camp.

When Selim E. Woodworth was a boy of twelve, he set out to cross the continent by himself on foot, carrying only a rifle. He traveled three hundred miles before he was caught and sent home. As a young man, he signed on a merchant ship as clerk, was shipwrecked off Madagascar, and spent three years living among the fiercely warring tribes of that island. In the summer of 1846 he crossed the plains to Oregon for the adventure of it. (Some sources say that Woodworth had been sent to Oregon by the government with dispatches telling the American settlers that the joint occupation with Britain had been terminated. Government commission or no, it was still no trip for the faint-hearted.) The very model of a danger-courting adventurer, one might think. But in the Sierras his spirit of adventure withered and died with uncommon swiftness. Well before the storm struck, Woodworth stopped at Bear Valley.

Woodworth believed that rank had its privileges, and he camped in comfort, at government expense. He had men to fetch water, make his campfire, and cook for him. He had a cask of French brandy, known to aid the digestion. All he lacked, apparently, was courage.

Eddy and Foster asked Woodworth why he had not proceeded over the mountain, as he was supposed to. Woodworth replied that his guides—Greenwood's mountain men—had gone ahead with Reed and that he couldn't risk his expedition in the mountains without a guide. The two veterans of the Forlorn Hope told him that he already had the best possible guide: the tracks of the men who had gone up ahead of him.

Woodworth, somewhat ashamed, said he would go forward the next morning, but not all the way to the pass, and he cautioned the two men not to attempt it themselves. They answered scornfully that they "had passed over it under vastly more difficult circumstances and would certainly attempt it again." (At least, that was how Thornton elegantly reported it.)

Woodworth set off in the morning—March 9—as he had promised. As commanding officer he felt it beneath his dignity to carry a pack, but to hearten his men by his example he did carry his own blanket. About 3 p.m. he became tired from this burdensome load and ordered the party to make camp.

The following morning Woodworth asked for volunteers to accompany Eddy and Foster on their risky and arduous trip across the mountains. The men, obviously inspired by their leader's example, did not raise a single hand. Eddy and Foster, in desperation, offered $50 apiece to anyone who would go with them. Even that got no takers. Some of the men objected cynically that neither Foster nor Eddy could be trusted to pay them because they had lost everything they had owned.

By now Reed's party had come down as far as Woodworth's campsite, and Reed and Miller offered to make good the pay if Eddy and Foster could not. No one trusted them either, except for one good-hearted man named John Starks, who volunteered to go without pay. Starks was as big and strong as McCutchen or Turner, but Reed, still haunted by his own near-disaster in the storm, warned him that his very size—234 pounds—was a danger, for he would almost certainly bog down if he hit a patch of soft, deep snow.

Eddy and Foster were about to set off alone and unaided, but Reed persuaded them that this would be suicidal, and everyone went back down to Woodworth's camp in Bear Valley. There the two fathers made another try at raising volunteers. This time Hiram Miller said he would go if Eddy would pay him $50. One can hardly blame him for wanting to be paid, since he had almost lost his own life in the recent storm and was still worn down and exhausted, with badly frostbitten hands. Once Miller had committed himself, Foster hired a man named Thompson for $50. Starks volunteered again, and this time nobody stopped him. A Mormon named Howard Oakley joined the expedition. Finally young Stone, somewhat redeeming his dishonesty and treachery to Tamsen Donner (or possibly going back for a crack at more loot), completed the crew. These last three men were to be paid from Woodworth's navy funds. The hastily assembled Third Relief was ready.

They departed from Bear Valley early on March 11, while Woodworth retreated to the comforts of Mule Springs to rough it in style. The men made good time, and they stopped only to examine the corpse of John Denton, still sitting in his useless blanket. They searched his pockets and found he had not touched the food that his comrades had left him—food they needed desperately themselves. The dying man had felt no hunger.

By Denton's side they found a little diary, a lead pencil, a piece of rubber eraser, and a sheet of paper. On the paper Denton had written a poem as he lay dying. He had taken some pains with it, for the men could see that he had erased some words and written in new ones.

The poem went as follows:

O! after many roving years,
    How sweet it is to come
Back to the dwelling place of youth—
    Our first and dearest home:—
To turn away our wearied eyes
    From proud ambition's towers,
And wander in those summer fields,
    The scene of boyhood's hours.

But I am changed since last I stood
    Upon that tranquil scene,

And sat beneath the old witch-elm
  That shades the village green;
And watched my boat upon the brook—
  It was a regal galley,
And sighed for not a joy on earth
  Beyond the happy valley.

I wish I could once more recall
  That bright and blissful joy,
And summon to my weary heart
  The feelings of a boy.
But now on scenes of past delight
  I look and feel no pleasure.
As misers on their bed of death
  Gaze coldly on their treasure.

The men hurried on past Denton's corpse and about four in the afternoon arrived at the snow pit where Reed had left the Breens and Graveses and Mary Donner. A bizarre and soul-scarring scene met their eyes.

The fire had melted its way clear down to bare ground, twenty-five feet deep, and the floor of the pit was twelve to fifteen feet across, bigger than the cabin where the Breens had spent the winter. Around the fire lay Patrick and Peggy Breen, sunning themselves comfortably and looking as if they had not a care in the world. Bones and other repellent remains of a human dinner lay scattered about, for Mrs. Breen's housekeeping had become very lax.

The worst of all was the body of Mrs. Graves. Almost all the flesh had been cut away from her arms and legs. Her breasts were cut off, and her torso had been opened to remove her heart and liver. These were at that moment stewing in a pot over the fire. Beside her sat her little girl, barely over a year old. The child had one arm on the mangled body of her mother, as if to seek comfort, and cried bitterly, "Ma! Ma! Ma!"

Eddy, thinking of his own dead child, hurried down the steps that the Breen boys had cut into the snow, followed by the other men of the relief party. He picked up the sobbing infant and held her close until she stopped crying. While the others distributed food, he made a thin soup for the baby, which seemed to do her some good.

Then he heard the story of the past six days from Mrs. Breen, who related it as calmly as if such things happened every day. After the rescue party had left, said Mrs. Breen, Betsy Graves's mind had snapped and she proposed that they kill and eat her baby. But that night she died instead, and her five-year-old son Franklin Ward, Jr., died with her. The cold was bitter, and the fire had melted its way so deep in the snow that the wretched survivors got almost no warmth from it. Then someone peered into the pit and saw the fire resting on the bare ground. One of the Breen boys, curious, climbed down and discovered that it was warm and snug down at the bottom of the pit. It was sheltered from the wind, and the walls of the pit reflected the fire cozily.

The boy called up to the others, and they cut steps in the snow so that everyone could get down. They were warm now, but they were only a few calories away from starvation. Mrs. Breen doled out her hoarded seeds and tea and sugar, a little bit at a time to make them last. Once it looked as if John Breen, the eldest son, were dying, but she pressed a lump of sugar between his lips, and this brought him back. It is not known whether she offered any food to Mary Donner or the three surviving Graves children, Nancy, Jonathan, and baby Elizabeth.

On the fourth day, Mrs. Breen reported, Mary Donner had suggested they eat the bodies of the dead. They started with the dead children, Isaac Donner and Franklin Graves; when they were finished they began on Mrs. Graves. This had kept them alive until Eddy's rescue party came.

It was obvious that these survivors had to be taken to safety without delay. Starks, Oakley, and Stone were chosen for this task. They planned to carry Mary Donner and the three orphaned Graves children. No one felt much like helping the Breens, who had stayed there by their own choice, or at least the choice of the parents.

But then Starks argued that it was not right to take some and leave others. He had come into the snow to bring out all the people who were left there, and that was what he intended to do. The others could do as they pleased. In the end, Oakley took charge of Mary

Donner, Stone took the Graves baby, and Starks took responsibility for the other seven survivors.

At dawn the next day they left the snow pit, which they named "Starved Camp," and reached Bear Valley without incident. Starks performed miracles of strength, good humor, and encouragement along the trail. He would carry a tired child until it was rested, put it down, and pick up one or two more. He laughed and told the children they were no trouble to carry; they were so thin that they were very light. Often he had to carry the children a mile or two, set them down on a blanket, and go back for others. Not once did he complain or lose his temper.

Starks cheered the children on by telling them that they would soon be out of the snow and have all the fat meat they could eat and get a long rest. Years later, John Breen remembered how good Starks had been to them all. In fact, he seemed to remember this more vividly than any other detail of the whole journey from Independence to California.

John Breen remembered also that when they got to Bear Valley there was only a little snow on the ground, and at Mule Springs there was none at all. "Here was an end to hunger and cold," wrote John thirty years afterward, and continued, " . . . I will ever remember the appearance of the country at Johnson's ranch. The grass was forward, and many flowers mingled through it. The weather was warm and clear, which gave a sensation to the tired emigrants that I cannot describe."

But no such happy sight awaited the four men who had headed for Truckee Lake that same morning at dawn. When they reached the Murphy cabin later that morning, Eddy and Foster looked for their children. Keseberg met them at the door and blandly informed the men that he had eaten their sons.

Eddy, horror-stricken, asked why Keseberg had not eaten the hides he had left, or a dead ox that the melting snow had uncovered. Keseberg replied matter-of-factly that he preferred human flesh because it tasted better and contained more nourishment.

The outraged Eddy decided then and there that such a man deserved to die, whether or not he had actually killed the children. But he could not bring himself to take the life of a man in Keseberg's helpless and wretched condition. Instead, he resolved to kill Keseberg if he ever met him in California.

So much for the man who had, without the least contrition or shame, admitted to eating Eddy's child. There was still old Mrs. Murphy to make comfortable and the three little Donner girls to rescue. Also, there was Tamsen.

Tamsen's first concern was to get her little girls to safety, and in her desperation she offered Eddy $1,500 to take them out. He replied that he would not take the extra weight of even $100 for all the wealth she had, but he would see the children safe or die in the effort.

Eddy urged Tamsen to come out with his party. Her husband would soon be dead, he pointed out, and then she would either die of starvation herself or be killed and eaten by Keseberg. But Tamsen's conscience would not let her leave her dear George to die among strangers—Jean-Baptiste and Clark. And little Sammie was still alive, too. Finally, she felt it would be wrong to leave Jean-Baptiste and Clark without warning. She asked Eddy if he could wait a day while she went back to Alder Creek and sent Sammie out with the two young men. Perhaps George would be dead by morning, and she would be free to go.

Eddy answered that he could not wait a day. He and his men did not have enough food, and they all knew how precarious was the balance between strength and starvation. And there was always the danger of a sudden storm trapping them at the lake.

Tamsen, remarkably, was in good health and even looked a little plump, thought the men. She could easily walk the trail to Bear Valley with the rescuers. And the thought of leaving such little children to face the world without a protector was hard—their older half sisters Elitha and Leanna were scarcely more than children themselves. But the thought of leaving her husband to die without her was harder still. It was a terrible decision, and she made it. She said good-bye to her children a second time and said to Eddy, "O, save! Save my children!" Then she turned and walked out of their lives forever. They said she never once looked back.

The Third Relief stayed only long enough to tend to Mrs. Murphy and get the children ready. They wasted no sympathy on Keseberg.

He seemed to be able to look out for himself. They left at noon, having stayed only two hours.

There was one child per man. Eddy carried Georgia Donner—he had taken a fancy to the frail child, who reminded him of his own dead daughter. Foster carried his little brother-in-law, Simon Murphy. Thompson took Frances Donner, and Hiram Miller carried little Eliza. Simon and Frances could walk part of the time, and Georgia could walk a little bit, but Eliza had to be carried all the way.

The party got only as far as the head of the lake that evening. There they found Jean-Baptiste and Clark, who had run off during Tamsen's absence—a truly handsome return for her loyalty to them. Clark had a forty-pound pack filled with stolen valuables, plus two pistols. The pack weighed a good deal more than little Sammie Donner, whom Clark and Jean-Baptiste had abandoned. Faced with the choice between easy gain and saving a child's life, Clark shouldered the booty and left the child to die. As for Jean-Baptiste, he was happy just to save himself.

The next morning, March 14, the group scaled the pass and began the long journey down. They were fortunate: The weather held good, and the journey was uneventful. But toward the end of the first day Miller, not yet recovered from his own recent ordeal, grew tired and put Eliza down to walk the last few hundred yards by herself. She didn't want to, but he bribed her with the promise of a lump of sugar when they got to camp. When they arrived, Eliza asked for her sugar and Miller told her there wasn't any. She cried herself to sleep

The next morning, Miller told Eliza to walk again. Still angry about the sugar, she sat down in the snow and screamed that she wanted to go back to her mother. The exasperated Miller spanked her. Frances Donner rushed to her sister's defense, and the noise brought Eddy and Foster. The newly bereaved fathers had some hard words for Miller, and he ended up carrying Eliza after all, slung in a blanket on his back like an Indian papoose. It was an uncomfortable victory for Eliza, though, for her head bounced wildly with every step that Miller took, and there were many steps before they made camp.

The next night Eddy found a bundle by the trail. It was the one that Cady and Stone had stolen and abandoned when their feet swelled with frostbite. In it were the fine silk dresses that Tamsen had made for her daughters, dove-gray for Frances, light brown for Georgia, and coffee-colored for Eliza. Thompson had to take out his pocket knife, needle, and thread, and do some trailside tailoring to make the dresses fit. Prudent Tamsen had made them a couple of sizes too large, so that the girls could grow into them.

The remainder of the journey went smoothly. The little party rested for a few days at Mule Springs, near the end of the mountains, and there the girls met the survivors who had come down with Reed and with Starks. Their cousin Mary Donner was there, with an old woolen stocking covering her badly burned foot. She was in tears from the pain, and her kind-hearted rescuer, Oakley, was trying to comfort her. In a few more days they were all at Sutter's. There the little girls were handed over to the care of their teenaged half sisters Elitha and Leanna, and they waited for news of their parents.

CHAPTER 22

The Last Survivor

The flesh of starved beings contains little nutriment. It is like feeding straw to horses. . . . It has been told that I boasted of my shame—said that I enjoyed this horrid food, and that I remarked that human flesh was more palatable than California beef. This is a falsehood. It is a horrible, revolting falsehood. This food was never other than loathsome, insipid, and disgusting.

—Statement of Lewis Keseberg, 1879

It was more than a month before the anxiously waiting Donner girls received news of their parents, when the final relief expedition came down.

Toward the end of March, Woodworth had been ordered to organize another relief expedition, and he raised a capable bunch of volunteers: John Rhoads, Reasin Tucker, Sels, Starks, Coffeemeyer, Foster, and Billy Graves. All were veterans of other relief expeditions in one way or another, and Foster and Graves had been members of the Donner Party. But the group got only as far as Bear Valley and then turned back.

They gave as their reason that the snow had become too soft and slushy to travel on. The real reason was probably that they could see a storm brewing in the mountains, and none of them was ready to risk his life once more. There was no longer any motivation for them: Foster's mother-in-law, Mrs. Murphy, was surely dead by now, and poor old Uncle George Donner and little Sammie likewise. It was too bad about Tamsen, but twice she had been urged to come down to safety and twice she had refused. She could not ask more of them. As for Lewis Keseberg, no one cared. Every other member of the Donner Party either had been rescued or was dead.

Not until April 13 did the last relief party leave from Johnson's Ranch, and it was in reality a salvage expedition. It was common knowledge that the Donners had brought many valuable goods in their wagons as far as Alder Creek, and everyone agreed that it would be a dreadful waste if spring floods carried the goods away or wandering Indians purloined them. The men were entitled by law to half the goods they brought back . . . and if they kept a little more than half for themselves, who was going to do anything about it?

The leader of this seven-man expedition, sometimes known as the Fourth Relief, was "Captain" William Fallon, a huge mountain man of the most thuggish type. He was also known as Le Gros, French for "the big one," and he was feared by everyone who knew him. Fallon's followers were John Rhoads, Sels, William Foster, Tucker, Coffeemeyer, and a man named Keyser, who was a settler at Johnson's Ranch.

Spring had by now come to the mountains, and the men were able to ride their horses as far as Bear Valley instead of slogging up on foot in the snow. They took ten days' rations and set off on foot from there. The route was all too familiar to five of them. The remaining snow was packed so hard that it gave firm footing, almost as good as bare ground, and the men made good speed. They reached the lake in four days from Johnson's Ranch. The snow that had trapped the emigrants in their cabins for so many weary months was almost gone, and there were patches of bare ground.

It was just after noon when the men reached the cabins. They saw no sign of life—only a welter of dismembered corpses. Legs, arms, and skulls lay scattered in every direction. They saw a body that Foster thought might have been Eleanor Eddy's, but it was hard to be certain. The arms and legs had been cut off, and the skull had a frightful gash in it. Most of the flesh on the bones had been eaten.

The men were sure that everyone at the cabins was dead, when they heard a sudden shout. They ran toward the shout, but it turned out to be three Digger Indians, so alarmed that they fled in haste, leaving their bows and arrows behind.

The men spent about two hours searching the cabins, finding horror after horror—things they thought too sickening to put down on paper. Then they started down for the Donner camp; when they had gotten about halfway, they saw tracks in the snow that did not look like an Indian's. They followed the footprints to Jacob Donner's camp, which the person who made them had apparently left that morning.

Inside the shelter they found books, bolts of calico cloth, tea, coffee, shoes, percussion caps for guns, and all kinds of furniture and kitchen equipment scattered on the ground. Most were lying in puddles of water, which ruined their value. At the mouth of the tent stood a large iron kettle, filled with chunks of human flesh. They had obviously been cut from the cadaver of George Donner, which was lying nearby. George's head had been split open and the brains taken out. He appeared to have been dead no more than three or four days. (Actually he had been dead much longer, but the cold had kept him fresh.)

Near the kettle stood a chair with three legs of an ox piled on it. The Donners had killed the ox last fall, but the snow had buried it before they could butcher it. If Jean-Baptiste had only been able to find the carcass, how differently the story might have ended! The men sniffed and tasted the beef, and found it still good. But the occupant of the tent had not touched it, except for a little chunk from one shoulder.

Fallon and his men spent the rest of that day, and the next one, gathering small, valuable objects they could take in their packs. Most of the things had to be dried in the sun. The men were bothered by the fact that the Donners' money was missing—what could have happened to it?—and by the mysterious tracks that led away from Jake Donner's tent. On the morning of April 19, Foster, Rhoads, and Sels set off to follow the tracks, while Fallon and the others stayed at the Donners' to cache what they could not carry with them.

The trail soon disappeared in the melting snow, so the search party, following a hunch, went directly to the cabins by the lake. There, on the floor of the Breen cabin, they found Keseberg, lying among a disorderly jumble of human bones, calmly smoking a pipe, with a large pan full of fresh liver and lungs beside him.

Keseberg, once so neat and vain of his appearance, was now haggard and revolting. His beard had grown grotesquely long, and his untrimmed nails had lengthened until they resembled the claws of a beast. The outraged men questioned Keseberg angrily: What had become of the other survivors? What had become of Mrs. Donner? He replied that they were all dead.

As Keseberg told it, Mrs. Murphy had lingered for about a week after the Third Relief departed. Keseberg remained in the cabin another week or so after she died, with only the dead for company. Even for the callous Keseberg, this must have been an unnerving experience. He lived on the flesh of the dead, which, he said, he could hardly bear to eat. His injured foot grew better, and he moved over to the Breen cabin, which had a proper fireplace. He went out only to get firewood, which took him two or three hours a day in his weakened state. At night the wolves would come and sniff and scratch outside the door; one night he awoke in terror, certain that the wolves would get in and eat him as well as the bodies of the dead.

Then, in the middle of one cold, bitter night, Tamsen Donner had come to his cabin. She had stayed with George until he died in her arms at nightfall. Then she laid him out, wrapped decently in a sheet, and left. Her one thought now was to reach her children. In the dark she lost the trail and wandered in the woods, falling into a stream. Her clothing was wet and ice-cold when she arrived at Keseberg's, chilled and exhausted. Tamsen told Keseberg that she was going to go over the mountains alone, never mind that she had no food and no one to guide her. She kept repeating, "My children! I must see my children!"

Keseberg tried to dissuade her, he said, but she insisted she must go. At last she let herself be persuaded to stay over until the morning. Tamsen remarked that she was very hungry. Keseberg offered her the only food he had—human flesh—but she refused to touch it. She finally lay down, and Keseberg spread a feather bed and a blanket over her. In the morning she was dead.

Keseberg told the men that he had eaten Tamsen and found her flesh the best he had ever tasted. He added that he had gotten at least three or four pounds of fat from her body. The three men could find no traces of Tamsen's body nor of Mrs. Murphy's. They became suspicious, since Tamsen had been in perfect health when Foster had seen her only a few weeks earlier.

They looked around the cabin and found two kettles containing human blood, about a gallon in all. Rhoads asked Keseberg where the blood came from, and he answered, "There is blood in dead bodies." The men, believing mistakenly that one could get blood only from a still-living body, were now sure that he had murdered Tamsen, and his behavior when they questioned him about her money only confirmed their belief.

Keseberg gave evasive answers, equivocated, and contradicted himself. He told them that Tamsen must have cached the money before she died and swore that he himself had nothing, not the property of any person, living or dead. But when they searched his bundle, they found silks and jewelry that Foster recognized as the Donners' property and worth, they judged, about $200. On Keseberg's person they found a pair of George Donner's pistols, and while they removed these someone found a lump in Keseberg's waistcoat. It turned out to be $225 in gold coins.

Before the men had set out, Keseberg's wife had told them that her husband had little or no money about him, so they knew he was lying when he claimed that the money was his. They told him so, and they added that they were sure he knew where Tamsen's money was hidden. Keseberg swore that he knew nothing about it. They told him it was no use to lie to them, for Fallon would not hesitate to hang him from the nearest tree if he did not come clean.

When Keseberg persisted in his denials, Rhoads took him aside for a private interrogation. Speaking in a kindly tone, he told Keseberg that, if he gave them the information they wanted, they would give him the best of treatment. If not, they would put him to death as soon as the other four arrived from the Donner camp. But Keseberg stuck to his story. The three men told him he could have the night to make up his mind, and they rejoined their comrades at the Donner camp.

The next morning the seven salvagers started back for Bear Valley, laboring under one-hundred-pound packs. They ate breakfast near Keseberg's cabin and then walked in to continue their inquiries. Keseberg turned pale and once again blurted out that he knew nothing of Mrs. Donner's money.

The huge and menacing Fallon turned toward Keseberg and said, "Keseberg, you know well where Donner's money is, and, d—n you, you shall tell me! I am not going to multiply words with you, nor say but little about it—bring me that rope!"

Keseberg heaved himself up from his pot of soup and human flesh and begged Fallon not to harm him. He insisted that he had neither the money nor the goods, and that the valuables and cash they had found in his pack and his pockets the previous day, which he had said were his wife's, really belonged to other emigrants down in California.

Fallon, annoyed, told Keseberg that he wished to hear no more, unless he revealed where he had hidden the money of the orphaned children. (What a treat it must have been for the gangsterlike Fallon to play the role of a righteous rescuer for once!) He held out the rope and approached Keseberg, who became very frightened. Fallon tied the rope around Keseberg's neck and threw the desperately struggling man to the ground. As the noose was tightened, Keseberg managed to gasp out that he would confess everything if Fallon would release him. Reluctantly, and after more argument, Keseberg led Rhoads and Tucker back to Alder Creek. They returned the next morning with $273, which Keseberg had buried under the projecting limb of a huge pine tree.

While they were gone, Foster went to the Murphy cabin on a final search for valuables. He found, instead, the mutilated body of his late brother-in-law, Landrum Murphy, with the brains, liver, and lungs removed. These had been Keseberg's breakfast when he was discovered. When Rhoads and Tucker came back—they had let Keseberg go when he showed them the treasure cache—they found him crouched in the Breen cabin devouring the remains of this gruesome meal.

Keseberg's own story, which he recounted more than thirty years later to a sympathetic journalist, was that Tamsen had made him promise to get her money and take it to her children in case she perished. Some days after she died, he felt strong enough to fulfill this promise, and made his way painfully down to Alder Creek. There he searched through the Donner belongings and found the money, part in gold and part in silver. The silver he buried beneath the pine tree; the gold he put in his pocket. On the way back he became lost in the gathering dark and fell through the snow into a hidden stream. The water was so deep that he could not stand, and he barely extricated himself. Just at dark, completely exhausted, he reached the Mountain Camp, his clothes frozen stiff from his fall into the water. He dragged himself to bed, too exhausted to make a fire, and eventually fell asleep. In the morning he awoke to find his trunks broken open and the contents strewn everywhere. His wife's jewelry, his own cloak, and his pistols and ammunition were missing. Then the three men from Fallon's party had walked in, "not with a 'good morning,' or a kind word, but with the gruff, insolent demand, 'Where is Donner's money?'"

Keseberg, terrified, thought they were robbers. When he asked them who they were and where they had come from, they replied by threatening to kill him if he did not give up the money. This, he said, was why he had tried to conceal it from them. Throughout, he complained, the men had treated him with the greatest unkindness.

Back now to April 1847. Rhoads and Tucker hurried the degraded remnant of a man away from his cabin and his horrid meal. But, before leaving, he insisted on gathering up the bones and putting them in a box that he had set aside for that purpose. He pronounced a blessing over the bones and the cabin and said, "I hope God will forgive me for what I have done, I couldn't help it! And I hope I may get to heaven yet!"

One of the men asked Keseberg why he had not eaten the meat of the ox, or a horse that was also uncovered when the snow melted away. With lunatic cunning he replied that he had not seen them. The men told him they knew better, and asked him why he had not eaten the meat they had seen on the chair.

Keseberg gave them his gourmet's opinion: "Oh! It's too dry eating! The liver and lights [lungs] were a great deal better, and the brains made good soup!"

Keseberg later denied that he had ever said any such thing. In 1879 he stated to his interviewer: "The flesh of starved beings contains little nutriment. It is like feeding straw to horses. I cannot describe the unutterable repugnance with which I tasted the first mouthful of flesh. . . . It makes my blood curdle to think of it! It has been told that I boasted of my shame—said that I enjoyed this horrid food, and that I remarked that human flesh was more palatable than California beef. This is a falsehood. It is a horrible, revolting falsehood. The food was never otherwise than loathsome, insipid, and disgusting." However, this statement was almost certainly the product of wishful thinking and of the thirty-two years Keseberg had had in which to ponder and regret the dreadful things that had happened in the Sierra snows.

That night of April 23, 1847, the Fourth Relief, with the wretched Keseberg in tow, camped at the head of the lake for the last time. In four more days they reached the lower end of Bear Valley, met their horses, and came in with no events of note.

Except this: Keseberg, lagging behind the others, stopped at an old campsite left by an earlier relief party to fix himself a pot of coffee. A scrap of cloth protruding from the snow caught his eye. Out of curiosity he gave it a tug—and pulled up the dead body of his little daughter, Ada, who had perished on the trail and been buried by the wayside.

So the last surviving member of the hopeful group that had made a decision on the banks of the Little Sandy came down to Sutter's Fort. The tragedy that began with the hyperactive ambitions and the easy, persuasive lies of a clever but irresponsible young Ohio lawyer had reached its end.

EPILOGUE

O Mary I have not wrote you half of the trubel we have had but I hav wrote you anuf to let you know that you dont know what trubel is but thank God we have all got throw and the onely family that did not eat human flesh we have left everything but I dont cair for that we have got through with our lives but Dont let this letter dishaten [dishearten] anybody but never take no cutofs and hury along as fast as you can. . . . We are all very well pleased with California particularly with the climate . . . it is a beautiful Country . . . it aut to be a beautiful Country to pay us for our trubel getting there. . . .

—Letter of Virginia Reed to her cousin
Mary C. Keyes, May 16, 1847

'There was one more death after the survivors of the Donner Party came down at last to California. The little Graves baby had lost its will to live and pined away. The others recovered and soon found their places in the booming new society of California.

Some of the survivors' subsequent stories are known, and they may be of interest. Let us begin with Lewis Keseberg and save the pleasanter reports until later.

When Keseberg arrived at Sutter's Fort, the men of the Fourth Relief wasted no time telling all and sundry that he was a murderer, a cannibal, and a thief. Sutter rallied to the defense of his fellow German (though some people said that Keseberg was blackmailing Sutter), and advised him to sue Coffeemeyer for defamation of character. The case was tried before Alcalde Sinclair, who found in favor of Keseberg and awarded him one dollar in damages.

After that, Keseberg began to work for Sutter as the captain of his river schooner, which plied between Sutter's Fort and San Francisco carrying wheat and passengers. He held this job for seven months but was never paid. Some said that Sutter fired him because so many passengers complained about Keseberg. They were afraid he would kill and eat them if the boat ran aground. But this story was probably started by Sutter himself. It was the kind of thing that was his idea of a joke. To add to Keseberg's punishment, his wife took to committing adultery with young boatmen while he was away.

In 1848, Keseberg followed the rush to the newly discovered gold mines. Then he opened a boardinghouse at Sutter's Fort, prospered, and graduated to a fine hotel in Sacramento. He sold it for a large profit, but the night that the deal was closed a terrible fire burned down most of the city of Sacramento, and the hotel with it. The purchaser was ruined, and Keseberg could not collect a cent. He started a brewery at Sutter's Fort and sold it for $50,000. A flood swept it away before the buyer got his money out of the bank. Again Keseberg lost his fortune.

Several other times he made money, only to lose it through no apparent fault of his own. He and his wife had nine more children; five of them died. The two youngest surviving children, both girls, were severely retarded and subject to frequent fits of violence. They were also grotesquely deformed, and one weighed more than two hundred pounds at age fifteen. No caretaker would stay with them for more than a few days. When Keseberg's wife died, he had to take care of them himself; when he went to work he had to take the girls with him and lock them in a room. In their spasms, the girls screamed so loudly that the neighbors complained, until Keseberg was forced to live in an isolated little house behind a brewery, where no one could hear them.

Did Keseberg murder Tamsen Donner? The truth will never be known. He was certainly in an abnormal state of mind when the Third Relief arrived at the cabins and he boasted to Eddy and Foster that he had eaten their sons. And even in better days on the trail his actions, such as abandoning Hardkoop to die in the desert and attempting to lynch Reed, suggest that he had little respect for the lives of others. Keep such a man imprisoned in a filthy little cabin for months, add the stresses of prolonged starvation and the ever-present fear of death, and he might very easily commit murder to stave off his own demise. The taboo against eating human flesh had been broken when Mrs. Murphy began on Milt Elliott, and one can easily imagine Keseberg thinking that there was no harm in hastening the deaths of his starved, suffering companions. Especially when that would help Keseberg, a husband and father himself, to live.

It is certain that he ate Tamsen Donner. We have his own word for it. Moreover, he ate her when there was plenty of other food available. Perhaps his crazed mind told him that human flesh would keep him alive longer, by some magical process, than dried-out beef from starved oxen. Perhaps he even ate Tamsen in some warped spirit of admiration, hoping to gain her good qualities by devouring her. For he had only good things to say of Tamsen afterward.

Keseberg was probably unbalanced for several years after he came down from the mountains, for he liked to boast of having been a cannibal. In the raw frontier society of California this brought him a great deal of attention, which he apparently enjoyed. (Jean-Baptiste also boasted of having eaten human flesh, for the same reason.) But at the same time Keseberg was afraid that people would think badly of him, and he made frequent pathetic attempts to excuse the fact that he had lived on human flesh.

> Keseberg made several attempts to turn the conversation to his lonely vigil in the mountains, and the hideous way he kept himself alive, but I changed the subject every time. … He noticed my attitude, and remarked that this episode had been misconstrued, and that he had been made to assume the role of a hyena [Heinrich Lienhard, *From St. Louis to Sutter's Fort*]

Then the gold rush passed, and many of the rough characters who had enjoyed Keseberg's tales of cannibalism disappeared, and people no longer found the idea entertaining. Good citizens began to shun Keseberg. In his later years, boys would yell names at him in the street and throw stones at him. Whatever crimes Keseberg committed, we may say that he suffered in full for them.

♦

Eliza, Georgia, and Frances Donner had a discouraging introduction to California. Soon after they arrived at Johnson's Ranch, settlers' wives stole the fine silk dresses off the girls' backs and gave them their own daughters' outgrown clothes instead. Poor Eliza ended up with a dress that was too small for her.

Then they learned that both their parents were dead. Foolish, pious women came to preach at them and tell them how much better off they would be if they had died with their mother and father and were not left alone in this wicked world. The girls' only defense was to run off and hide, but they knew that these morbidly religious ladies were wrong. Their mother wanted them to be safe and happy, not dead.

Not long after, fourteen-year-old Elitha married Perry McCoon, the ex-sailor, and went off to live with him at his new ranch. Elitha did not want little sisters on her hands to interfere with her exciting new life as a grown-up woman—and a bride!—and the family was split up. Frances went to live with the Reeds; Eliza and Georgia were taken in by a kindly old Swiss couple named Brunner. Georgia was too frail to do much work for her keep, but Eliza helped with the family dairy business and tended the vegetable garden. She also learned German and helped Grandma Brunner with the bookkeeping. Eventually the girls were sent off to school and were reunited with Frances. All of them grew up, married, and lived long and comfortable lives. Georgia, whom everyone expected to die in childhood, surprised everyone by living to a ripe old age.

The Reeds loved California. Soon after the family was reunited, Virginia wrote a long letter to a cousin back in Springfield, in which she recounted the troubles they had suffered in getting there, but concluded it was worth it all. The letter, now a classic document of Western history, is included in the Appendix of this book.

Virginia soon grew into a young beauty, kept her vow to become a Roman Catholic, and when she was sixteen eloped with another recent emigrant, John Murphy, who had come across the mountains with the Stevens-Murphy party in 1844. They had nine children.

Always independent, Virginia took over her husband's real-estate business after he died, did very well for herself, and became a well-known local character. She died in 1921 at age eighty-seven.

Patty Reed was permanently marked by her ordeal in the mountains. Her father remarked that she was old in mind, small for her age, and would never be a beauty (he seemed to feel that was the worst blow). Nevertheless, she married at eighteen, had a large family, and lived to be quite old.

The Reed boys, Jimmy and Tommy, grew up normally and went into the mining business. According to family tradition, Jimmy rode a horse and never walked if he could help it, while Tommy could never eat calf's-foot jelly or any other dish that reminded him of the hides they ate in the Sierras.

Margaret Reed regained her health when she reached California, and her headaches disappeared completely. So at least one of Hastings's promises—renewed health—came true. She and her husband adopted Jacob Donner's surviving children, Mary and George, and had two more of their own. Margaret died in 1861 through a doctor's error in administering medicine.

James Frazier Reed plunged zestfully into California life. He invested very profitably in land and became one of California's first subdividers. He owned farms and wrote letters to his favorite brother-in-law in Springfield to brag about the wonderful melons and other crops he grew. Reed also located a vein of silver in the coastal mountains near his home in San Jose and opened a mine, but soon had to close it when his workers rushed off to the Sierras to pan for gold. Reed himself joined the parade to the gold diggings and did fairly well.

Later he lost most of his money in a business crash, but managed to save some. To the end of his life (he died in 1874), Reed was constantly speculating in far-flung ventures, including farmland in Kansas and silver mines in Nevada. In California, too, he fulfilled his ambition of becoming influential in politics.

Patrick Breen got himself a farm and prospered. The family went into local politics, and one of the sons, John, became a judge. Baby Isabella Breen, who was only one year old when she crossed the plains, achieved the distinction of becoming the very last survivor of the Donner Party. She died in 1935, aged about ninety.

William Eddy, to my mind the greatest hero of the Donner Party, had lost everything: wife, children, and property. But he married again and had a new family. One day in San Francisco, standing by a pier, he spotted Keseberg on Sutter's schooner. Eddy went for his gun to carry out his vow of vengeance, but Reed and Bryant, who were with him, prevented him. That was fortunate, for public opinion was no longer favorable to the Donner Party's survivors.

For a few months, they had enjoyed general sympathy; they were even treated as heroes. But the public tired quickly of them—what was so special about these Donner Party folks, anyway? They were no different from anyone else.

Ugly stories began to circulate among people who didn't know the survivors personally. Weren't those the folks who got themselves into trouble by quarreling all the time, until they were so late they got caught in the snow? And when they were there, didn't they eat each other even when they had plenty of beef? And that Jim Reed, he had a terrible temper. They say he killed his own hired man and had to run away from the wagon train to escape being lynched!

The press coverage they got did not improve matters. The reports in *The California Star* dwelled on the cannibalism to titillate the newspaper's readers. Even Thornton and Bryant, who were friends of the survivors, devoted a good deal of space to that sensational topic in their books, which came out a mere year or two later. So the survivors found it best to put the whole horrifying experience out of mind and not discuss it with strangers.

Attorney Jessy Quinn Thornton came down to San Francisco in the summer of 1847, and there he ran into Reed and some of the other survivors and got their stories. Later he became a judge in Oregon. The book he wrote about the Donner Party, though confused and chaotically organized, remains one of the best original sources.

Passed Midshipman Selim E. Woodworth settled in San Francisco and did exceedingly well in business. In 1851 he was chosen to head

the Vigilance Committee (the original vigilantes), a group of citizens
who banded together to put down the vicious gangs that ruled and
terrorized the city. It was a job that required courage, although of a
different kind from that required to face starvation and snow in the
Sierras. Durng the Civil War, Woodworth re-enlisted in the U.S. Navy
and served with credit under Admiral David Farragut (the man who
said "Damn the torpedoes! Full speed ahead!").

Lansford W. Hastings managed to stay on good terms with the
emigrants with whom he had blundered through the Wasatch and
across the desert, and he achieved his mini-moment of glory as a
captain of volunteers under Frémont in the California uprising. When
told of the Donner tragedy, he said that he was very sorry to hear of
such misfortune, but that he had told them to hurry on and it was
not his fault that they didn't heed him. Not once did he show any
sense of his responsibility for the tragedy.

After his fling at playing soldier, Hastings opened a law office in
San Francisco, where he specialized in real-estate claims and litiga-
tion. During the Civil War he supported the pro-slavery side, and
traveled to Richmond with a plan to seize California and Arizona for
the Confederacy. When his dreams of a slave-holding aristocracy collapsed, he went to South America with a plan to found a colony for
Southern expatriates in Brazil. He died in 1870, of a tropical disease.

In June 1847 "Captain" Fallon, the mountain man, guided General Stephen W. Kearny and his troops through Truckee Pass on their
way east. The snow at the summit was still fifteen to twenty feet deep.
On June 22 they reached the cabins of the Mountain Camp. The
general left a detachment of men to gather the bones and give them
decent burial in a mass grave. They were then to burn the cabins to
the ground. Apparently neither the men nor their commanding officer had any stomach for this sort of work, because at least one cabin
remained standing for several years, and passing emigrants and gold-
seekers looked with mingled horror and titillation at bits and pieces
of human skeletons.

Despite its difficulty, Truckee Pass became a major route during
the Gold Rush. Eventually a stagecoach road was built, and later the

Southern Pacific Railroad came through there. Someone built an inn for wagon teamsters and stagecoach passengers, and well before the end of the century a resort hotel catered to tourists where the Donner Party had starved and huddled in the cold. Nowadays a modern interstate highway, U.S. 80, follows fairly closely the route of the Donner Party along the Hastings cutoff and then the old emigrant road along the Humboldt and the Truckee and across the pass to Sacramento, where a historical park commemorates Sutter's Fort. Truckee Lake has been renamed Donner Lake, and Truckee Pass is now Donner Pass. A state memorial park by the lake draws thousands of visitors each year. Snow still closes the pass in winter, and trains are occasionally trapped in the drifts.

Why did the Donner Party fail when so many other emigrant parties came through unscathed? Almost certainly, the cause was a chain of mishaps, none of them fatal in itself, but cumulatively leading up to disaster.

First, they were lied to by Hastings, Bridger, and Vasquez, people they had reason to trust. Then a series of decisions turned out badly: to cut their own passage through the Wasatch, to banish Reed from the wagon company (with his intelligence and organizing ability he might have been able to pull them through), and the emigrants' refusal to abandon their wagons at Truckee Lake and cross the pass on foot while there was still time. Yet each of these decisions appeared reasonable at the time.

Hastings had warned them that his passage through the canyons of the Weber River was too difficult and dangerous for wagons, and the alternate way that he indicated to Reed was indeed shorter. Banishing Reed was vindictive and unfair, but the alternative was to lynch him. Stopping to rest the oxen at Truckee Meadows was a considered gamble—it was almost certain that the worn-out animals would drop in their tracks long before the pass was reached if they did not get a brief respite and some fodder. The refusal to abandon the wagons at the lake may appear motivated by unthinking greed, but we must remember that the emigrants had their entire fortunes—or what was left of them—in their wagons, and one did not abandon one's last resources lightly, especially when going into a strange country.

Reed's carefully planned rescue expedition was wrecked by the irresponsibility of Woodworth and by the frightful snowstorm, neither of which Reed could possibly have foreseen. The weather itself seemed to be against them. The winter of 1846–47 was one of the worst the Sierras had experienced in years. The snows came early and stayed late, and there were nine great storms from the time the Donner Party stopped at the end of October until the Fourth Relief went up in the spring.

As early as 1847, many people wondered why the women of the Donner Party survived so much better than the men. One contributing factor may have been biological: The women had more body fat and less muscle mass then the men and so could survive longer on the same meager rations. But the main reason was surely psychological: The men were indoctrinated with the philosophy that a real man should be able to conquer every obstacle and provide for his family. When it became painfully clear that they could not do this, many lost self-confidence and the will to live. The women, schooled for a role of submission and adaptability to men's and Fate's strange whims, were far better able to take their adversity in stride.

Historians have pointed out that the members of the Donner Party were, for the most part, ordinary, decent citizens. Even their mishaps were not unique. Other emigrant parties also got into serious trouble. The group with which Thornton continued to Oregon that same summer ran out of food in the canyons of the Cascade Mountains; many of their wagons were smashed or abandoned; and Thornton depicted their guide, Jesse Applegate, as competing with Lansford W. Hastings in villainy. The Bartleson-Bidwell party of 1841, the first to take the overland trail to California, were forced to cache their wagons at the end of the Salt Lake Desert. They blundered onward the rest of the way on foot and nearly lost their lives.

The Bennett-Arcane party in 1849 got lost in an out-of-the-way desert valley in Southern California; their sufferings gave it the name Death Valley. Even the great "Pathfinder," Frémont, got an expedition stuck in the San Juan Mountains in 1848, and one of the sections had to resort to cannibalism to survive.

Yet, when all is said and done, there was something special about the fate of the Donner Party that struck a chord in the hearts and imaginations of their countrymen, a chord that still vibrates down the years. It has inspired—and continues to inspire—poems, plays, television specials, magazine articles, and books. Like this one.

FINIS

REQUIESCANT IN PACE

APPENDIX

Virginia Reed's Letter

Napa Vallie California May 16th 1847
No 1 My Dear Cousin   May the 16 1847

I take this oppertunity to write to you to let you know that we
are all well at presant and hope this letter may find you all
well, My Dear cousin I am a going to write you about our
trubels geting to Callifornia; We had good luck till we come
to big Sandy thare we lost our best yoak of oxen we come to
Birdgers Fort we lost another ox we sold some of our provisions [&] bought a yoak of cows & oxen they pursuaded us to
take Hastings cutoff over the salt plain thay said it saved 3
Hundred miles, we went that & we had to go a long drive of
40 miles without water or grass Hastings said it was 40 but I

think it was 80 miles We traveld a day and a night and a
nother day and at noon pa went on to see if he Coud find
water he had not bin gone long till some of the oxen give out
and We had to leave the Wagons and take the oxon on to
water one of the men staid with us and the others went on
with the cattel to water pa was a coming back to us with Water
and met the men thay was about 10 miles from water pa said
they [would] get to water that night, and the next day to
bring the cattel back for the wagons and bring some water pa
got to us about noon the man that was with us took the horse
and went on to water we waited thare though [thinking] thay
[would] come we waited till night, and we thought we
[would] start and wlk to Mr doners wagons that night we took
what little water we hade and some bread and started pa
carried Thomos and all the rest of us walk we got to Donner
and thay were all a sleep so we laid down on the ground [we]
spred one shawl down we laid down on it and spred another
over us and then put the dogs on top it was the couldes
[coldest] night you most ever saw the wind blew very hard
and if it haden [hadn't] ben for the dogs we would have
Frose as soon as it was day we went to Miss Donners she said
we could not walk to the Water and if we staid we could ride
thare wagons to the spring so pa went on to the water to see
why thay did not bring

No 2 the cattel when he got thare thare was but one ox
and cow thare none of the rest had got to water Mr Donner
come out that night with his cattel and braught his wagons
and all of us in. we staid thare a week and hunted for our
cattel and could not find them so some of the companie took
their oxons and went out and brout in one wagon and cashed
the other too and a grate many things all but What we could
put in one Wagon we had to divied our provisions out to
them [Virginia meant with the rest of the company] to get
them to cary in [it] We got three yoak with our ox & cow so
we went on that way a while and we got out of provisions and
pa had to go on to callifornia for propisions [provisions] we
could not get along that way in 2 or 3 days after pa left we

had to cash our wagon and take Mr graves wagon and cash
some more of our things well we went on in that way a while
and then we had to get Mr Eddys Wagon we went on in that
way a while and then we had to cash all of our close except a
change or 2 and put them in Mr Bri [Breen's] Wagon and
Thomos and James rode the 2 horses and the rest of us had
to walk we went on that way a while and we coome to a
nother long drive of 40 miles and we went with Mr Donner
We had to walk all the time we was a traveling up the trucke
[Truckee] river we met [Stanton] and to [two] Indians who
that we had sent on for propisions [provisions] to Suter Fort
thay had met pa, not fur from Suters Fort he looked very bad
he had not ate but 3 times in 7 days and the [last three]
without any thing his horse was not abel to carrie him thay
give him a horse and he went on so we cashed some more of
our things all but what we could pack on one mule and we
started Martha and James road behind the two Indians it was
a raing [raining] in the Vallies and snowing on the montains
so we went on that way 3 or 4 days tell we come to the big
mountain or the Callifornia Mountain the
    No 3
    snow then was about 3 feet deep thare was some wagons
thare thay said thay had atempted to croos [cross] and could
not well we thought we would try it so we started and thay
started again with their wagons the snow was then way up to
the muels side the farther we went on the deeper the snow
got so the wagons could not go so thay packed thare oxons
and started with us carring [carrying] a child a piece and
driving the oxons in snow up to thare wast [waist] the mule
Martha and the Indian was on was the best one so thay went
and broak the road and that indian was the Pilet so we went
oon that way 2 miles and the mules kept faling down in the
snow head formost and the Indian said he could not find the
road we spoped [stopped] and let the Indian and man
[Stanton] go on to hunt the road thay went on and found the
road to the top of the mountain and come back and said thay
thought we could git over if it did not snow any more well the

Weman were all so tirder [tired of] caring [carrying] there
Children that thay could not go over that night so we made a
fire and got somthing to eat & ma spred down a bufalorobe &
we all laid down on it & I spred somthing over us & ma sit up
by the fire & it snowed one foot on top of the bed so we got
up in the morning & the snow was so deep we could not go
over & we had to go back to the cabin [and] build more
cabins & stay thar all Winter without Pa we had not the first
thing to eat Ma made arrangements for some cattel giving 2
for 1 in callifornia we seldom thot of bread for we had not
had any since Pa left & the cattel was so poor thay could not
get up hadley [hardly] when thay laid down we stoped thare
the 4th of November & staid till March and what we had to
eat i cant hardley tell you & we had that man {Stanton] &
Indians to feed to [too] well thay started over a foot and had
to come back so thay made snowshoes and started again & it
come on a storme & thay had to come back it would snow 10
days before it would stop thay wated tell it stoped & started
again I was a going to [too] with them & I took sick & could
not go. thare was 15 started & thare was 7 got throw
[through] 5 woman & 2 men it come a storme and thay lost
the road & got out of provisions & [those] that got throwe
had to eat them that Died not long after thay started we got
out of

No 4

propisions & had to put Martha at one cabin James at
another Thomas at another & Ma & Elizia & Milt Eliot & I
dried up what littel meat we had and started to see if we
could git acroose & had to leve the childrin o Mary you may
think that hard to leve theme with strangers & did not now
[know] wether we would see them again or not we could not
hardle [hardly] git a way from them but we told them we
[would] bring them Bread & then thay was willing to stay we
went and was out 5 days in the mountains Eliza giv out & had
to go back we went on a day longer we had to lay by a day &
make snowshows & we went on a while and coud not find the
road so we had to turn back I could go on verry well while i

thout we were geting along but as soone as we had to turn
back i coud hadley [hardly] git along but we got to the cabins
that night & I frose one of my feet verry bad that same night
thare was the worst storme we had that winter & if we had not
come back that night we would never got back we had nothing to eat but ox hides o Mary I would cry and Wish I had
what you all wasted Eliza had to go to Mr Graves cabin & we
staid at Mr Breen thay had meat all the time & we had to kill
little cash the dog & eat him we ate his body his feet & tale
and every thing about him o my Dear Cousin you dont now
what trubel is yet & many a time we had in the last thing a
cooking and did not now wher the next would come from
but there was awl wais some way provided there was 15 in the
cabon we was in and half of us had to lay abed all the time
thare was 10 starved to death them [then?] we was hadly abel
to walk we lived on little cash a week and after Mr Breen
would cook his meat we would take the bones and boil them
3 or 4 days at a time ma went down to the other cabin and
got half a hide carried it in snow up to her wast it snowed one
time and cover the cabin all over so we could not git out for 3
or 4 days we would have to cut pieces of the logos [logs] in
sied to make fire with I could hardly eat the hide we had not
eat anything 3 days Pa stated [started] out to us with provisions and thear come a storm and he could not go he cash his
provision and went back to on the other side of the bay to git
a compana of men and the San Wakien [San Joaquin] got so
hye he could not crose well thay made up a Compana at
Suters Fort and sent out we had not ate any thing for 3 or 4
days & we had onely half a hide and we was out on top of the
cabin and we seen them [the First Relief] a coming

No 5

O my Dear Cousin you dont now [know] how glad i was
we run and met them one of them we knew we had traveled
with them on the road thay staid thare 3 days to recruit us a
little [so that we could regain some strength] so we could go
thare was 21 started and went a piece and Marth and Thomas
giv out and the men had to take them back ma and Eliza &

James & I come on and o Mary that was the hades [hardest]
thing yet to come on and leiv them thar [We] did not [k]now
but what thay would starve to Death Martha said well ma if
you never see me again do the best you can the men said thay
could hadly stand it it maid them all cry but they said it was
better for all of us to go on for if we was to go back we would
eat that much more from them thay give them a littel meat
and flore [flour] and took them back and we come on we
went over great hye mountain as strait as stair steps in snow
up to our knees little James walk the hole [whole] way over
all the mountain in snow he said every step he took he wasa
gitting nigher Pa and somthing to eat the Bears took the
provision the men had cashed and we had but very little to
eat when we had traveld 5 days travel we met Pa with 13 men
going to the cabins o Mary you do not [k]now how glad we
was to see him we had not seen him for 6 months we thought
we woul[d] never see him again he heard we was coming and
he made some seet [sweet?] cakes to give us he said he would
see Martha and Thomas the next day he went in tow [two]
days what took us 5 days some of the compana was eating
them thar that Died but Thomas and Martha had not ate any
Pa and the men started with 17 peaple Hiram Miller Carried
Thomas and Pa caried Martha and thay wer caught in [a
storm] and thay had to stop one day it stormd so thay could
not go and the Bears took their provision and thay were 4
days without nay thing Pa and Hiram and all the men started
one of Donner boys Pa a rarring [carrying] Martha Hiram
caring Thomas and the snow up to thare wast and it a snowing so they could hadly see the way they raped [wrapped] the
children up and never took them out for 4 days thay had
nothing to eat in all that time Thomas asked for somthing to
eat once them that thay brought from the cabins some of
them was not able to come

    No 6

    and some would not come thare was 3 died and the rest
eat them thay was 10 days without any thing but the Dead Pa
braught Thoma and pady [Patty] in to where we was none of

the men was abel to go there feet was frose very bad so they was a nother Compana went and braught them all in thay are all in from the mountains now but for [four] thay was men went out after them and was caught in a storm and had to come back thare was nother compana gone thare was half got through that was stoped thare thare was but 2 familes that all of them got [through] we was one Mary I have not wrote you half of the truble we have had but I hav wrote you anuf to let you now that you dont now what truble is but thank god we have all got throw and the onely family that did not eat human flesh we have left every thing but i dont cair for that we have got [through] with our lives but Dont let this letter dishaten [dishearten] anybody and never take no cutofs and hury along as fast as you can

My Dear Cousin

We are all very much pleased with Callifornia particulary with the climate let it be evr so hot a day there is all wais cool nights it is a beautiful Country it is mostley in vallies it aut to be a beautiful Country to pay us for our trubel giting there it is the greatest place for cattel and horses you ever saw it would Just suit Charley for he could ride down 3 or 4 horses a day and he could learn to be Bocarro [vaquero] that one who luses [lassos] cattel the spanards and Indians are the best riders I ever saw thay have a spanish sadel and wodon sturups and great big spurs 5 inches in diameter they could not manage the Callifornia horses witout the spurs thay wont go atol [at all] if thay cant hear the spurs rattle thay have littel bells to them to make them rattle thay blindfold the [wild] horses til ther [they] sadel them and git on them and then take the blindfole of and let run and if thay can sit on thay tie themselves on and let them run as fast as thay can and go out to a band [of] bullluck [bullocks] and throw the reatter [riata] on a wild bullluck and but [put] it around the horn of his sadel and he can hold it as long as he wants a nother Indian throwes his reatter on its feet and throws them and when thay take the reatter of of them thay are very dangerous

No 7

thay will run after them hook there horses and run after any person thay see thay ride from 80 to 100 miles a day some of the spanard have from 6 to 7000 head of horses and from 15 to 16000 head of Cattel we are all verry fleshy Ma waies 10040 pons [this was Virginia's way of writing 140] and still a gaing [gaining] I waigh 81 tel Henriet if she wants to get Married for to come to Callifornia she can get a spanyard any time that Eliza is a going to marrie a a spanyard by the name of Armeho and Eliza weighs 10072 [172] We Have not saw uncle Cadon yet but we have had 2 letters from him he is well and he is a coming here as soon as he can Mary take this to uncle Gursham and to all that i know to all of our neighbors and every girl i know and let them read it and tell Dochter Maniel [MacNeil?] Mary kiss little Sue and Maryann for me and give my best love to all i know to uncle James aunt Leida and all the rest of the famla [family] and to uncle Gursham and aunt Percilla and all of the Children and to all of our neighbors and to all she knows so no more at present

My Dear casons
Virginia Elizabeth B Reed

BIBLIOGRAPHICAL NOTES

For the general reader, the best sources are George Rippey Stewart's *Ordeal by Hunger* (Boston: Houghton Mifflin Co., 1960 ed.) and Bernard DeVoto's *The Year of Decision: 1846* (Boston: Houghton Mifflin Co., 1961 ed.). Stewart, a fine and prolific writer of history, was the recognized modern authority on the Donner Party, which was one of his lifetime interests. The 1960 edition contains much valuable material that was not available when Stewart wrote the original version, in 1936. DeVoto, though more opinionated than Stewart, is an incomparable writer, and he gives a multifaceted, panoramic view of the events of that year and the following one, in which the Donner story is one of several simultaneous themes.

Both *Ordeal by Hunger* and *The Year of Decision: 1846* are generally available at public libraries. At the time of this writing, some bookstores carried them in paperback.

The original sources from which I drew are, unfortunately, not readily available to the general public, as the few copies extant are in special reference collections of a few major libraries, notably the Bancroft Library of the University of California at Berkeley, the Illinois State Historical Society at Springfield, and main branch of the New York Public Library at Forty-second Street. The principal ones are listed below, in approximate order of usefulness.

BOOKS

Jessy Quinn Thornton. *Oregon and California in 1848*, 2 vols. (New York, 1849) (no publisher listed in front matter). Thornton gives a colorful, detailed, highly opinionated account of life on the trail with the Russell-Boggs wagon company in Vol. 1, and in Vol. 2 picks up the story of the Donner Party again. Unfortunately, as Thornton explains in a prefatory note, his New York publisher rushed the book into print from a first draft, and Thornton had no opportunity to correct it. Apparently the publisher dispensed with the services of an editor, except for spelling and grammar. As a result, the narrative sequence is often confused, and there are a number of errors of fact. In addition, Thornton shared the tendency of his generation to put flowery conversations of high moral tone in his characters' mouths in rather unlikely circumstances. Still, all in all, Thornton supplies the most complete of the contemporary accounts.

Edwin Bryant. *What I Saw in California*. (New York, 1848) (no publisher listed). A well-written book by a professional journalist. Bryant traveled with the Donners and Reeds as far as Fort Laramie and met the survivors of the Donner Party again in California the following year (1847). Although the Donner Party is not the major subject of his book, Bryant gives many interesting details of life on the trail and is a good cross-check for Thornton. Bryant also furnishes much good information on crossing the Great Salt Desert and the Sierras on muleback, as well as on events in California during the fall of 1846 and the winter/spring of 1847. It is to Bryant that all later historians are indebted for the pungent portrait of the old mountain man Caleb Greenwood, most of which I have omitted to avoid repeating what appears in Stewart and DeVoto.

Heinrich Lienhard. *From St. Louis to Sutter's Fort.* (Norman: University of Oklahoma Press, 1961). Translated from the original German. Lienhard was one of the "Five German Boys," young Swiss and German bachelors who pooled their resources to buy a wagon and team and try their luck in California. Lienhard and his companions traveled across the plains to Fort Bridger at approximately the same time as the Donners and Reeds, but with a different wagon company. Having met Hastings's messenger on the trail, they decided to join the party that Hastings was forming at Fort Bridger. They arrived a little too late to meet him there, but caught up with him at Bear River and followed him along the Hastings cutoff, which, Lienhard commented, might better be called the Hastings long way around. In his memoirs, written in his old age, Lienhard depicted the passage down the Weber canyons as difficult and full of annoyances, but by no means impossible, as Hastings had claimed. In some aspects, he recalled it as almost a picnic, for example, the evening when the Five German boys dined sumptuously on fresh crayfish caught in the Weber River. The journey across the Great Salt Desert, so disastrous to the Donner Party, is graphically described. Interestingly, Lienhard describes Hastings as dashing back and forth on horseback among the emigrants' wagons, offering advice but giving no real leadership.

Lienhard's descriptions of the journey down the Humboldt and over the Sierras are also excellent source material. My description of the Humboldt Sink is based on Lienhard, supplemented by personal observation.

A second volume drawn from Lienhard's voluminous memoirs is *A Pioneer at Sutter's Fort,* ed. Margaret Wilbur. (Los Angeles: The Calafia Society, 1941). In this volume, among many other matters, Lienhard tells of his acquaintance with the Kesebergs, who lived temporarily on a farm that Lienhard was managing for Sutter. Mrs. Keseberg cooked Lienhard's meals, and the three German-speakers usually ate together. At dinner, Keseberg made several attempts to turn the conversation to his sojourn in the Sierras and his cannibalistic diet. Lienhard, although disgusted, was forced to listen, since Keseberg could not be turned off. He concluded that Keseberg was innocent of Tamsen Donner's murder. Lienhard also gives a fascinating portrait of Sutter, whom he served as a trusted employee for years. Beginning with great admiration for Sutter, Lienhard ended up disgusted with him. Lienhard's easy, informal style and spicy gossip make both volumes highly entertaining.

Lansford W. Hastings. *The Emigrant's Guide to Oregon and California.* (Cincinnati: George McConclin, 1845). (I used a facsimile edition at the New York Public Library.) The little book that caused so much tragedy. It is useful as a source document and interesting in its own right. Hastings was a master at dramatizing himself.

Charles F. McGlashan. *History of the Donner Party*, 2d ed. (San Francisco: A. L. Bancroft & Company, Printers. 1881). McGlashan, the editor of a small-town newspaper, was approached in 1878 by Judge James F. Breen, one of Patrick Breen's children, who offered to help McGlashan write the real history of the Donner Party. Breen was not able to give much actual help, but McGlashan, his interest kindled, went on to interview all the survivors who were still alive and willing to talk to him. Not all were willing—their memories were too painful. From these reminiscences, more than thirty years old, and from various printed sources such as *The California Star* and the books of Thornton and Bryant, McGlashan compiled his own history.

Unfortunately, McGlashan felt that he had to portray everybody in a favorable light and make excuses for bad behavior, which resulted in grave inaccuracies. He was further handicapped by the fact that after thirty years the survivors' memories were far from completely reliable. Not only were they confused about dates and places and what happened when; they also tended to remember things as they felt they should have been rather than as they actually were. Nevertheless, it is from McGlashan that later historians have obtained such details as the Forlorn Hope's crossing ravines on bridges of snow, and the Reeds' Christmas dinner at the Mountain Camp—the sort of thing that makes a profound impression on the mind of a child or a young adult.

Carroll D. Hall, ed., *Donner Miscellany.* (San Francisco: The Book Club of California, 1947). An extremely valuable collection of diaries and documents that includes the journal begun by Hiram Miller in May 1846 and continued by Reed after Miller left the wagon company at Fort Laramie, and the journal that Reed kept during the Second Relief. Some of the latter document was apparently written a day or two after the events described actually took place, as Reed was too busy keeping his fellow travelers alive to find time for his journal. However, this detracts but little from the probable accuracy of the journal, and Reed's on-the-spot description gives the reader a sense of immediacy that no other source can equal.

Eliza Donner Houghton, *Expedition of the Donner Party.* (Chicago: A. C. McClurg & Co., 1911). Since Eliza was only three when the Donner Party began their ill-fated journey and barely four when she was rescued, her recollections of what happened are necessarily limited. For her facts she depends mainly on printed sources such as McGlashan and Thornton, plus anecdotes that older siblings and cousins told her at one time or another. However, she is an excellent source for the personal details that would stay in a small child's mind, such as the daily routine at the campsite at Alder Creek, the frightening stay at Mrs. Murphy's cabin with the menacing Keseberg, and the incident of Hiram Miller's spanking her on the way down to Bear Valley. Eliza's book is also a mine of information on the precarious life she and her sisters and half sisters led during the first months after they were rescued, but that is really another story.

George Rippey Stewart, *Donner Pass and Those Who Crossed It.* (San Francisco: The California Historical Society. 1960. A concise, well-written account.

Moses Schallenberger, *The Opening of the California Trail,* ed. George R. Stewart. (Berkeley: University of California Press, 1953). Especially interesting for its account of Mose's lonely winter at Truckee Lake.

Jacob Wright Harlan, *California, '46 to '48.* Harlan, then a sickly youth of not quite 18, was one of the party that Hastings led down through the Wasatch and across the Great Salt Desert. His book is therefore of interest, although Harlan's recollections, affected by the passage of many years, are very often inaccurate. To a modern reader, it may be most valuable for its bitter portrait of life on a farm with unloving parents and relatives; nineteenth-century farm life in America was not always like a Currier & Ives print.

Kristin Johnson, ed. *Unfortunate Emigrants of the Donner Party.* (Logan, Utah: Utah State University Press, 1996). An anthology of material relating to the Donner Party, including extracts from Thornton, the Miller-Reed Diary (begun by Hiram Miller and continued by Reed), Reed's account in *The Pacific Rural Press,* and statements by other survivors, such as William Graves and his sister Mary. Also included are extracts from such peripherally related narrators as Eliza W. Farnham, Jacob Wright Harlan, and the early revisionist writer Francis H. MacDougall. There is even an extract from a letter by ex-Governor Lilburn Boggs, who had heard of the Donner story from the other emigrants. The variance among viewpoints is striking. A critical commentary precedes each selection; there are also maps and photos.

ARTICLES IN PERIODICALS

David E. Miller, "The Donner Road through the Great Salt Desert," *Pacific Historical Review,* vol. 27, No. 1, (1958): 39–44. Based on firsthand exploration by the author and others.

"The Journal of James Frazier Reed," *Utah Historical Quarterly* XIX (1951): 186–223. Extensive commentary and footnotes supply valuable information on the chronology and the route taken by the Donner Party between July 31 and October 4, the day before John Snyder's death, when the journal is broken off.

DIARIES, LETTERS, AND PERSONAL REMINISCENCES

(Reed's journals have already been cited under Donner Miscellany and Utah Historical Quarterly; so there is no need for repetition.)

Patrick Breen, *Diary.* Breen turned his diary over to Sheriff George McKinstry when Breen reached Sutter's Fort. The original was subsequently lost, but not before a number of printed versions had been made. I used a photocopy of a handwritten copy made in 1871 by Henry L. Oak; the copy is now in possession off the Bancroft Library. Of the printed versions, the one edited by Frederick Taggart (Berkeley: University of California Press, 1910) is regarded as the most authentic.

James Frazier Reed. "The Snow-Bound, Starved Emigrants of 1846," *The Pacific Rural Press,* (Mar. 25 and Apr. 1, 1871). The principal source for Reed's nightmare journey down the Humboldt and across the Sierras as well as the abortive rescue attempt in November 1846. Reed, in fact, covers his experiences from the time he left Springfield to the end of the Second Relief. A very useful source. However, Reed rather disingenuously omits any references to the killing of John Snyder—perhaps he felt that the incident was best forgotten so long after it occurred.

——— "Sports of the West. Letter from the South Fork of the Platte," *The Sangamo Journal,* Springfield, Ill. (July 30, 1846). This was Reed's boastful letter about his buffalo hunt, dutifully printed without corrections. I have quoted from it at length.

———"Narrative of the Sufferings of a Company of Emigrants in the Mountains of California, in the Winter of '46 and 47." Letter in *The Sangamo Journal,* (Dec. 9, 1847).

———"California Correspondence." Letter from San Francisco. *The Illinois Journal,* Springfield, Ill. (Dec. 23, 1847).

———Letter to his brother-in-law, James Keyes, from "3 miles west of the Kansas or Caw" (May 20, 1846).

William McCutchen. "Statement of William McCutchen," *The Pacific Rural Press* (Apr. 1, 1871). Details of his and Reed's encounter with the Curtises and of the Second Relief.

Virginia Elizabeth B. Reed. Letter to her cousin Mary C. Keyes (May 16, 1847). Reproduced in this book.

———Letter to Mary C. Keyes, (July 12, 1846). Reprinted in *Manuscripts,* VI, no. II, pp. 86-96 (Winter 1954): 86-96 and in *The Masterkey,* XVIII, no. 3, (May 1944): 81-89. This is the letter from Independence Rock describing the Fourth of July celebrations.

———"Deeply Interesting Letter," *The Illinois Journal* (Dec. 16, 1847). A highly edited version of the above-mentioned letter.

Virginia Reed Murphy. "Across the Plains in the Donner Party (1846)" *The Century Magazine* (July 1891). Virginia's recollections thirty-five years after the fact.

James Clyman. "James Clyman, His Diaries and Reminiscences." *California Historical Quarterly*, 4: 105-41, 272-83, 307-60; 5: 44-84, 109-38, 255-82, 378-401; 6: 58-68. The source for details of Jim Clyman's journey East with Hastings in the spring of 1846. Page 395 recounts Clyman's conversation with Reed at Fort Laramie.

John Breen. *Pioneer Memoirs.* Written for the Bancroft Library (Nov. 1877). Handwritten memoir, very difficult to decipher. Tells of the heroism and kindness of John Starks of the Third Relief, plus matters not relevant to this story.

David Campbell. "A Pioneer of 1846," *The Porterville Weekly Review,* Porterville, Calif. (July 28, 1899). Of interest because Campbell traveled with the Russell-Boggs Party over the regular trail via Fort Hall and so had some contact with the Donner Party.

Tamsen Eustis Dozier Donner. Letters to her sister dated June 28, 1831, Jan. 20, 1832, Nov. 22, 1832, Jan. 16, 1838, Feb. 3, 1838, Jan. 12, 1840, and May 11, 1846 (originals at Illinois State Historical Society Library at Springfield). All but the last long predating the fatal journey, these chatty letters give an idea of Tamsen's personality. The letter of Jan. 12, 1840, gives a picture of her happy marriage to George Donner and the comfort in which they lived. The last letter, a short note, is written from Independence, Mo., on the eve of departure.

————Letter dated June 16, 1846, *The Sangamo Journal* (July 23, 1846).

George Donner. Letter dated June 27, 1846, *The Sangamo Journal* (Aug. 13, 1846).

NEWSPAPERS (OTHER)

The California Star, Feb. 13, 1847, Feb. 27, 1847, Mar. 13, 1847, Apr. 3, 1847, Apr. 10, 1847, May 22, 1847, and June 5, 1847. The last number contains Fallon's account of the Fourth Relief and the encounter with Keseberg.

GENERAL BACKGROUND

History of Sangamon County. (Chicago: Inter-State Publishing Company, 1881). (no author credit given)

Joseph Wallace. *Past and Present History of the City of Springfield and of Sangamon County, Illinois.* {Chicago: S. J. Clarke Publishing Co., 1904).

Paul M Angle. *Here I Have Lived: A History of Lincoln's Springfield.* (Chicago and Lincoln's New Salem, Ill.: Abraham Lincoln Bookshop, 1971).

Mary A. Jones. *Recollections of Mary A. Jones.* Written for the Bancroft Library in 1915. Mrs. Jones crossed the plains in 1846, although in a different party from the Donner-Reed group. Mrs. Jones got her facts about the Donner Party quite muddled, an interesting illustration of how the victims themselves were blamed for their misfortunes.

John Bidwell. "Echoes of the Past," *The Century Illustrated Magazine* (Nov. 1890, Dec. 1890, Jan.1891). Reprinted by State of California, tthe Resources Agency, Department of Parks and Recreation, (1974). Bidwell was a member of the first emigrant party to reach California overland, in 1841. He knew Sutter well and worked for him off and on for several years.

Richard H. Dillon. *Fool's Gold.* (New York: Coward-McCann, 1967). A good biography of Sutter.

Irwin Gudde. *Sutter's Own Story.* (New York: G. P. Putnam & Co., 1936).

LATEST GLEANINGS FROM THE INTERNET

Although I discovered these sources too late to make use of them in this book, I recommend the home pages of Kris Johnson, a librarian by trade, and by avocation a Donner and anthologist. Her Internet address as of this writing is http://metrogourmet.com/crossroads/kjhome.htm. Also very useful is Daniel M. Rosen's *The Donner Party,* an exhaustive log of the party's progress. This can be "downloaded" from the Internet at http://members.aol.com/DanMRosen/donner/index.htm. Rosen, a self-described amateur historian, welcomes comments and sharing of information by E-mail. He can be reached at DanMRosen@aol.com.

MAPS

T. H. Jefferson. *Map of the Emigrant Road from Independence, Mo., to St. Francisco, California (1849)*. The most accurate contemporary map of the emigrant trail, with distances and information on road condition, water, etc., noted. It was a pity that the Donner Party did not have this map!

INDEX